Whispers of the Spirit

Whispers of the Spirit

Ann Albers

Published and distributed in the United States by:

Ann Albers • Phoenix, Arizona • (602) 485-1078

www.VisionsOfHeaven.com

Email: angelann@cox.net

©1996, 2007 by Ann Albers

Albers, Ann, 2007 –

Whispers of the Spirit / Ann Albers

1. Spirituality 2. Personal Growth I. Title

1st Printing, October 2007

Printed in Phoenix, Arizona

ISBN: 978-1-4357-0262-2

Dedication

This book is dedicated to God, my dear angels, and to all who have helped me during my journey of awakening.

Table of Contents

Acknowledgements

I could not possibly thank everyone who has contributed to my life and therefore to this book. A lifetime is the culmination of thousands of relationships, and I owe a huge debt of gratitude to so many people for helping me become who I am.

God bless my parents not only for all they gave me throughout my childhood, but also for the lessons they provided, their unconditional love, and their willingness to grow with me throughout the years. I love you both so much.

With all my heart, I bless my former husband John for giving me both roots and wings. Without his love and understanding, I would not have had the security I needed to blossom into the person I have become.

I want to thank Jessica, my first spiritual teacher, without whom I might still be a stubborn, angry, overly mental engineer. God bless you for your love, your patience, and your willingness to guide me into the light.

Thank you to James Braddock who taught me to journey into unseen worlds, and to Lynn Andrews who, at the time of this writing I have not met in waking life, but whose works served as guidance to me in the early days of my shamanic awakening.

Thank you to Carol and Jeff whose teachings and playful willingness to explore healing modalities helped me journey deeply into my own heart.

A huge thanks to all the engineers, managers, and support people at Honeywell and Boeing who gave everything they had to the 777 aircraft program and, on a more personal note, gave me incredible love, support, and encouragement. You live in my heart forever.

I am also eternally grateful to my dearest friends, Debbie and Daniela, who always support me when I withdraw from the world in order to work on my books, laugh with me when I am learning from the trickster, and love me beyond reason.

Thank you to Heather Clarke for your wonderful editing skills and for your commitment to service as well. I love your beautiful spirit.

I also want to thank Doreen Virtue, although I do not know her personally, for reading this book. When the angels woke me up late one night in 1998 and urged me to ask her this favor, I never thought she would be able to spare the time. Doreen, you are a blessing to this earth—loved and adored by God, angels, and millions of us who have benefited from your work.

To all my friends, I love and adore you. Many of you met me long after this book was originally written. I hope you have a good laugh reading about who I used to be, and are able to give thanks that you didn't know me back in the day!

To my clients, students, and colleagues—you know who you are—God bless you for being willing to walk the path. You are my inspiration on the journey.

I love you all.

Preface

I never intended to be a psychic when I grew up. Who does? I thought I would be an average woman with a husband, a normal career, two kids, a house, dogs, vacations, retirement, and a few adventures scattered here and there. I graduated from the University of Notre Dame with a B.S. in electrical engineering, got married, climbed the corporate ladder, and was well on my way to "having it all." *God had other plans.*

Several years into my dream life, I admitted to myself that I was not happy. I had done everything that my parents, school, religion, and society told me I should do in order to be content, and still I was not. In a desperate search to claim the life that was really mine, I turned to heaven and prayed.

Spirit answered in a myriad of different voices including dreams, coincidences, synchronicities, and conversations with an unseen angel. The whispers of Spirit tore apart my notions of reality and rebuilt my notions of myself. I learned a completely different way of looking at life and began to discover the truth of my soul. In visions, I met spirit guides who helped me journey into other realms of reality. During bodywork, I released the pain of my past. At the pinnacle of an eight-year engineering career, I quit.

Soon after, I met shamans and teachers who became my guides, and in a mind-expanding mystical experience, I touched God and knew myself as one of His many faces. My entire life changed.

I am now a spiritual author, instructor, and angel communicator. Some say "psychic." Others call me a "channel." It does not matter. I talk to God. I talk to angels. I talk to souls and learn what they have to say. The journey began when I tuned into the *Whispers of the Spirit* in my own life.

I offer you this book, and my life, as a gift. If you would like to shed some light on your own path, sit back, imagine we're sitting in a coffee shop, and allow me to share my story. These are the baby steps on my spiritual path. My prayer is that my experience can help you recognize the *Whispers of the Spirit* in your own life, so you too can come to know the beautiful essence of your soul.

With much love,
Ann Albers

Chapter 1
Lost in the Labyrinth

Before we begin our journey, let me tell you a little story. When I sat down to write this book, I was at a loss for words. Where does one start to share the mysteries that change our lives?

I stared at the computer that sat on the antique wooden table in my living room and waited for the machine to give me an answer. No such luck. My gaze wandered past the dining room shutters, into the garden where a friendly hummingbird was feeding on some bright red flowers and the bees were happily buzzing around the rose geranium. I turned back to the screen in front of me and closed my eyes in frustration. "Oh for goodness sake!" I exclaimed to no one in particular, feeling foolish with my own insight. "I'm writing a book about the *Whispers of the Spirit*. Perhaps I could ask for some help!"

"Dear God, I need a good metaphor for the process of our spiritual evolution, please." I prayed easily knowing a response would be forthcoming. Immediately, in my mind's eye, I saw the symbol of the labyrinth. I suspected my prayer had been answered.

Equipped with symbol dictionaries and reference books, I researched the vision. Still not satisfied that I understood the message, I drove to the local library where I found the story of the mythical Greek labyrinth in ancient Minoan Crete. I felt as if I had finally stumbled on the answer I was seeking. I settled into a comfortable chair by the windows that overlooked the library lawn and read further. I had no idea that I would find so many themes from my own life in the echoes of the ancient tale. The myth goes something like this:

Poseidon, the sea god, presented Minos with a beautiful white bull in answer to his earnest prayers. The bull was a symbol that Minos was to be king of Crete. Like so many of us, Minos became attached to his possession. The bull became a sign of his success and power, and he refused to slaughter the bull as Poseidon had instructed. Little did he know that holding on to something whose usefulness had passed would only bring him destruction and pain. The gods punished him by rendering him sterile.

Adding insult to injury, it so happened that Minos' lovely wife, Pasiphae, was smitten with the virile bull. Having very different moral standards than our own, she believed her behavior to be quite acceptable as she contrived a scheme to sleep with the bull and conceive the beast's child. She had Daedalus, one of the city's finest artisans, design and build her an artificial cow in which she hid during the brief but torrid bovine encounter. Hideous! The child resulting from their union was a man with a bull's head—a beast with a voracious appetite that was fearful to behold.

Minos was furious. (Wouldn't you be?) He ordered Daedalus to construct a labyrinth, a maze from which no man or beast could possibly escape. The bull-headed child—the Minotaur – was cast into its own hell, a lifetime of solitude spent retracing its steps within the tangled pathways.

Every eight years, Minos required the city of Athens to sacrifice seven young men and seven virgins to feed the angry, trapped beast. Theseus, a young Athenian, bravely volunteered, hoping to heroically save his city from future sacrifices. Lucky for Theseus, Minos' young daughter, Adriadne, had a huge crush on him. Adriadne, young and starry-eyed, stood by the door of the labyrinth as her beloved Theseus entered the twisting paths. She held in her hands a skein of golden yarn, which Theseus unraveled slowly as he made his way into the inner realms of the maze. At long last, Theseus found the bull, faced it, slaughtered it, and followed his trail of gold yarn back to his love. With Adriadne, Theseus left the city to follow his own fate.

Back at the scene of the crime, Minos wasn't thrilled. He cast Daedalus and his son, Icarus, into the maze that had been designed so well, that even Daedalus couldn't find his way out. Daedalus, ever the clever one, knew he had to rise above the maze to escape the pathways he had fashioned. He built wings of wax for himself and his son. Together they flew, soaring above the labyrinth toward freedom. Unfortunately, Icarus got a bit heady with his own power and flew too close to the sun. His wings melted and he plummeted to his death. Daedalus landed safely and was finally able to get on with his life.

So, what was the moral of the story? Ever the comic, I laughed. "Never sleep with a horny creature or you'll have a bull-headed child?" I grinned impishly and turned my attention to the words of Joseph Campbell, one of the late, great modern mythologists. Campbell tells us that myths speak to us of our common human experience and teach us how to live. They give us glimpses into the mystery behind our existence. I was intrigued. With more seriousness, I considered my own experiences in light of the myth.

—— § ——

You might not realize you're on the road to

heaven when you feel you're lost in the maze.

Early summer: Dear journal - What a lousy, rotten day. Nothing really went wrong I guess, except I threw up after breakfast and have been painful, bloated, and nauseated since dawn. It's that-time-of-month and I'm totally depressed. My boss just called to see if I would fly to California for a quick meeting Thursday. Of course I can. What else could I tell him? Some days I wish I could just fade out of existence.

The job is really getting me down. I don't feel any sense of self-worth here. What am I contributing to the greater good of humanity? Nothing. I feel trapped. Maybe I could win the lottery, stay at home, and have kids. At least then I would feel needed and worth something in my occupation. Well this is a huge pity party, isn't it? I'm just complaining because I feel low and I hurt. I don't really want to travel this week either. Hopefully there won't be any earthquakes while I'm out in California. I would hate to screw up my life before it really begins.

I feel like I'm searching. Is this a mid-life crisis hitting early? Why am I here? What purpose is my life? What is my life task? I wonder if I even have one. I just don't know. I don't love engineering. I watch my friends who do, and I become more and more convinced I don't. I wish I did. I wish I could. Maybe I'm just whining. What else would I do? I used to love writing. I guess still do, but I'm horribly out of practice. What would I write about? What do I have to contribute anyway?

Tears ran silently down my cheeks and onto the keyboard as I typed. I was having yet another bad day. They seemed to be coming with greater frequency as of late. As I wrote in my computer journal, I could barely sit up straight due to the shooting pain in my abdomen. I wanted to fall in an exhausted pile on the floor and give up. I hated feeling this way. I hated being out of control of my body and my mind. In more humorous moments, when the pain wasn't so bad, I joked that I felt like Sybil, the woman who had become famous in the early seventies for her multiple personality disorder—happy one day and in the depths of depression the next. "Poor John," I whimpered, feeling even more miserable and sorry for myself. I wondered how my husband could stand me. I hunched over and tried to breathe deeply as another wave of the ferocious menstrual cramps struck me. I wondered if something was wrong with me. The doctors seemed to think I was fine. "Take aspirin," one told me casually. "I'm allergic to aspirin," I reminded him with a tinge of sarcasm in my voice. "There are plenty of good substitutes," he told me curtly. No matter—on days like these no drug would touch the pain.

I trudged into the kitchen and opened the fridge. The day was a warm and beautiful Sunday afternoon but I was inside, dressed in my old baggy sweats, and a large comfortable shirt. My hair was an atrocious mess, and I wasn't wearing any makeup. I looked as awful as I felt, and I didn't even care. I'd spent the entire day alternately sleeping to escape the pain, and walking slowly around the house to relieve the cramps. I wasn't especially proud of myself in these moments.

"If they could only see me at work now," I thought grimly, wondering how I had inadvertently managed to fool so many people into thinking I "had it all together." I wonder if all those folks who thought I was such a great engineer would feel the same respect if they could see me standing here now with glazed eyes searching for some scrap of food to make life better, if only for a minute. I was disgusted with myself. In less than a week, I would be Ms. Systems Engineer again, sitting around a huge conference room table in California at a meeting with all the other big players in the commercial avionics business, designing future aircraft systems. At home alone today, I was nothing, numb.

The fridge was well stocked but there wasn't anything that looked appetizing. I walked over to a cupboard and stared inside, as if the contents might offer some answers. There wasn't much there. That's how I felt—empty, devoid of nourishment for my soul. "Soul?" I thought sarcastically, "Did I even have one left?" I didn't feel like I had any heart or soul lately. I went back and lay down on the couch, flipping channels on the TV, and hoping to find something to dull my thoughts.

With my teeth clenched and jaw locked, I braced myself each month and staunchly stuffed the pain and the anger inside, lest anyone see the emotions that stirred within me. Every now and then, I couldn't contain them. A spackled mark in the living room wall covered by fresh paint was a painful reminder of the time I had picked up a pair of scissors in frustration and hurled them. I never let John or anyone else see the seething emotions that broiled inside my internal furnace. They were embarrassing, and worse yet, illogical. Anyway, I wasn't mad at anyone in particular. I was just mad.

As soon as the anger passed, I felt incredibly stupid for having allowed myself to feel that way at all. After all, I had a good life... didn't I? I chalked up the rash of emotion to PMS and wondered if I was weak for being a woman. I worked harder than ever to appear strong. I didn't realize at the time that Spirit was whispering in my life, giving me an opportunity in the pain to wake up and be honest with myself. I wasn't really happy and yet I was doing everything possible to prove I was. Subtly, yet persistently, Spirit was rocking the very foundation of my beliefs in the hope that I would allow new growth to spring up through the cracks.

Pain can be a great teacher. I've learned that if you watch yourself in your weaker moments, you'll find the inner beasts that hide in the labyrinth of your own psyche. How do you react when you're ill? When I was down, I found I could no longer contain the bottled-up emotions that stirred inside of me and begged for release. I was faced with my own worst fears and my deepest sense of inadequacy. Stripped away of the mechanisms that helped me ignore my own feelings most days, I found myself faced with an ugly truth. I didn't really love my life. In fact, I didn't even like my life any more.

At age 28, I was deeply lost in the labyrinth. The beast inside me begged to scream out, "Isn't there more to life than this?" No one told me life would be this hard! No one told me I would feel alone, stressed-out, and empty at the end of each day! No one told me that this promise of success was just a façade that was really empty and useless. Then perhaps more quietly, wistfully, the poor bull-headed child would whimper, "Why me? Where did I go wrong? There has to be more." The beast was kept deeply buried in the maze of my own mind with the exception of the few days every month when the cramps broke down the barriers. The rest of the time, I would have never admitted to feeling these things. In fact, I worked very hard to keep from feeling at all.

On the surface, I appeared successful, bubbly, energetic, and happy. To others, John and I seemed happily married. We never fought, we went out together every weekend, and we owned our own home in Arizona with a pool, two cars, and a small but abundant garden. We had two furry, fun-loving dogs and anything else we wanted. We looked like the great American Dream.

We were busy too, always busy. John had left his first job at the military aerospace firm a few years ago and was now working at the same company where I worked. Despite the long hours, he enjoyed the challenge of designing hardware for the computers that would eventually fly and maintain the new Boeing 777 airplanes. Looking in from the outside, I had a "glamorous" job too. I traveled, worked with the leaders of major airline flight operations departments, and was involved in designing a computer system that was on the leading edge of commercial avionics technology. My career demanded most of my time and energy, as did John's, but we didn't mind. We knew we were lucky to have such good jobs.

Unwittingly, we had allowed ourselves to drift apart. Without ever realizing the cost, I had allowed my own dreams for a bright future to fall by the wayside, scattered in bits and pieces over the last several years of my life. Most days, I managed to keep busy enough to prevent myself from having to think about the situation, or worse yet, to feel the loss. I was content with my hectic daily schedule. The fast pace gave me a sense of accomplishment—a sense of being needed and useful. I dove into every aspect of my life with seemingly great zeal. I measured my worth by the results I produced, both at home and on the job.

I did feel good about all I managed to accomplish, but something still bothered me. Something wasn't quite right with my life. I could never seem to put my finger on the cause of my growing discontent. The beast raged deep within me and I didn't even realize the beast was there.

Every now and then, I tried to figure out the unrest that was gnawing at the edges of my consciousness until the fury erupted each month demanding to be faced once again. Unlike some people, I didn't have any great tragedy in my own life. Of course, I had some pain and sickness from time to time, but nothing compared to the terrible illnesses other people endured. "Sure, my parents argued a great deal while I was growing up," I admitted, "but didn't everyone's do that?" I didn't have the trauma of abuse, or neglect, or any of a hundred thousand other horrors that I heard other people report. I didn't feel like I had an excuse to be anything less than thrilled with my little fairy-tale-by-other-people's-standards life. Still, in times of truth, I was unhappy with myself, tired of my career and despondent about my marriage. In times when I could think clearly and honestly, I wondered where I had gone wrong. Looking back, I now know there was no "wrong."

All roads can lead to heaven. Some are just
more challenging than others.

— § —

I had always been a dreamer. As a kid, I had grandiose notions about what I would accomplish and what life would be like. I was playful, imaginative, sensitive, and infinitely joyful during my youngest years. I had imaginary friends, and with my younger brother, we took imaginary journeys to the far reaches of the earth. We built tents under tables and "went camping." In our young minds, we created sea-faring vessels out of wooden blocks and sailed through the "underwater" caverns of our small apartment. I made my brother sit through imaginary lessons while I played "teacher."

My carefree days didn't last long. Even at an early age, I became aware of the tensions that beset our young family. I didn't know at the time that I was an empath who felt other people's feelings. My father, a physics graduate in his late twenties, was working long hours to provide for us, while also attending night school for an advanced degree. "Don't bother Daddy. He's working on his thesis," Mom reminded us. "What's a thesis?" I asked, giggling like little girls do, while making myself a pest.

My mother was also busy. She graduated from college with a business degree but was now employed full-time watching over her two young children. My parents married in their early twenties, shortly after their college graduation. I arrived on the scene ten months later and my brother came after a three-year break. Instead of having a chance to use her degree, Mom plunged straight into motherhood and domestic life, while Dad worked hard to pave the way for our future.

When I was twelve, we moved from our small apartment into a new house. I was a very responsible child by that time. I worked hard in school and got good grades. I hurried home each day to do my homework and finish my chores so I could play outside with my new friends. Three boys and three girls in the neighborhood formed a happy little gang—we climbed trees, rode skateboards and bikes, played with our walkie-talkies, and innocently mauled each other in a variety of contact sports in the backyard. I could have been any young child growing up in middle-class America in the seventies.

By this time, my mother was also employed, which gave her a chance to get out and do something commensurate with her education and experience. My younger brother and I were happily ignorant of the mounting financial pressures in our small family. My parents had a mortgage and two kids approaching high school age. Always eager to give us their best, they were both working long hours to make sure we could attend a private school.

At the time I never knew the price they paid for their sacrifice. As a young teen, all I knew was that the arguments were getting more frequent. Always sensitive, I felt their pain, and as a result, spent considerable time worrying about how I might smooth things over and make life better for them. Instead, I often found myself in the middle of a discussion that originally had nothing to do with me.

My parents must have been tired from working so hard. Still thinking egocentrically as a child, however, I didn't know this. I felt betrayed and unloved. "They don't care about me," I cried. "Can't they see I'm doing everything I can to make their lives easier?" I took on their pain and adopted their struggle as my own. I weeded the huge garden in the back yard, cleaned the basement, organized the garage, and fixed things around the house. I baked birthday cakes, gave them presents on the holidays, and listened as they told me their woes. What more could I do? I spent long, lonely nights in my bedroom, staring at the moon crossing the panes of my window through tear-stained eyes. I started talking to my pet rabbits, crying to them sometimes when no one else was there to listen. In return for the dried banana chips I fed them, they sniffed and stared at me as if they understood. I filled pages of my journal each night, and found writing to be the only outlet for emotions that were unacceptable in public.

I worked harder than ever in school. Good grades brought good words. Yet, the cycle would happen again. There would be another argument and inevitably, I believed myself to be at the root of the problem. Thus were planted the seeds that bred an ugly beast within— a voice that constantly told me I wasn't good enough. Although no one ever said this to me directly, I started living as if I had an inner recording playing constantly. "Work harder. Work smarter. Listen more. Fix things. Make their life better. Doesn't matter, you'll never succeed. Ha ha." The voice was so subtle I didn't notice its insidious effects.

My rage was building throughout these years as well. No matter how hard I tried to mollify the arguments, my actions or words were never good enough. Something deep down inside told me this wasn't my problem. Something I couldn't face was trying to tell me that my feelings were valid. I stuffed the anger down deep in my psyche. "Damn!" The words escaped from my lips with a vehemence that surprised me. I was fifteen and I wasn't supposed to cuss, so I did so anyway, a small secret rebellion. "How dare they yell at me?" I tightened my jaw, lest I explode. "How dare they come apologize to me one fight after another." The thought made me sick. I ran into my room, shut the door, and slammed my fist into my pillow silencing the tears, lest they hear me cry and know they had gotten to me. I clenched my teeth vowing not to let them see my pain. I would hide the hurt, bury the anger, and never let them know.

I stormed silently until the anger was so great I grabbed a hairbrush and beat my own arm leaving huge red welts. I couldn't stand the thought of hurting anyone else. "If I hurt myself, then they'll be sorry. Then they'll stop fighting and be nice to me," I vowed. Logic had no voice when buried by such intense emotion. "Something has to pay for this hurt!" I burst into tears, dropping the brush and falling into my pillows, sobbing the heart-wrenching tears of an overly sensitive young woman who didn't understand life much less herself. In less than an hour, I would dry my eyes and go back downstairs, a fake smile painted smugly across my face. The Cheshire grin was so real that even I was beginning to believe in the masquerade.

I didn't know, at the time, the pressures that were involved with being a dual-career family when the idea wasn't altogether socially acceptable. I didn't realize that my mother was working to give us the extras in life while living with criticism from other women for not being at home with her children. I didn't understand that my dad had to choose between spending more time with his family and providing for them. I certainly didn't see my own part in the explosions. I didn't realize my smart-alecky sarcasm managed to push their hot buttons. Years would pass by before I would completely understand how I had a hand in creating my own pain.

My brother and I had every material thing we ever needed and then some: our own rooms in a large house, furniture we'd been allowed to choose, plenty of toys, bikes, skateboards, bats, balls, music, and three healthy meals every day. Furthermore, my parents made every effort to raise us as well-rounded individuals. We attended church regularly, enjoyed concerts, went to the park, visited museums, and read books together. We gardened, explored nature, and went on vacations that we would never forget. I enjoyed all the benefits and the good times that came from living in a family that was successful by every one of society's standards. Our every physical, mental, and spiritual need was met.

Nonetheless, when angry words and frustrated comments stung me like wasps, I felt emotionally impoverished. Focusing on their perceived injustices, I ignored my parents when they told me they loved me and felt unlovable. Watching them come home from work tired more often than not, I didn't believe them when they said they had a good life. My fifteen-year-old ideal of married love didn't match the drama I saw enacted before me. Adamantly, I promised myself that my own life would be better. During those so-called "confusing" adolescent years, I was perhaps more sure of what I wanted from life than I would be for years to come.

The seeds of my hopes and dreams were sown during my high school years. Even then, Spirit was laying the foundation for the life I would eventually come to know as my own—only after living through struggle myself. I did my first science fair project on crystals, marveling at their organization and meticulously repetitive structure.

I did a second project on memory. "How does our brain work?" I wondered. During my senior year, I did yet another study, this time on dreams. "What was really going on during those nightly flights?"

I developed an avid interest in consciousness, and read everything I could find on the subject. I raided my father's bookshelves and digested the information as quickly as I could find something new and exciting. During the time I was shopping for my first prom dress, I was also learning how a sodium-potassium pump carries electrical signals along the long nerve cells in our brain. While listening to the rock and roll on my first stereo I marveled at the number of neurotransmitters that must be taking the leap from neuron to neuron, just to give me the pleasure I called "music." Sometimes, staring at the stars late at night, I tried to figure out how science fit in with my religion. I was a mystic, a geek, and an emerging young woman all rolled into one.

Still the dreamer in spite of life's up and downs, I entered college with a huge idea of whom I was going to become. "I am going to be a leading expert in brain research and unlock the mysteries of human consciousness," I told my younger friends as I packed my belongings in the family station wagon. Long ago, I had given up any notion of pursing my interest in writing. That wasn't even an option I considered as I left my home in Virginia for my freshman year at the University of Notre Dame.

Instead, I formed other dreams that were equally exciting. Unfortunately, they were equally short-lived. I signed up for the freshman program in pre-medicine, intent on pursuing a long-term career in neuro-physiological research. Reality hit me like a brick wall only one semester into my higher education when, after a talk with my guidance counselor, I actually understood what life would be like if I were in school for another eight years after college. Even after graduating from medical school, I imagined, I would have massive debts to pay off, clients to treat, and only in my spare time would I be able to do the occasional research project. "Ugh!" I thought ahead. Didn't I want a family, children, and a life without such "round-the-clock" intensity? Not yet, of course, but some day. Wasn't that everybody's plan?

My seemingly clear direction was clouded once again. I stood with my hands on a spinning dial of choices for my life. I weighed my options rationally, with all their pros and cons but still had no answer. Spirit whispered again. Who knows how the thought was planted in my mind, but I soon found myself thinking along lines that resulted in my switch to an electrical engineering major. "Hm... the brain, neurons, electricity... hey, electrical engineering." I hopped on the roller coaster that would be my life for the next several years. Little did I know that precisely eight years after college would pass before I would reclaim my dream. I'm sure Spirit smiled.

Having made my career decision, I was no longer required to think about my future. I was on "cruise control." I loved my life! College afforded me an opportunity to pour equal amounts of passion and energy into my studies as my social life. After a late night of cramming three chapters in physics, my friends and I would wake up early on a Notre Dame football Saturday to feast at the tailgate parties with alumni we had never met, and then we would head into the stadium to see the famed Fighting Irish go for the gold. That night we would celebrate the victory, dancing everywhere that campus security would allow us. We danced on radiators in crowded rooms, on pool tables in the dorm halls, on tables in the dining hall, and in the reflecting pool in front of the massive library with the huge mosaic that we affectionately called "Touchdown Jesus." I felt like I was finally dancing through life.

In freshman Physical Education class during my second semester, I met the young man who would later become my husband. John was indescribably cute in my estimation, about 5'9" and blondish with bright sparkling eyes. He looked so alive and playful. I noticed him on the first day of our ice-skating rotation, and contrived a way to meet him.

As we laced up our skates, we traded essential freshman information. "Hi, I'm Ann. Where you from?" "Phoenix, Arizona" he replied. "I'm John." Score! I was planning to live out west after school. "What's your major?" One by one, we went through the standard list of "getting-to-know-you" questions, following the unwritten protocol of freshman small talk. "Chemical engineering," he replied. "A shame," I thought. I was already hoping that we would have more classes together. The instructor called our attention and we gingerly made our way onto the ice rink.

As we skated by each other, playing a version of broom-ball, something inside made my stomach do a quick flip-flop, or my face flush every so slightly when he passed me, racing by with that "come-if-you-dare" look. Those eyes! They were deep blue sparkles of life that invited me to stare. Playing opposite one another, we would lock gazes, grin wickedly and block the shot, or smack the ball with a vengeance. I was never really an extraordinary athlete, but I played like a champion now that I had someone to impress. I couldn't have cared less about the score. I was extremely fascinated by a specific member of the opposing team.

Early sophomore year, I was delighted to find that John had switched his major from chemical to electrical engineering. When he showed up the first day of my electronics class, I could not have been more thrilled. His face lit up when he saw me, and he came to sit by my side. We compared our rosters, and my stomach flipped once again when I saw that we had all of our first-semester classes together. Was fate at work? I felt my face get warm at the thought and tried to conceal my sudden embarrassment by asking about his summer.

John and I spent many hours together. We started saving each other seats, sharing our notes, and studying as a pair for all our exams. We waited for each other after class and ate lunches together. Occasionally, I saw him in the dining hall at dinnertime and our smiles would betray our feelings. We became close friends and companions—so close in fact, that we were the last two to acknowledge the fact that our friendship had slowly blossomed into love. One day late in the winter when John stopped by my electronics lab to give me some notes, I looked at him a little differently and I realized I could no longer imagine my life without him. Feeling a bit queasy for the next few days, I admitted to myself that he was much more than just a friend. My stomach was churning all the time now as fear set in. I kept my feelings hidden well, not wanting to mess up our friendship. By the time John kissed me for the first time, on a warm spring night, I was so starry-eyed that I was getting my first "C" in a college class, day-dreaming all the time, and unable to get whole sentences out of my mouth without great effort when he was around. His kiss melted away my needless concerns. This feeling! This was what I'd been waiting for all my life. Never before had I felt so special, and best yet, so loved. My "C" paled by comparison to the vast reservoir of emotion that I was beginning to enjoy, and my world revolved ecstatically around John.

Notre Dame was a magical place at night. John and I took moonlit walks past the small stone grotto patterned after the famed grotto of Our Lady of Lourdes. Candles flickered in front of old stone walls and iron crosses, while the smoke sent many a student's prayer for a passing grade or an alumni's wish for a football victory toward the heavens. We watched the flames as they danced hypnotically, silently whispered our own secret prayers for the future, and then strolled onto the dirt path that wound around the shores of the campus lakes. As we walked, tiny waves kissed the banks of the lake, while the ducks quacked in a cacophony of sound that echoed across the quiet waters. We held hands and shyly shared our hopes and dreams. We stopped every now and then and stood very close while watching the stars twinkle brightly in the night sky. I wrapped my hands inside his warm jacket on the cool fall nights and felt a blush of warmth that would last for days. He made my heart so happy I could barely think of anyone or anything else. We were young and naive and we were deeply in love.

Time passed quickly. Two years later, on a rainy day in South Bend, Indiana, John and I graduated from the University of Notre Dame with our Bachelors of Science degrees in Electrical Engineering. The rain didn't even begin to dampen our moods. At long last, real life was just around the corner, and we couldn't wait to begin. Two weeks before graduation John had asked me to marry him and I had accepted with all my heart. Although the wedding was over a year away, we were already newlyweds in our dreams, anxiously awaiting the magical life we were planning together. We moved to Phoenix and dove into our new careers with great zeal.

Phoenix appeared to be one constant vacation destination with its mountains looming up in the midst of the city and the palm trees swaying in the warm starry nights. In the evenings, after work and after dinner, John and I drove high into the Phoenix Mountain Preserve and sat perched over the city, watching the sparkling lights beneath us. As we held each other, his warm breath on my face held the promise of sunny days forever. Life was all so wonderful. The new jobs were interesting, the money infinitely more abundant than our cash flow had ever been in our young adult lives, and the times so much simpler than they were soon to become. We spent our first year after college playing, getting accustomed to our new roles as young professionals, and working on our wedding plans. We bought a house and filled the place with our dreams.

After a fairy-tale wedding in June of 1987 and a beautiful honeymoon in Bermuda, we returned to our lives in Phoenix. We cooked our first married meal in the bright and shining kitchen of our new home. We served ourselves on a small card table covered with some brightly colored fabric that I'd found on sale and feasted on tacos that tasted as good as if they'd been prepared in the world's finest restaurant. Love cast its magic on all that we touched. We didn't know that in a very short time, "real life" would cast a cruel shadow on the brightness of our married bliss.

Most nights I beat John home from work by at least ten or fifteen minutes which gave me just enough time to change clothes and start dinner. Cooking for a man I loved was a joy. In fact, doing anything that made him happy gave me great pleasure. I liked my new role as wife, and I loved my new life. Without fail, just after I set the table, I would hear the garage door opening, hear the key in the lock, and rush to the door to meet him. I kissed him every evening as he returned home, happy to be together again after spending eight hours apart.

Today, something was wrong. I sensed trouble when I came bounding to greet John and in place of his usual smile, I saw a somber countenance. I was immediately alarmed. I had never seen him this dejected and despondent. "What's wrong? What happened?" I questioned. "You're not going to like this," he said, and buying some time, told me he would explain over dinner. I went back to my preparations, wondering what on earth could dim that endless smile. "Had he been transferred?" That was the only thing I could think of. "It doesn't matter," I told myself. I would follow him to the ends of the earth.

We sat down and I stared at him expectantly and uneasily. He took a deep breath. "I have to work second shift every other two weeks. We won't see each other awake. I don't have any say in the matter." The words hit me like a lead balloon. A heavy feeling formed in the pit of my stomach as we watched each other across the table. Second shift. Every two weeks. That might be no big deal to some people, but to two newlyweds the thought of being apart for several hours was painful enough. Two weeks seemed to be an eternity. "How long do you have to do this?" I asked slowly, playing with my fork and not knowing what else to say. "I don't know." He turned away. "It could be for up to two years."

"Years?!" I was incredulous. This wasn't right. This couldn't be happening to us. We were supposed to be living happily-ever-after, and now we wouldn't even see each other awake fifty percent of the time? The situation didn't make any sense. "Why?!" I practically shouted. I wasn't mad at John. I just felt utterly and completely helpless. He explained patiently. He had struggled with the question himself. "There's limited lab equipment at work, and we don't have enough daylight hours remaining before the deadline to finish our testing. The people in my group are going to have to work around the clock." He became silent. "Two years." Two years seemed like such a long time.

We faced each other again waiting for someone to offer an alternative. "I could quit my job," John said at long last. I knew he didn't really want to do that either. We didn't even know if that was feasible. We had been lucky to get jobs in the same city. We were only just beginning to establish ourselves. We finally felt as if we were starting to know something about our work and to fit in. I couldn't ask him to give all that up. Besides, we had house payments and car payments too. We couldn't afford for either one of us to be unemployed for long. We considered our options until late into the night when we finally gave up and resigned ourselves to the situation. "Two years?!" had turned into a quieter, "Well, it's only for two years. We'll make it. We'll survive. Love conquers all, doesn't it?"

The days and nights without seeing each other awake passed slowly and painfully. Coming home to an empty house that had been for a few weeks filled with conversation and deep caring was a cruel letdown. There were days when I was OK with the situation. I would microwave my dinner, visit the health club, and sink into a novel. Then there were other days when the arrangement wasn't OK. I would bounce through the door happy from a good day at work and longing to share my good news with John. Instead, the silence pounded as loudly as clanging gongs through my head. I sank to the floor and cried tears of loneliness and frustration. I was too new to the area to have made any friends yet. John was everything to me and he wasn't here. "This is pretty close to hell," I thought vehemently. I had known the feeling of being loved for the first time in my life, and now I felt robbed of the experience and cheated out of the first few years of my marriage.

I made my first quilt during those times, waiting up every night until 1:00 a.m. so I could visit with John for a brief half hour when he got home. Then, I would collapse exhausted, only to face my own alarm clock ringing at 5:30 a.m. the next morning. The quilt was a beautiful queen-sized patchwork pattern covered with hearts. I poured my love into my stitching because my new husband wasn't there to receive the emotion. I tried not to let him see the sadness and the tears. I tried not to feel the pain of the separation. I buried my feelings and wondered if I was destined to always feel as if love were just around the next corner. John and I became players trapped in our own private tragedy. Love was so close and yet so far. Surely, Romeo and Juliet, even separated by death, were closer than we were in real life.

When we were together, we bore the sadness of our separation stoically, reminding each other that we had a good life. Neither one of us wanted to tell the other how much we hated the situation. "It isn't John's fault," I told myself time and again, trying not to feel so angry. The hours were already hard enough on him without me complaining. "We're so lucky to be in love and have good jobs," we told each other over dinner on the weekends. "We really can't complain." We repeated the vicious lie over and over again until we actually believed the statement to be true.

Slowly but surely, we built a trap in our own thinking that would erode away the closeness we once shared and keep us imprisoned for years in the darkness of our own private labyrinths of emotion. Fearful of sharing feelings that might make life even more difficult, we buried our thoughts, becoming more resentful of life and each other. Silently, separately, we allowed our frustration to fester. I would get angry with John for not changing his situation then immediately feel guilty because I knew he couldn't. He got frustrated for the same reasons. I waited up for him only to find he was too tired at that late hour to think of anything but resting. He never knew how desperately I wanted to be held. I interpreted his late-night hands-off policy as disinterest. My mind began to weave elaborate tales that told me I was no longer attractive to him. He began to feel inadequate. I worked harder than ever to be a "good wife" and buried myself in my work so I could avoid the feelings of increasing loneliness.

I should have learned the lesson my garden had to teach me before the weeds grew too tall in my own marriage. Love may be the seed, but a relationship requires care and tending. If you don't take time to thin out the practices that don't work, nurture the good habits, and enjoy the fruits of this labor, a marriage begins to wither or at best simply doesn't grow. The odd shifts at work weren't driving us apart; instead, the lack of sharing and nurturing between us was the subtle killer. Instead of being honest with ourselves and each other, the fears of exposing our feelings of loneliness and frustration were simply making them all the worse.

By the time John returned to regular shifts two years later, our new habit patterns were so deeply ingrained that we no longer remembered the joy of new love. Our schedules were never quite synchronized. When one of our positions demanded massive overtime, the other somehow ended up working forty-hour weeks. We actually convinced ourselves that this was a good thing.

At least one of us could be home to "man the fort" and take care of the chores.

We still loved each other, but we had no time. Once vibrant youths, filled with the joy of first love, we became pragmatic adults working to pay for the life we were buying, forgetting that there were things that were more important to us than money, and wondering all the time if "real" life weren't just around the corner.

We were in cruise control, going quickly on a path without a firm destination, not quite knowing what we really wanted but hoping something good awaited us. Like Daedalus, we were trapped in a labyrinth of our own design. We had been there so long, we didn't even notice. Not until we were temporarily removed from the distractions of our busy lifestyle did we realize the great loss we had allowed ourselves to suffer.

— § —

The moon shone brightly overhead like a giant luminescent pearl in the dark clamshell dome of the night sky. The sea lapped up and back, tickling the shores of the white sand beach only one hundred yards from where we sat. Balmy breezes carrying the passionate perfumed fragrance of plumeria rustled through the palms, making them dance as frivolously as the skirts on a Tahitian hula dancer. Meanwhile, in sharp contrast to the bustling palm dance, soft strains of piano music filtered toward us from somewhere in the open-air courtyard of the stately hotel.

The buffet spread before us was a feast fit for a king and queen: fresh seafood fettuccine, just-picked-today ripe island fruit, a huge salad, cheeses and meats of every kind, and tempting desserts. The spread tantalized our senses, while our table awaited us on the open-air terrace of the restaurant, lit only by a single candle and the full moon. John and I should have been in heaven.

For months, we had been saving our money and planning, in intricate detail, this fifth anniversary dream vacation to Hawaii. We charted a fourteen-day, four-island trip to paradise that could have been any couple's fantasy. We had looked forward to the trip and eagerly counted the days, feeling sure that once we had some quality time together in a romantic and tropical atmosphere, we would be able to instantly rekindle a flame that had been waning without fuel for years.

Only three days into the fantasy we were surrounded by everything we had wished for and so much more. We had a hotel room with an incredible view of the crystal-clear waters of Waikiki. Upon our arrival, we were given a bountiful fruit basket that served as our breakfast in heaven the next day. On our second day, we traveled to see Pearl Harbor and the windy cliff side views offered by Nu'u anu Pali. Today we had driven around the island exploring beaches that each offered us a different treat. We snorkeled at the marine preserve in Hanaumu Bay, napped after lunch on an idyllic strip of sand on the eastern shore, body-surfed in the afternoon at the famous Waimea Bay, and then watched the sun melt below the horizon at aptly-named Sunset beach. Tired now and a bit sun-washed, we piled our plates high before the buffet closed for the night, and sank into the comfortable chairs beside our table.

We ate in silence. I looked around and tried to ignore the dark thoughts that had been haunting me for the past two days. I savored the sweetly scented air and tried to allow the gentle sounds of the waves and the music to drown out my growing dissatisfaction. I waited for the wind's caress to clear the foreboding thoughts from my mind. The exotic moon shone overhead, brightly illuminating the darkest shadows of night and, in a setting where romance practically begged to blossom, the moon was also shedding light into the dark recesses of my soul.

I looked at John and said something. He replied quickly and became immersed once again in the delicious pasta. I stabbed a piece of papaya on my plate a bit too vehemently, and started to get angry. "Why was it," I wondered, "that we never seemed to have much to talk about?" Oh, we were fine during the days when we were active. We talked and laughed about our adventures, and held hands, looking outwardly like a couple deeply in love. At night, however, when we had already talked about the day's activities, when we had time alone and nothing to do, there was a strange silence between us, thick and syrupy, that seemed to prevent any meaningful conversation.

"What was wrong with him? Why weren't we this happy couple anymore? How could we act so close and feel so distant?" The thoughts I had been avoiding for the past few days swirled through my mind in an angry torrent. "I spent so much money on this trip. I planned every detail. And here we were on the date from heaven and he was taking all of this for granted!" I fumed inside as I quietly ate my dinner and stared at the handsome but impassive face of the man sitting across from me.

A pang of sadness and longing, sharp as a knife, twisted through my heart. "Where was the man with whom I had fallen in love," I wondered desperately, no longer angry. I could no longer ignore the fact that our relationship wasn't the happy and carefree bond we had once shared. I could no longer lie to myself and say things were fine. I couldn't even admit that I liked my so-called wonderful career. I was working so hard, but for what? When I got what I wanted I still wasn't satisfied. The thoughts pounded me like stormy waves.

Then and there, in the midst of heaven on earth, an ugly insight struck me with the force of a sharp blow to the gut. No! No. Oh no. "Better to ask where is the woman with whom John fell in love?" The thought I hadn't asked for popped into my mind, and I choked back sudden tears. "Oh God, who was I anyhow, any more?" I really didn't know myself. Playing with food that no longer looked so good, I realized that the success I had worked so hard to achieve hadn't even brought me close to the happiness I desperately sought. I blinked my eyes quickly as a single tear fell, and in that flash, I saw John and myself five years earlier, discussing the bright dreams we had for our future together. A dashed and crumpled script for our lives that was never played out, those dreams now taunted me seeming as cruelly frivolous and foolish as they had once seemed real.

"John," I said, and he looked up at me. "I love you. I really do." I wanted desperately to feel once more the truth of that statement. "I love you too," he said. We both felt the empty feeling behind the words spoken with as much sincerity as we could muster. After dinner, we walked, and then sat side by side on the sands of Waikiki. We talked long into the night, wondering aloud how we could be so much in love and yet feel so distant. Like two marooned victims of a shipwreck, we knew we were survivors and yet we didn't know how to get back to where we had been before. We doodled idly in the sand, avoiding the pain in each other's eyes, each feeling at fault for the situation but not knowing exactly why. At one point we stared at each other, our eyes moist with tears uncried. I reached for his hand, and for a brief instant, our once-forgotten dreams of a better life became real again—a tantalizing glimpse into a future that still held promise. I leaned on his shoulder and for the first time in a very long time, he put his arm around my waist. Reaching for words, grasping for the right thing to say in order to verbalize the feeling that was about to spill over, I vowed that I would make whatever changes were necessary to find satisfaction in my life. I was blissfully ignorant of the changes that would be required for me to fulfill that promise. We kissed—a real kiss—and I realized for the first time that heaven was not what surrounded me, but rather what I found inside. I wondered why the realization had been so long in coming.

In retrospect, I know that Spirit had been whispering to me for some time before that difficult night in Hawaii. Like a spring stretched too far from center, I had felt the tension gradually building. I found myself expending more and more effort to maintain my position that life was fine—"just fine, thank you"—exactly as it was. I felt pulled in many different directions by conflicting demands on my time and energies. Spirit was the force that called me to stop the struggle and return to my center. Spirit guided me to a place and time, on my vacation in Hawaii, where I would be forced to admit the truth of my longings and the lie I had been living.

Each of us has hidden monsters. They're the things about ourselves that we don't want to face and wouldn't want to admit: feelings of inadequacy or unworthiness; aspects of our life that don't quite work the way we would like them to; dreams that have been forgotten; careers we don't love; relationships that don't fulfill us. Ever fearful of looking incompetent, ungrateful, or worse yet, weak and out of control, we lock these fears deep within our own minds—so deep that, for the most part, we forget they even exist. Every now and then, however, the beast demands to be fed, causing us to react in ways that surprise ourselves: sinking us into a sudden depression, or having us roar uncharacteristically in sudden anger. The beast causes us to repeat pathways in our own labyrinth of life until, like Theseus, we are brave enough to go within and face the monster; or like Daedalus, we are willing to rise above the dead-ends and twisted pathways we've created to view our lives from a slightly higher perspective.

Life is the mythical labyrinth. We cruise through our days calmly and contentedly, happy to be in motion, but not worrying too much about our destination. Sometimes we settle for mediocrity and resign ourselves to a "pretty good" life. Other times we find ourselves living brilliant lives that fulfill everyone else's hopes, dreams, and expectations while ignoring our own. When we find ourselves seemingly lost in a situation we can no longer tolerate, we finally begin to question our choices. Through the pain and confusion, Spirit is finally granted an opportunity to let its voice be heard in our lives.

In some of our darkest moments, Spirit speaks. I've come to learn that if I'm frustrated, feeling stuck, or at the end of my rope, chances are I've wound myself too deeply in the maze. These are the times when I need to trust that Spirit, who holds the mythical golden cord, will guide me back to the light, or like Daedalus, will help me rise above the situation and see the big picture. These are the times when our questions begin to open the doors of our consciousness, to welcome the whispered answers that were always there.

Chapter 2
Whispers in the Night

Feeling drunk and heady from the kiss, I watched the silver shaft of moonlight reflect off the undulating black-glass surface of the midnight ocean. The motion was hypnotic. Back and forth, the waves crashed up on the shore then slid into the darkness of an eternal sea. The stars above glittered brightly—tiny points far away in time and space. For a split second I felt... something... centered between the sky and the land and the sea, dancing with the motion of the ocean, sliding with the earth as she whirled around the sun in the void of endless space. The feeling of being in motion with all of creation was almost palpable. The feeling of being an integral part of a much larger whole was overwhelming. Then, as quickly as I felt the sensation, the moment was gone and John and I sat alone on the beach—two tiny humans who were microscopic compared to the larger view all around us. "My problems," I thought, "are insignificant compared to the immensity of life." I snuggled closer to John. The sand was cool underneath us, but my beating heart was warm again and my soul was joyful. I was grateful to be alive. In that moment, for just an instant, my future seemed clear, my dreams attainable, and my marriage deeply fulfilling.

— § —

Two weeks after the trip I sat at my desk at work with my head propped up in my hands. I was reading

DO-178B—the government publication written by the Federal Aviation Administration that regulates the production of software intended for use in commercial airplane computer systems. This document was destined to save lives, but at the moment, it was doing a fine job of lulling me to sleep. I sighed, shifted my posture, and let my mind wander. "What was I doing with my life?" In Hawaii, my priorities had seemed so clear. I felt strong and confident that I would go back home, shift my attitude, love my job, and have plenty of time to enjoy with John. Immersed once again in the demands of every day living, I experienced the familiar confusion and doubt as I considered my options for the future. What on earth was wrong with my life?

I didn't share the same lust for my profession as did many of my peers. Solving a complex software problem or creating an intricate new design just didn't give me any inner satisfaction, other than feeling good about a job well done. "What would I do if I weren't an engineer?" The question that plagued me seemed absurd. "I am an engineer," I reminded myself, as if I were explaining an obvious fact to a very young child. I couldn't imagine throwing away four years of college to pursue another line of work. I couldn't even entertain the thought of giving up the high salary and prestige that I enjoyed by virtue of being a woman in my profession. How many times had I introduced myself to someone and then immediately told him or her that I worked in the avionics industry? How many times had I bragged excitedly about the test flights where I stood behind the pilot for five hours at a time answering questions and making sure that the computers worked properly? How many times had I used my career as a means of earning automatic respect? "Every time I met someone," I answered my own question glumly. Invariably, when I told people what I did for a living, their eyes widened and they automatically treated me as an intelligent and successful woman. How could I give that up? Who would I be without this career?

"I don't have to leave engineering," I reassured the portion of myself that always cringed in fear at this line of thinking. "I could always change jobs." My current tasks were interesting but the corporate politics were driving me crazy. Five engineers and I comprised a small research and development team responsible for designing an Electronic Library System that would store pilot and maintenance data on optical disks onboard the airplane. We had prototyped the system, demonstrated the concept to various major airlines, and were now considering the technical and legal details of putting the real system together.

The job sounded wonderful, but the behavior of corporate management had dampened my enthusiasm considerably. Publicly, at air shows and trade conventions, the marketing folks and upper level managers bragged endlessly about our new product. Internally, our small group had to fight the bureaucracy to buy the equipment we needed and to prevent upper management from making promises to the airlines that would create an engineering nightmare for us. With my rather one-sided perspective at the time, I felt like we were being paid lip service in the upper echelons of the corporation while being asked to create a miracle with one hand tied behind our backs.

"I could switch companies," I reasoned, adding pragmatically, "but I doubt that would solve anything." Surely there were no perfect workplaces. Plus, I had done all I could to develop an excellent reputation in my current position. In return, I received above-average performance reviews, good raises, and sufficient recognition for my efforts. If I left, I would have to start all over again. "Wouldn't that be a waste of five years?" My logic spun in the same endless circle each time I considered the matter. "Maybe you should just be happy with what you have," answered the voice of my upbringing.

The voices of my own truth were becoming more insistent. I could no longer ignore the fact that I went home most days tired and frustrated, feeling devoid of purpose. I wondered if anything I did at work really mattered in the larger scheme of life. My negative outlook, hidden well beneath a cheerful countenance, wasn't helping me find a solution to my problems. "What can I do?" I got a headache every time I tried to puzzle out the answer that useless question. I couldn't stomach the thought of living in a future that promised only more of the same confusion and futility that I currently felt, but I saw no other choices. Doing what many of us do when every other resource fails to answer our life's toughest questions, I turned to God and prayed fervently. "Please, please help me improve my marriage, love my career, and figure out a way to feel like something I'm doing is worthwhile," I implored. "I want to wake up happy, go to bed grateful, and make a decent living." I felt as if I was asking for a miracle.

Spirit hears every prayer, fulfills every intention, and answers every question—but typically not in the ways we might expect.

— § —

As far as I knew, the miracle never came. Day after day I waited faithfully for some insight to strike me, some feeling of, "Ah ha! That's what I need to do to be happy." I wanted God to give me a checklist of things to do and a road map that would lead me step by step into my ideal future. Instead, work continued as usual. Although John and I were conscientious about spending more time together, we still felt as if the spark between us was missing. I angrily questioned whether or not my prayers were being heard then, feeling utterly despondent, conceded that God must have bigger problems to deal with than making some spoiled engineering woman's already-good life better. If I could have seen through my soul's eyes at the time, I would have laughed at my own despair. While I was busy bemoaning the fact that God must be punishing me for being so ungrateful, events were transpiring that would eventually lead me to live a life that was more fulfilling than I could possibly imagine at the time. I didn't realize that I would first have to embark on a path of spiritual growth in order to allow the very things I desired to come into my life.

Well-meaning friends knew of my struggle and lent me all sorts of self-help and personal growth books. Being a voracious reader, I traveled often to the new bookstore in town and wandered up and down sections I had never considered before. New types of books attracted me now, beckoning me to explore ideas and concepts that shocked me and caused me to question the assumptions I had always believed to be fact. Could there really be unseen dimensions of reality? Did we as souls, really have the option to chose the fates that befell us here on earth? Was the benevolent Grandpa-in-the-Sky figure of God that I worshipped a mere metaphor for a more mysterious force that was the creator, source, and substance of all life? The more I learned, the more I questioned.

During this period of my unrest, a series of "chance" coincidences motivated me to maintain a journal of my nighttime dreams. A friend called to relate a particularly vivid dream that had been haunting him. A homework assignment in a seminar I was attending involved recording my dreams. At the bookstore, the cover of a book attracted me from several feet away and I was hardly surprised to find that I had selected a treatise on dream interpretation. I was beginning to discard my belief in chance. Perhaps there really were no accidents in life. I bought the book and began to record my dreams for the first time since high school.

My dreams were a curious mixture of life experience and bizarre fantasy. Some were random pictures strung together as haphazardly as a bad collage, but many more were complete stories with themes or mythological overtones that echoed the issues I faced in my everyday life. Despite what I had learned in high school science class, I found the symbology in my dreams too rich to attribute solely to the chance firings of nerve cells, and too meaningful to simply be a by-product of my brain's filing system. My sense of hopelessness and desperation with life gave way to a tentative sense of adventure. Within my dreams, I received curious insights and whispers of truth that hinted at changes soon to occur in my waking life.

"Huh?" I gasped. "Oh." I rolled over in bed and hit the alarm clock that sounded like a large chainsaw cutting through the thick curtain of sleep that had been drawn over me after the first alarm rang only ten minutes ago. "Oh boy," I mumbled, trying to open my eyes, "another long day ahead." I laid back on the bed, closed my eyes and replayed a strange dream that still danced through my mind:

In the dream, a woman and two men were searching through the halls of an institution for a large nun who was the establishment's proprietor. When they found her, they asked her if they could borrow some jackets because the weather outside was cold in the pre-dawn hour and they wanted to watch the sun rise from the rim of the nearby Grand Canyon.

The nun became frightened, convinced that these people intended to hurt her. The two men and the lady assured the nun that they meant her no harm, but she didn't believe them. Backing away in fear, she stepped through the glass window of her second-story office and crashed to the ground where she broke and shattered as if she were made of a thousand pieces of glass.

I awoke and thought to myself, "What does this mean?" Immediately the words, "The last bastions of the establishment are crumbling," popped into my head and echoed loudly as I rubbed the sleep from my eyes.

The last bastions of the establishment were indeed crumbling within the structure of my psyche. Spirit was whispering in my dreams, calling me to recognize the truths that my conscious mind was not yet ready to accept. My assumptions, attitudes, and beliefs about myself, my life and others were thought forms living in a glass house—an old establishment that I had built in my mind over the years. The walls of this mental establishment were about to come crashing down.

— § —

A month passed and my dream was all but forgotten. I sat in an uncomfortable straight-backed chair, crammed into a room with over one hundred other people who most likely, like me, been talked into taking a miserable personal development seminar. I wondered if they had all been sold a too-good-to-be-true story of having major revelations about their life over the course of a weekend. "What the heck am I doing here?" I asked myself squirming impatiently in my seat. The air-conditioning was set a little too low and I was chilly. I sat on my hands to warm them. Outside, the weather looked perfect. Through the tiny slats of the blinds in the narrow windows of the second-story room I could see cotton clouds drifting through the turquoise sky. I could have been hiking, gardening, or doing a thousand other things on this rare weekend away from work. Instead, I was sitting in the same room with the same people for two days. "I must be an idiot," I chastised myself. "I should just walk out."

My mind drifted with the clouds. I was still searching for the unnamable something that would make my life worth living. I was still grasping at straws and wishing desperately that I could find someone or something that would give me a peek at a better future than the one that currently lay before me. A few days after my dream about the establishment, a good friend called up raving about this great seminar he had taken. "It'll change your perspective on life," he told me. "You'll love it." I trusted my friend's advice and registered for what now seemed like a three-day mental marathon rather than a period of spiritual enlightenment.

As the cloud drifting by the window passed out of my view, my attention snapped back to the present moment. Time seemed to stretch on into infinity. The seminar moderator was having yet another brutal dialog with one of the participants. "Will this never end?" I grimaced. I was getting a headache. "She's so almighty arrogant." I secretly wondered how anyone else could stand to listen to her for so long. She seemed so triumphant as she relegated one person after another to tears after making them see that their life was a big play act based on some assumptions made in early childhood. I couldn't stand her. I thought I would burst if she delivered one more harsh statement. The word "bitch" came to mind.

Even the melodrama was getting old after twenty hours of this stuff. "Why don't you leave?" I asked myself for the twentieth time. A faint glimmer of honesty told me that a fainter glimmer of hope was keeping me glued to my chair. I really did want to learn something from all of this.

I thought about the points the leader was trying to make during the course of each conversation. "Yeah sure, we all made decisions about ourselves in early childhood," I thought. "I know that. Everyone who's ever read any basic psychology or self-help book knows that. Big deal." What was causing these proud professionals to break down in tears, sighing with relief as they found out they didn't have to keep on acting the way they had been acting? "Maybe they had never read the books or examined their own lives," I thought. "I guess I would be having a religious experience too if, all of a sudden, I figured out that I could do anything I wanted to do." My thoughts were becoming ugly and sarcastic. "I know I can do anything I want to do. I just don't know what I want to do. I'm not here to get some almighty revelation or mystical insight that I can do whatever I want. Besides," I told myself contemptuously, "anything I've ever set my mind to do, I've done!"

"And furthermore," I thought, contemplating another point that the moderator had made repeatedly as she reminded participants not to blame their failures on their childhoods or their parents, "I've been through all this stuff about forgiving your parents." I had read so much about "releasing childhood emotions," that I was tired of the topic. I had already examined my own past to see how my earlier days affected my present. I already had my eye-opening insights. Unlike the others in the room who were sharing their stories, I didn't have any huge trauma or skeletons in the closet. I had never been abused. "Things are just fine between my parents and me now," I thought, a bit defensively. "Yeah, so they weren't at one time, but we're on good terms now. So, things still aren't perfect. So what? Life isn't perfect. That's normal, isn't it?" The smallest doubt inside betrayed my confidence. The conversation outside droned on. "I can't take any more of this." My head pounded.

My thoughts turned venomous as I shifted in my chair. I glanced at my watch and wondered if we were ever going break for dinner. I didn't see where my current train of thought was leading. My anger gave way to frustration. I felt cheated. I had paid good money for this seminar that was supposed to help me figure out what I wanted out of life and I was determined to get my money's worth. "I'll make that woman tell me what I can do to clarify my goals," I thought caustically. "If she can," I added. My hand shot up in the air signaling that I wanted to speak.

I waited with my arm stiff as a wire antenna. My face became hotter, and my jaw tightened. I realized I was struggling to remain civil. I was tired, uncomfortable, and cranky, and I really wanted to lash out at this venomous woman who seemed to be dishing out nothing but pain to the people who conversed with her. Never mind their seeming gratitude at the end of a discussion. They were probably just relieved to be done with her. I was seething, but I held myself in check. I was going to get that woman to tell me just exactly what the heck I was paying her to do. She glanced my way and indicated I could speak. I played according to the seminar "rules" and stood up in front of my chair, while accepting a microphone from one of the "helpers." I wondered what on earth had possessed the young woman to volunteer for three long days of work without pay. I looked around as the people in the packed room looked my way.

I took a deep breath and with as much decency as I could muster said slowly and deliberately, "I would like you to tell me just what I am paying for. I feel like this whole thing is a waste of my time and money. You aren't telling me anything new. This stuff is in all the books." The microphone whined. My boldness and the edge in my voice startled me. I was never, ever this rude even when I was angry. "Too much sitting and too little sleep," I thought, wondering what she would come up with. Underneath the surface of my words was the desperate challenge. "OK, look at me. Tell me what's wrong with my life if you're at all worth what I paid you."

On her podium at the front of the room the moderator stood still as a statue. She looked at me and I felt her eyes as if they were steel clamps gripping my gaze and forcing me to focus all my attention on what she was about to say. She inhaled just slightly before she delivered me a verbal one-two punch, telling me in few words that I was self-righteous, arrogant, and a jerk. I felt like she had breathed fire on me. She turned as if that was all she had to say.

I was furious now. Hair was standing up on the back of my neck. I could feel my face getting hotter by the minute. The woman was going to leave me alone after making that statement? I couldn't believe what I just heard. I was paying for this? Ready to vent my frustration I opened my mouth to tell the woman just what I thought of her affront. Instead, my words and the tone of my voice betrayed my lack of self-confidence and hinted at the despair lying just beneath the surface of the conversation.

"Then tell me what you see!" I choked out, surprised to find that in my frustration and exhaustion I was near tears. "Sure my parents yelled at me but I wasn't abused. I didn't have trauma like all these other people." I couldn't believe what I was spewing aloud. "You don't want to hear it." I wasn't sure if the moderator spoke the words aloud or if they simply emerged from the depths of my own mind.

I was broken now, in tears like everyone else. I didn't want to hear what she had to say. Deep, deep down, I probably knew the truth that was about to hit me in the face, and I wanted desperately to avoid the facts, run from them, and hide. Using the same tone that I had considered harsh and arrogant, she finished me off, telling me bluntly that I was the type who always had to be perfect, who never felt good enough, and who refused to accept even my own human nature. Her voice softened just a bit and in her eyes I saw a flash of deep compassion before the mask of harsh honesty reappeared. "And," I finished the conversation in my own mind, "I have lived my whole life based on those assumptions."

She was finished. I sat down in my chair as the roomful of people was dismissed for dinner. I hated that woman so badly. I hated her for ripping open the curtains of illusion I had worn before the world. "She's right," I cursed inwardly. I wanted everyone to leave me alone so I could crawl like a wounded animal into some corner and sob. My eyes were still seeping as I held my breath and braced my chin to stop the tears. I ran to the restroom and splashed cold water on my face. I didn't want that woman to see how much she had gotten to me. I didn't want to let her know how much I hurt. I didn't want to believe what I knew to be true.

I choked back more tears and joined the others for dinner. No one said much. No one could. We were all in the same boat. There were no secrets in this crowd and yet I still didn't feel safe. I felt as if I had been stripped naked before the world and hung out for all to see. "Hi, I'm Ann. You're right, I never feel good enough. I work so hard. I do everything I can. I succeed at everything I try and still I don't do enough. They never loved me," I cried inside, surprised that I still felt that way about my parents. Where did *that* thought come from? I was over that feeling, wasn't I? I knew better—my parents and I had discussed the incidents in my childhood that made me feel unloved. They had explained to me how they did love me in spite of circumstances that had made me think otherwise, and I understood them, or so I thought. Yet here I was, heart aching again with the pain of over a decade of my childhood still unhealed. "Will this never end?" A lump formed in my throat as I choked, trying so hard for the millionth time in my life not to cry. Anything to distract me, anything. "How dare she call me names?!" I thought of the moderator and got angry again. Anger helped me to escape from feeling the old pain. I was so tired.

I suffered silently through the remainder of the seminar and left enraged. I still didn't understand how the revelation that I always assumed I "wasn't good enough" would make my life better. Not until I walked into work the next day did I see just how much my perspective had shifted. As the months after the seminar passed I began to realize just how much of what that woman had said was true. I learned by observing myself in day-to-day interactions that many of my mannerisms, habits, and ways of reacting were a defense mechanism put in place years ago to prevent others from seeing how deeply insecure I was and how desperately I wanted love.

I was sickened to see just how much of my behavior was designed during my early teenage years. When people argued at work I was subconsciously reminded of my childhood. I did everything humanly possible to appease the opposing parties. I found myself wanting to "help" anyone with a troubled relationship, and as a result, I often became way too deeply involved in other people's problems. I felt like a trapped animal when anyone raised his or her voice in front of me during meetings. I lost most of my inner self-control and wanted to lash out in a rage. Instead, I lost my voice suffered in ineffective silence. In those situations I felt like the teen I once was, who ran to her room afraid of sticking up for herself lest the argument become worse.

I noticed with disgust that I expected everyone I loved to eventually disappoint me. When I found myself getting upset at a small thing said or done by my husband or a friend, I would examine my behavior and attitudes and find that I carried within me a basic assumption that no one could be trusted with my heart. At some level, deep inside, I believed they would all betray me. Worse yet, like the child wanting praise for good grades, I worked hard to be perfect at everything I did. I judged my very worth as a human being by the results I produced. I reminded myself often that I was very lucky to have the background and the education that I did, and I worked hard not to "waste" it. I apologized for the slightest imperfections in my own work, preferring to criticize myself before someone else did. On the outside I was the perfect worker, a great wife, and a good human being. On the inside I was a desperate child, screaming out for love and yet pushing love away because I was afraid love wouldn't last.

At first, I felt worse than I did before I had all these "insights." "Life was truly easier when I was ignorant," I told myself at times when I noticed the tenth instance on a given day when I was re-enacting my past rather than responding to the present moment. I began to notice that I wasn't alone. Other people were acting out their childhood mini-dramas in their adult lives as well. I saw the principle of past-affects-present in people all around me. Some were like me—perfectionists who could never please anyone, least of all themselves. Others believed themselves to be victims of circumstance, convinced that life owed them something so much more, but not willing to do anything to further their goals. Still others worked hard to maintain an image that was socially acceptable, even if that meant making others look bad. "We're all like this," I thought, "each of us wearing many masks to conceal the secret vulnerable faces that hide underneath the layers we've built for protection."

This understanding gave me hope that perhaps I wasn't hopeless after all. I learned to see myself with a little more compassion—human foibles and all. I practiced observing my behavior and attitudes with diligence. I questioned why I was acting a certain way when I felt upset or powerless. I didn't realize that I was doing the kindergarten exercises that would one day enable me to create magic and miracles in my own life.

In the midst of the turmoil and confusion that resulted from my newfound insights, new life and new hope was springing forth in my consciousness. My earlier dream had been right. The last bastions of the inner establishment of my identity were crumbling; indeed, they had been shattered. I was watching the dawning of a new day in my life from a higher perspective, and I was cold and frightened at times in this pre-dawn hour of my new life. Nonetheless, even before I learned to consciously listen to the voices of Spirit in my waking life, the messages were getting clearer in my dreams.

Last night I dreamt I was in a house with Belle, the young heroine from Disney's movie "Beauty and the Beast." She and I were racing through the rooms, moving incredibly fast, as if our lives depended on how quickly we could run. We dashed through an open doorway and breathlessly bolted the door shut behind us. As we caught our breath, we looked around the room in which we were trapped. We had cornered ourselves in a dungeon with walls that were made of cartoon-like bright blue stones.

I heard a deep compassionate voice coming out of nowhere that remarked, as if to someone else, "The cartoon stones are being used in this picture to make the dungeon seem less real. We don't want to scare the children." Shivers ran up and down my spine in the dream. For just a moment, my thoughts were coming from a different perspective. I knew the voice was referring to Belle and me when it talked about "the children." I understood that the dream scene was being concocted to teach me something, and they, whoever "they" were, didn't want to scare me. Unfortunately, "they" didn't have names or faces.

Meanwhile, Belle and I knew we couldn't go back the way we came, so we searched for an alternate way out of the room. A small window high up on one wall appeared to be our only means of escape. Gingerly we climbed up cold stones until we were close enough to break the glass and step through the tiny window. Instead of being on solid ground again, we were dismayed to find ourselves on the rooftop in the pouring rain. Belle jumped down to the ground easily but I hesitated and cowered as I peered over the roof's edge. Visibility was poor, the roof was slippery, and the ground was far below. My stomach was knotted with fear. I looked over the edge again and pulled back, but as I did so, the key to my house dropped out of my pocket and landed beneath me. I was faced with a dilemma—I was afraid to jump and afraid that if I did not, I would lose my key. The alarm clock rang and I bolted awake, rubbing my eyes to erase the feelings of unease that lingered beyond the dream.

The story replayed itself over and over in my mind long after I showered and ate my breakfast. Driving to work, the images still haunted me and begged me to examine them for a deeper message. "Maybe this one will uncover a few more answers," I thought. I still had plenty of questions.

My life had recently taken yet another unexpected turn. At work, rumors were flying fast and furiously that our small research and development team would be dissolved. The airline industry, which lags the U.S. economy by about two years, was in the process of entering an economic slump. Airlines were becoming more competitive for business and fare wars were cutting into their profits. The resulting cutbacks in airline spending translated into financial losses for the avionics industry. Managers at my company appeared to be doing what they could to forestall the impending layoffs, but as the financial situation became grimmer, the people in my group knew that it was only a matter of time before the funds supporting our project would be cut. We worked, waited, and wondered what would happen to us.

There were daily murmurings in the lunchroom that said we would be transferred onto different projects. As a result, there were daily grumblings within our small team. "Why do anything if we're just going to be disbanded?" I heard my peers say the same thing almost every morning. Tense and belligerent about the situation, two of the guys complained regularly that we were pawns in a corporate game in which only we would be the losers. "We're useful," one of them would say, "but expendable." The biting sarcasm was almost palpable. I wish I could say that I rose above the negativity and complaining, but I too harbored a grudge against those managers who, with a single stroke of a pen on paper, could alter my future without ever considering my opinion.

One night a week, I attended seminars that taught me about taking control over my thoughts and assuming more responsibility for my future. The timing could not have been more perfect. Truth is truth, I learned, available in many different guises. I found I could apply the same principles to my life that I took for granted as part of the engineering process: design first, take action to build your vision, reassess the situation to make sure you've created what you wanted, then repeat the process all over again.

So, what was my current vision? I didn't know until one night when I stood in front of a classroom filled with people and told them what was important to me. The thought had come to mind suddenly and easily, despite my hesitation to participate in the exercise. "My vision is that people communicate, cooperate, and work together to create great things," I declared in a voice so loud and powerful that it shocked me. The feeling of standing tall, thinking clearly, and speaking with confidence was exciting. I raised my eyebrows in surprise and handed the microphone to the next person in line.

Communication and cooperation had always been very important to me. I realized that I was already living my vision at work. When I joined my group, there was serious tension between some of the strong-willed, albeit extremely intelligent people on the team. I consciously worked to smooth over the harsh words, to get the guys to understand one another's viewpoints, and to forgive each other's quirky mannerisms. Now we operated together like a well-oiled machine, teasing each other about the habits that used to infuriate us. We truly were "working together to create great things."

We already played an integral role in changing the way airlines would handle information storage and retrieval in the future. The insight struck me as powerfully as if someone had just flipped on a switch in the pitch-black labyrinth of my mind.

Suddenly I saw that I could be satisfied in a career where I had previously seen no higher purpose. At work the next day, I knew for the first time that my worth went far beyond my technical achievements. I felt that I was a much more important part of my team than I had ever allowed myself to believe. My life, in light of my personal vision, did have a meaning and a direction. My engineering work might pass away into obscurity some day, but at least I was making a difference in lives of the five people I worked with.

A week later, I received my transfer notice.

Mark's expression and the sinking feeling in the pit of my stomach told me that my worst nightmare was about to come true. "I need to talk to you," he said, avoiding my eyes. Mark had been my immediate boss for three years. I liked and respected him a great deal. "I've been transferred, haven't I?" I asked. I must have looked like I was about to become ill. "It's not all that bad," he said. "You've been loaned. We'll get you back in October." October? Nine months? Nine months on a program that the engineers in our group had sarcastically labeled "the black hole?" My heart sank.

The 777 Aircraft Information Management System project was one of the largest computer systems in aviation history designed and built by a single company. Over seven hundred engineers were employed on the project. They had been working sixty to seventy hours a week on average and were still worried about meeting what seemed to be impossible deadlines. We called the 777 program the "black hole" because management appeared to be "sucking" every available engineer from other departments onto the project. Even people who were loaned seemed to remain on the project forever. Now I had fallen into the "black hole."

"I tried to keep you in the group as long as I could," Mark apologized, "but this was inevitable. They need people over there very badly." I felt my face flush. All those times in the past when I had angrily sworn I would never let the company change my career direction without my permission flashed before my eyes. "Would I put my money where my mouth had been?" Mark watched me, and I became conscious of the fact that he knew how much I hated being transferred. He was concerned about my reaction. Actually, he looked like he was dreading the backlash. I softened a bit. I didn't want to take out my frustration on a man who had been a pleasure to work for and who had been so kind as to ask us earlier in the month where we preferred to work in case we were transferred. He had done all he could. "It's OK," I told him, trying to be reasonable.

"This could be a great career move," Mark said. He seemed visibly relieved that I hadn't become upset. "We picked you because you were best qualified for the job." "What job?" I asked. "You'll have to talk to your new boss, but I understand you'll be coordinating something over there in the test group." "Great," I thought, "I hate testing. Oh great." "I'll schedule an appointment with them next week," I said aloud. "I would like to wrap up my last project here." "That would be good," Mark said, "At least it's only nine months."

I walked slowly back to my desk where my peers waited to hear the details. Their faces wore a mixture of genuine sympathy and relief that they hadn't been the ones to go. "The new job won't be so bad," I said with a false smile. "I'm only on loan and besides, this will look great on my resume." The humor was faint and feeble. The underlying sarcasm was not. The smile remained plastered on my face until I escaped to my car at the end of the day. There I allowed my clenched jaw to quiver until I burst into angry tears driving out of the parking lot. "Just when I decided I liked what I'm doing..." I stormed. "What right do they have to move me to a new job that I'll probably hate, without even asking me first? What right?! If they had *asked* me and *explained* their reasons, I would feel a little better." Mark had asked, but he wasn't the one who was ultimately responsible for the 777 understaffing. "How can they just move lives around without even caring? Don't they know this screws up our productivity and motivation in a big way?" I raged and I cried until, on a long stretch of road that ran past the mountains, I saw myself from a higher perspective and realized I was making a bad situation worse. I couldn't change my current fate at the office, but I could change my attitude. "For all I know, the new job could turn out to be the best thing that's ever happened to me." I finished sniffling and wiped my eyes. Using all the tools I could recall from my recent seminars, I reluctantly talked myself into making the best of what I perceived to be a very bad situation.

The conference room in which I sat was jokingly called the "ice box" because it was small, square, and freezing cold. I waited nervously for the three men who would be my new supervisors, while methodically gnawing at my left thumbnail. I had scheduled this meeting to learn about my new job, but in spite of my resolve to be open-minded and professional, my thoughts were growing as chilly as the room. Three men filed into the tiny conference room, assessing me with a glance as I did the same with them. "The situation isn't their fault," I told myself. "They're just people like me who are trying to do their best on a project in which they're grossly understaffed." Now they were sitting with this highly recommended young woman who had a bad attitude the size of Texas. I felt like I needed to speak the unspeakable and address the underlying currents in the room before we could move on to our work. Feeling generous for saying so, I told them I wasn't upset with them; instead I was upset with "Them"—the invisible managers, "those" folks at the top who moved us around like numbers on a child's puzzle, never considering our life interests or goals. Yes, I resented the career change, but I promised that I would put my feelings aside and do my job well. They looked at one another as if they were trying to figure out whether or not I was speaking the truth.

One of the men shrugged and went to the white board. He drew two milestone triangles. The first represented today's date and the other, nine months from now. A line connected the two. "Your job," he told me with a sympathetic grin, "is to figure out what needs to happen in the department between these two dates and then do what it takes to make it happen." My nervousness was turning into stark terror. "I don't understand," I said slowly, shaking my head and breathing deeply to remain calm. The description was too open-ended. I didn't even understand the department's purpose or product.

"We have developers designing and writing software for the 777 cockpit displays at a very rapid rate," someone explained. I wasn't even looking to see who was talking. "At some point in the very near future they're going to be finished with their first assignments and we have to figure out how all the pieces come together. We need to form an integration team to merge the different pieces of software, and we need to make sure the integrated program is tested and then delivered on time. We also need to make sure we're consistent with the program-wide schedules. "And," someone else laughed nervously, "there are many factors outside our department that have to fall into place as well. We're relying on hardware being delivered to us on certain dates and our lab being operational in time for us to test. You need to figure out the big picture and turn it into a coherent plan." I was incredulous. There was no big picture two years into the department's work? There was no understanding of how software would come together to meet delivery deadlines that were less than a year away? This couldn't be. "I must be missing something," I told myself. I asked if there wasn't already some plan in place. "There is a high level schedule, but we're at the stage where we need to show Boeing that we really understand how the details are going to work out." "Don't you want to know too?" I asked a bit too quickly. I was almost ready to burst into hysterical laughter. "We did have someone working on the plan, but he, uh, left the company," somebody replied.

"Why don't you come to the meeting with Boeing tomorrow and then stop by my office afterwards," one of the men said quickly. I saw compassion written in his expression. "I'll help you out for starters." "Thank you God," I prayed, inwardly grateful for one human being who seemed to care about how I felt.

— § —

The next day I was calmer. I reassured myself that I was just feeling overwhelmed and within a few weeks I would know what I was doing once again. I promised myself that I would make new friends and talked myself into believing that I would do as well here as I had in all my previous jobs. I still wasn't quite sure where I fit in. I was no longer doing engineering work, and yet I wasn't in management either. "I guess I'm a freelancer," I chuckled, glad to be laughing about something. I located the conference room indicated on my meeting notice and helped myself to a pastry and a cup of hot coffee while waiting for the others to arrive.

Equipped with a new notebook and pen, I felt like I used to feel on the first day of school—apprehensive and a little excited. In general, I liked customer meetings. I always learned more about airplanes when I talked with an aircraft manufacturer. This was the part of my job that had teased me into hiring on with my firm in the first place. Airplanes had always fascinated me. When I was young, my mom and dad often drove my brother and me to Washington National Airport to see the planes takeoff and land. Flight seemed so freeing and so exciting through the eyes of a three year old who vividly remembered her experiences of flying during her nightly dreams. The door opened and I snapped out of my reverie. One by one, the managers I met the day before filed into the room along with several people I didn't recognize. I wiped the icing off my hands and waited expectantly, hoping to figure out exactly how the schedule I would be creating fit into the overall program plan for the 777 airplane.

For two hours, I sat listening to various topics on the agenda while feeling utterly clueless. There was so much for me to learn. I was nervous again, by the time we began to discuss the schedules. "Ann's going to be taking care of this now," somebody said. The Boeing manager took one look at me, half-smiled, then looked at my new supervisors with an obvious question on his countenance. "Now how's she going to pull this off when no one else has been able to do the job yet? We're getting a little short on time here." His voice was cordial, but under the surface I heard a challenge and a doubt. "How dare he question my abilities?" I thought. "He doesn't even know me." I started to fume irrationally, conveniently ignoring the fact that I had asked myself the same question. I held my tongue and watched the curious reactions in the room. My supervisors looked pained. Obviously, this topic was a sore spot for them, but why? "Probably because the man previously assigned to the task quit and left them with a big problem," I thought wryly.

The Boeing manager waited for someone to respond, a clear challenge still written in his expression. I got the impression that he had asked for this plan before and the answer hadn't been to his liking. Something snapped inside of me. Was I going to let fear and insecurity get in the way of my doing this job? They had no idea who I was or what I was capable of accomplishing! Anger ignited a commitment that would push me past any and all of my perceived limitations over the next year and half. Feeling my nervousness being replaced by a sense of personal power, I looked straight into my customer's eyes and slowly but deliberately said, "You have my word." Period. He smiled, amused, I supposed, at my tone, and raised his eyebrows. "We'll see next month, won't we?"

My new boss teased me later without mercy, finding my fuming incredibly funny. "Don't let him get to you," he said. "We've been working like crazy and yet it's never enough. That's why we're so glad to have *you* over here." He smiled and pulled a pile of papers out of his desk. For the next two hours he explained the overall program and flight test schedules, the dates on which our department was supposed to receive test hardware, the due dates for the interim deliveries to Boeing, the testing regulations, and the structure of the department.

By the time I was ready to leave his office, my head was swimming in facts, but I felt a sense of relief once again now that I knew more about what I would be doing. "You sure you won't consider staying here permanently, now that you know all about this wonderful program? We might just have to keep you." My new supervisor was trying to be lighthearted. "Wrong thing to say," I thought. My good mood disappeared quickly and I reacted without engaging my brain. "If I'm not returned on October 15, I will quit," I replied without humor. "Oh, wrong thing to say to your new boss, Ann," the voice of censure was a little too late. I left the office feeling terrible about my harsh words and wondering why on earth I would be so obnoxious to the one person who seemed to believe in me more than I currently believed in myself.

I didn't see that I was getting exactly what I had asked for. I had no higher perspective yet to tell me that I was receiving the opportunity of a lifetime to learn about working with large numbers of people, living with complete integrity with regard to personal commitments, and discovering what I was capable of accomplishing. This was a chance to expand my sphere of influence and to foster communication and cooperation in a group of people twenty times larger than my last. Little did I know as I walked back to my desk, head hung in sheer exhaustion from the thought of my new workload, that I had asked for this task and Spirit had been all too happy to oblige me. The next two years in my life would be ones of great challenge and change, causing me to dip into the depths of my own personal hells, only to emerge in a heaven I couldn't have anticipated and certainly would not have believed at the time.

—— § ——

One month later, I sat at my desk thinking about the dream of "Beauty and the Beast" while trying to concentrate on my work. I had been moving awfully fast lately. "Dear Journal," I wrote only a few days before the dream, "The yard is blooming, but I don't take time to smell the flowers. I feel like the days and weeks are passing by but my busy lifestyle doesn't afford me much time to think about where I am heading."

I learned a great deal in very little time. After determining the basic nature of my task, I spent several days figuring out exactly what the hundred engineers in my department were working to produce. Each person, I learned, was designing, writing, and testing a piece of the large software program that would display airplane flight and maintenance information in the cockpit of the new Boeing 777 aircraft. Glossy artist-rendition photos showed the slick eight-by-eight inch flat panel displays with the various display formats. On the PFD, or personal flight director display, the pilot would be able to check his position relative to the horizon and track other information such as altitude and airspeed. The ND, or Navigation Display, would depict "en route airways" that were invisible highways in the sky and diamond-shaped "waypoints" that were latitude and longitude intersections with names that linked the various airways together. Maintenance pages would display readouts about the state of various aircraft systems, while engine pages would show engine thrust and pressure data, as well as many other variables.

The specifications defining the system were written in over two feet of paper volumes stacked end-to-end. Writing the software according to specification was only the first part of a long process that had to occur before we could deliver our product to the customer. Each engineer in the department was responsible for testing his or her piece of the program before submitting the computer files to our local integration group. The integration group would then merge the different segments of software into one big program, which we would load onto the computers in our lab and test with real cockpit displays. After satisfying ourselves that the department's software worked correctly, we would submit our files to the program-level Systems Integration Department. They would merge our work with the software written by other departments. We would then test again to make sure that the displays software responded correctly to requests from the flight management and maintenance functions and then make sure that our displays accurately represented their information in the cockpit. The end product was a set of computer files that comprised the program our company would deliver to Boeing for testing in their simulated aircraft labs and eventually on a real airplane.

If errors were found in any stage of the process, we would have to start all over from the beginning. In order to avoid costly mistakes, we had to make sure that we were communicating within our department and working in well-orchestrated synchronization with the hundreds of other engineers on the program. To compound the issue, there were several such deliveries to Boeing planned throughout the upcoming months. Each time, we would have to add more functions to the software until our company delivered all that we had contractually promised.

I had just completed my first assignment—a seventy-page document showing in great detail how and when the various pieces of software would come together and when they would be incorporated into our customer deliveries. The project had been a planner's nightmare. I started by interviewing each of the design teams, innocently telling them when their software files were due. A few people told me they could make the dates. The rest weren't so optimistic. The polite team leaders told me that they were aware of the program-level delivery dates, but not the dates by which our internal integration group needed the files in order to adequately merge and test them. Other people told me I was crazy and laughed when I told them the task I had been assigned. "Good luck." "There's no way." "Too much to do in too little time, and I just lost another person in my group." I was given one really good excuse after another telling me why I had been given an impossible task. I went back to my desk and buried my face in my hands.

Never one to give up so easily, I returned the next day and asked the team leaders what dates they thought *were* feasible. "It doesn't matter what we think, does it?" I was surprised by the degree of cynicism. "Just tell me what dates you can make." I tried to reply without answering the sarcasm. Using their inputs, I sat for days arranging the pieces of the puzzle on paper, trying to find a way to meet deadlines that were approaching all too quickly. Iterating the process, I showed the team leads my plan and made changes according to their comments. Via the grapevine, I heard the remarks that some of them made after I left their cubicles. "Another paper pusher," or from the kinder folks, "I feel sorry for her. She's got a thankless job."

In spite of the gossip, I tried to figure out where we could work in parallel with one another, streamline tasks, and cut out work that wasn't absolutely necessary. To the surprise and satisfaction of my customers and supervisors, I finally arrived at a plan that appeared to be workable. "Appear is the operative word," I thought apprehensively as I handed in the assignment. The complex schedules were based on a hundred things all happening perfectly, and I knew chances of that were slim. One wrong move, one slipped deadline, one piece of hardware delivered late to our lab and then we would be in big trouble. I wondered if I wasn't simply proposing a pipe dream to make management happy. What if I was the scapegoat who would be blamed when the plan went awry? Who was going to help the teams make the dates they had given me? There was no room for error. The dream was right. I did feel trapped.

What about the room in which I bolted myself in the dream? Rooms in my dreams often symbolized states of consciousness. "Yes," I thought honestly, "I have recently locked myself into a new way of being." The harder I worked, the more praise I received. The more praise I received, the harder I worked. My overtime was increasing, as were my responsibilities. As the dream indicated, there really was no turning back. I couldn't say to my boss, "Sorry, I want to work forty hour weeks so I can spend more time at home. I guess I won't be able to get my job done." I didn't even know if I wanted to say that anymore. I felt alive again, satisfied with how quickly I had shifted my attitude about the transfer and how much I had managed to accomplish as a result. I didn't realize how quickly I had forgotten about my dreams of working in a field I genuinely loved, spending more time with John, and being able to pursue my other interests. Whereas a hopeless sense of desperation once trapped me in a life that wasn't realizing my deepest desires, this time my intoxication with success had me feeling safe, but approaching another dead end. The dream seemed to tell me that I had cornered myself into a situation and a state of consciousness that would eventually leave me searching for another way out.

The rest of the dream appeared to be a clear message. When you feel trapped, there's always a window of opportunity. Your means of resolving a seemingly impossible situation might not be what you expect, and you might have to expend some effort to alter your circumstances. Even after you've found the way to resolve your dilemma, you might have to make a leap of faith to reclaim the key to your own happiness and success. This teaching would be incredibly valuable in my future. During the next eighteen months I would be required to make many leaps of faith, fearful each time, yet like Belle in the dream, courageous enough to jump. Time and time again I would relearn the lesson that only I could claim the key to my desired future. As the dream predicted, I would jump into the unknown many times in order to reclaim that key.

— § —

Two weeks after I turned in my first plan, the schedule slipped. The prototype hardware wasn't delivered on time. The test facilities wouldn't be ready until a month later than they were originally promised to us. One of the software development teams had an unexpected problem with a workstation, and as a result, they were three days behind schedule. My house of cards was falling quickly, and to my dismay, nobody seemed overly concerned. Maybe they were just confident that I could come up with a solution. I wasn't. "Well, you just need to do a replan," I was told when I asked for advice on solving the cascading problems we faced. "What?" I stormed inside. The grapevine was right. I was a paper pusher. Replan after replan wouldn't solve the problems. Barring a miracle or some additional effort on someone's part to manage the troublesome obstacles to progress, there was no way our department would meet our deadlines. What were our alternatives? Who would stand up and tell the customer the truth? Who would come up with an acceptable compromise? Did anyone care? I looked around and realized everyone was too busy fighting the current brush fires to think about the impending bomb.

I calmed myself and faced the first serious moral dilemma I had been presented in over six years of engineering. No one seemed to think we could make the deadlines anyway, so they certainly didn't expect me to make that happen. I had a feeling that as long as I could provide good reasons for the schedule slips people would be satisfied with my work, even if they weren't pleased with what I had to say. After all, there were many valid reasons why we couldn't succeed. "Do what it takes to make the plan happen." I remembered the words spoken to me on the first day of my job in this department. "Do what it takes." "That shouldn't be my job," I argued with myself, thinking the task more appropriate for "them." I remembered something I had learned in one of my seminars about how "shoulds" get you in trouble. Real life doesn't always work the way you think life "should." I gave up the complaint.

My conscience fought an inner battle with the portion of my mind that argued to keep me safe. The latter voice told me, "Just keep making them happy. That's all you have to do." The louder more persistent voice said, "You can't live with yourself knowing you're simply making excuses for a living. Jump in. Take the leap. Take the challenge and see if you can make this impossible program work. This is your chance to learn what you are capable of doing. This is your opportunity to rise above the cynicism and resignation that you see all around you. Go for it. What are you waiting for?" What would life be like if I really did decide to assume total responsibility for making my department's portion of the program work?

For starters, I thought wryly, I would feel as ill equipped for the task as if I were climbing Mt. Everest with no training and no supplies. I considered my situation. How would I act if I really *were* in charge of the department's success? While the paper plan was a start, I knew much more would be required. First and foremost, better communication was necessary. We would only succeed if every person in the department was aware of what was expected of him or her. I would need to set deadlines for submitting the software to the integration group, let people know when the integrated program was ready for testing, make sure the people responsible for the labs had the equipment working adequately, and schedule lab usage. I would have to find a way to let the teams in the department know what the others were doing and make sure they were aware of the program goals and issues. I would have to make sure everyone knew where he or she fit in the larger picture of the entire airplane program.

Secondly, cooperation was key to our success; somehow, I would have to smooth over disagreements and mediate situations where both parties seemed to be at odds. Some of the people in the department were extremely tense after working long hours and being placed under a great deal of stress. Issues that normally would have been resolved peacefully were escalating into noisy arguments. I would need to step in and make sure the solution was for the good of the program and not just for one individual. I would also have to make sure that the compromise met the individual's needs or I would soon be the target of much resentment. I sighed.

Removing barriers to progress would be equally important. I thought of all the complaints I heard from the engineers and the infinite reasons why they couldn't do their jobs without interruption. They weren't simply whining either; their complaints were valid, and if they were addressed, we could operate more efficiently. If I took my commitment seriously, I would have to expand my job description to include everything from fetching lab supplies to taking up the engineers' concerns with people in other departments and with our upper management.

As I weighed my decision, the voice of inner wisdom taught me the things I would need to know in order to succeed. I would have to get really tough with myself. I would have to give up my own complaints with management and with some of the other engineers. I wouldn't have time to wallow in pity for myself being given an "impossible task." Instead, I would have to focus solely on success, doing whatever would be necessary to meet my commitment. I wondered if I could do this alone. "No," came the answer. I would have to make my needs clear. I would have to find out who was already responsible for various coordination tasks, and then ask my managers to help me find people to fill in the gaps. I would have to ask the engineers to meet difficult commitments. "Who am I to ask them to work?" I wondered. "Nobody," came the answer. "Do it anyway." I had been a group leader several years ago, responsible for coordinating five people on a team doing input/output software for a flight management system, but I had never even considered the scope of the job I was about to undertake. I was accustomed to succeeding as an individual, but I had no experience in leading and motivating large groups of people.

Faced with a task so huge, I felt for a moment that I would be insignificant and powerless to effect the necessary changes. In fear, I wavered and wondered if I was insane to even consider such a choice. I wanted to ignore the dilemma and to assume a "don't care"

WHISPERS OF THE SPIRIT

attitude, but once I considered the problem, there was no turning back. I could never be satisfied dreaming up paper plans that I knew wouldn't work without some additional effort. I drew in a deep breath, bit my lower lip, and made the decision. I resolved that day to do everything in my power to ensure the department's success. From the depths of my being arose a new sense of courage and personal power that I hadn't known before.

With commitment comes the strength

equal to the task.

—— § ——

At 8:15 on a Friday morning I stood in the department conference room with a doughnut in one hand and a marker in the other while I listed the day's goals on the white board. One of the engineers had suggested that we hold brief daily meetings with the team leads and anyone else who was interested in order to align our efforts. Glad for another way to improve communication in the department, I had followed his advice. The Friday meetings were the most popular due to the two-dozen doughnuts I purchased on the way to work.

"Files are due to integration next Tuesday by noon," I started with the reminder. Eyes rolled and a few people stopped sucking the cream filling out of their pastries to groan. "Come on guys," I pleaded. "This is no surprise."

I saw heads bobbing. Good, I wasn't imagining the fact that I mentioned this deadline the four previous days this week. A snide comment shot from the far side of the room, undermining any authority I had just managed to assume, "Yeah we better hurry so we can get laid off quicker." The comment was followed by suppressed laughter. I looked at the faces around the table and read their mixed reactions. "Boy that was rude." "What's she going to say about that one?" "Well?" They waited for my reaction. I counted quietly to ten. "You have more control over that than I do," I snapped back, frustrated at how powerless I felt to fight the growing wave of despair that was threatening to drown even the most positive individuals. What use were my efforts to lighten up the place and motivate people when the company atmosphere was so grim?

The economic downturn had worsened over the last few months, prompting management to take more drastic measures in order to prevent serious financial loss. Cutting discretionary funding hadn't saved the division enough money; now management was telling us that layoffs were likely to occur in the near future. Already we had more work than people to accomplish the tasks. The news was a slap in the face. I heard snide remarks wherever I turned. "If I get laid off, I'll be without a job. If I don't I'll have two more." More snickers. I could barely walk down an aisle without hearing someone poking at the inconsistency between layoffs and the continuous requests from "above" to work harder. Personal integrity and ethics compelled most people to do their jobs well, but the continuous threats to job security were slowly eroding even the most dedicated individual's efforts and will to succeed of. I had to do something, but what?

"You need to let upper management know what is going on down here." Another one of those thoughts from nowhere zipped into my mind as I walked away from the morning meeting. "Yeah, right. Me? Go marching into the Vice President's office and tell him the layoff talk is undermining every management effort to

motivate the work force? That's not my job." I was arguing with myself again. Meanwhile, the committee of voices in my head was having a panel discussion and ignoring my input. "*What this company needs is a sense of direction. People need to know there are more projects after this one, so they have a reason to be motivated.*" "Oh shut up. I've got enough to worry about with my own job," I tried to suppress the inner rebellion. "*The company who offers your personal development seminars has a corporate course. You could recommend that.*" My thoughts were really crazy now. "Recommend that my management take a class? Oh right, sure." The thoughts were insistent and relentless. No matter what I did, I couldn't get the idea out of my mind that I had to stop complaining and do something about the negativity that surrounded me. Feeling possessed by a will stronger than my own, I picked up the phone and dialed the VP of engineering. His voice mail message answered me and with a sigh of relief I heard myself saying that I knew something that would "put the spark" back into the organization. I hung up the phone, appalled at the message I just left. With my hand still clenched on the receiver, I sat with my jaw hanging open and wondered who had spoken those words.

The VP returned my message a few days later. With my stomach churning, I scheduled a meeting with him the following week. I had met the man before and he seemed nice enough. "What the heck am I doing?" My doubts tangoed with my desired to make a difference. "Who am I to talk to him about our perception that the company lacked vision. Fine thing to do while they're considering layoffs. Real smart, Ann." I thought of all the things I had read and learned over the past several months. "Decide what you want and act in spite of your fears," I reminded myself. I thought about the type of company that I would be proud to work for and I wrote my own sample vision statement for the division. A vision, I knew, was a useless collection of words unless they became words to live by. Nonetheless, an airplane didn't arrive at a destination without a flight plan, and our company wouldn't get where management wanted us to go without some similar sense of direction. I worried about what I would say.

Spirit whispered in my sleep quelling my fears and telling me I was on the right track. A dreamtime "dress rehearsal" gave me the confidence to have a conversation I never would have considered a few months before. The dream in which I talked with the VP and he listened with polite and careful consideration was so realistic that by the time I walked into his office two days later, I already knew that the outcome of our discussion would be positive. We had a wonderful talk and before the morning was over, he invited me to participate on a team of senior managers whose charter was to make the company a better place for people to work. "They—the influential ones—now had names and faces, and to my chagrin, I had unexpectedly been accepted as one of "their" peers. I no longer recognized the woman I was becoming. I wondered if my leaps of faith had me falling helplessly out of control.

I woke up remembering a brief dream in which I passed the VP in the hallway. He told me to arrange a conference call so he can set up the course I recommended. Interesting.

Next, I dreamt I was hiking up my favorite mountain when I saw our VP once again. He was really excited because this was his first time "climbing the mountain." I was concerned that I might hike too fast for him since I had traveled this path before. I decided that I didn't want to interfere with his journey so I left. Driving away, dark clouds gathered and I became worried that the man I left on the mountain would be upset because of the storm. Something I couldn't see in the dream calmed me and reassured me that he would be just fine.

Imagine my surprise later today at work when the management team watched a Stanford Video about creating a corporate vision. The video, and later the managers on my team, continuously referred to the need to "climb the mountain." We also talked about setting up the class I've been promoting. It looks like the dream is going to become reality. I hope that the impending storm that my efforts have initiated won't be too frightening.

In June, forty-five of my division's upper level managers attended the seminar I had recommended. There were no sudden miracles but I noticed that some of the managers seemed to think more often of the long-term goals instead of focusing on the current crises of the day. There were no radical changes in personality, but I did see people who had taken the class listening to one another with greater respect and showing more tolerance for diverging opinions. Managers who had once been concerned about expressing their opinions to their own supervisors now spoke more freely. Our meetings became more volatile, and yet much more potent.

I worked with the managers on my team to improve communication between the people at their levels and the rest of the workforce. We disseminated communiqués with leadership tips and techniques. We worked with Human Resources to change the management review process so employees' comments affected their manager's appraisals, and we instituted an employee survey so the managers could better understand the concerns of the engineers. We encouraged managers to become more liberal with praise, to give employees more power and support, and to reward people for noteworthy efforts. We felt as if we were chipping away at an iceberg with a pick ax, and yet little by little progress was being made. "Rome wasn't built overnight," I wrote in my journal, "and the entrenched behaviors of corporate America will take years to change."

Meanwhile, in my "real" job on the 777 cockpit displays project, I was going crazy and loving the fast pace. Like a woman possessed, I did everything humanly possible to make sure obstacles were removed and lines of communication kept open. I kept the department informed and made sure the customer received regular updates detailing our progress. Our department manager left the company and a new gentleman took his place, but at the levels where the nuts and bolts of the engineering work was taking place, we didn't miss a beat.

I was busier than ever, but strangely more satisfied. At work I was finally making a difference consistent with the vision I had created for my life. At home, I started enjoying and appreciating the time John and I spent together rather than wishing I had more. Like a curious child, I continued my path of personal exploration. I was eager to explore new ideas and see how they fit in with my swiftly changing life experiences. Themes in my new education began to emerge. Again and again I found myself attracted to books on energetic healing and shamanism—two topics that I would have been embarrassed to express an interest in only a year or two before. Idly, I wished that I could meet a real shaman someday, and I wondered what life might be like if I became a healer instead of an engineer. The thoughts were passing curiosities. Changing careers was the farthest thing from my mind. At long last, I felt alive with purpose and satisfied with my life choices.

As if another chapter in my life had come to a close, John and I traveled to Kauai for our sixth anniversary vacation. We were shocked by what we saw. The island's changes mirrored my own. Nine months ago, Hurricane Iniki, whose name means "sharp, as in wind or pangs of love," had taken only five hours to uproot ancient trees, whip the roofs off houses and shatter the structures of the major resorts. Around the same time, pangs of love had led me to take a seminar that shattered my own belief structures with a quick and devastating blow to the ego.

John and I drove to the south shore, afraid of what we would find. The room where we stayed last year was gone; the patio on which we had dined watching a sunset wasn't there. The windswept beach had claimed the lawn where I had fond memories of sipping tropical rum drinks, and the pool was now an empty concrete basin with a puddle of murky water lapping back and forth in the bottom. Rusted bathtubs that had been recovered from the few rooms left standing were piled in a fenced-off area and only the concrete structures of the buildings remained. Farther down the beach the seaward faces of the neighboring resort had been stripped away. A surfboard still thrust through one of the wooden walls was a grim reminder of the ferocious strength of the hurricane's winds. We felt as if we had stepped into a different reality.

In sharp contrast to the man-made rubble, the squeaky-clean beach glistened as white as the inside of the polished seashells, as if the sand was happy to have reclaimed its territory from the ravaged resorts. The lapis-colored ocean was so calm that you couldn't imagine angry waves gripping steel girders and wooden planks in the tight curl of their watery fists. Wild sea grapes were beginning to grow back along the shoreline and the palms that had been able to bend and flex in the storm's blast remained untouched. The raw power of Mother Nature as she took form in the hurricane's blast had only made the island's wild beauty all the more vivid and surreal. I felt similarly, that the "real me" was finally beginning to emerge from beneath the rubble of my shattered assumptions about life. I sank into the soft sand and let my musings drift away with the tide. Beside me, John sat reading contentedly. Life seemed magical.

I didn't know at the time that spiritual growth occurs in cycles. Like one of the ocean waves, I had reached a crest and was resting briefly before I would soon be called back to explore the vast ocean of my consciousness. Again, my dreams were the portent.

— § —

Dear Journal - Last night I dreamt of visiting my elderly "aunt" in Hawaii. John and I had been driving together on a dirt road that spiraled up toward the top of a mountain. At one point, we stopped the car and got out. I left John waiting on the road and started walking alone along a path covered with living roots and sheltered by wide-leafed trees. In the dream I could practically smell the damp earth and feel the moistness of the tropical jungle. I emerged from the dark canopy of the trees and vines into an area where the light shone on a small clearing. My "aunt" stood there—a small oriental woman with a warm smile and a lively countenance. Wasting no time, she began to question me about my life and what was important to me. Looking pointedly into my eyes, she asked me if I would be willing to give up life as I knew it and move to paradise.

I don't recall what I answered, but I woke up still swimming in the feelings of love and beauty exuded by this tiny woman standing with her herbs and flowers in a clearing protected by the friendly tropical trees.

"John." I didn't want to move much farther, but I needed to wake him up. "John. Look at this." Right under my body, directly under the base of my spine, under all the covers, three rose petals lay in a triangular pattern where I had just been sleeping. "How did they get there?" I demanded. "I don't know," he mumbled sleepily. This was too weird. I looked at the wall three feet away and shook the heart-shaped floral wreath that hung there. No petals fell. In fact, no petals had fallen from my wreath in the three years since I had created the decoration from the roses I loved in my own garden, and none have fallen since. I thought of the woman in the dream and her beautiful flowers. Was there a connection? The feeling of standing in the presence of an unconditional love lingered into my morning and gave me the uncanny feeling that I had just been visited by an angel.

The same day I received a brochure in the mail that invited me to attend a local conference with seminars on healing the mind, body, and spirit. I never stopped to wonder why an engineer had been invited to an event that was typically reserved for therapists and health care practitioners. I didn't realize until a few months later that the dream and the brochure for the conference were not random events, but rather a synchronized series of incidents that would radically alter the course of my life. I had no idea that I would soon be branching off on my own path. Instead, as I thumbed through page after page of the flyer that described the latest modalities in therapy and healing, I felt only that curious sense of intuition that I was beginning to recognize every now and then as a hint of direction. Knowing, without knowing why, that I should go to the conference, I dialed the number on the back of the brochure and registered myself.

Every night my dreams hinted that big changes in my life were just around the next corner. I now respected the messages I was receiving in the dark, knowing that even before my conscious mind was ready to grasp the reality of a new idea the concept would come to me silently and stealthily in my dreams. Like a burglar creeping into the corners of my securely bolted conscious mind, Spirit slipped into my sleeping psyche, planting the seeds of a new reality while surreptitiously stealing the underpinnings of my old one.

Chapter 3
Signposts and Symbols

The grasses carpeting the hills on the side of the highway were baking in the relentless desert sun. Heat shimmered off the scorched blacktop on the road ahead and there was no hint of a breeze. Driving in the comfort of our air-conditioned car, John and I were oblivious to the sweltering heat. We talked animatedly, looking forward to the hike and the swimming hole that our friends had promised we would absolutely love. On a 115° Saturday, about an hour north of Phoenix and an hour shy of our destination, we were daydreaming of a cold clear creek when we noticed that the car was overheating.

John groaned and pulled off to the side of the road, muttering under his breath like a snorting rhino about to charge. "Why do cars always pick the worst times to break down?!" "Don't ask me," I replied quickly, just as frustrated with the situation as he was. I opened the car doors and windows and watched him lift the sizzling hood while I gulped the last few drops of water from the jug in the front seat. Thank goodness, after living in the desert so many years we knew enough to carry extra gallons of water. I suspected we would need them. John hauled a large jar around to the front of the car, refilled the radiator, and then wiped off his greasy hands before sitting back down behind the wheel. "Let's hope that will fix the problem." He looked doubtful.

Ten minutes later the engine temperature gauge crept up over the red line. "Shoot!" John pulled off the road again, visibly upset. With his hands on the wheel, staring straight ahead, he considered our predicament in silence. I sat in the passenger seat stewing about the situation until he was ready to share his thoughts with me. "We could open the windows and go on. I think the air conditioning is putting too heavy a load on the car." He paused. "Or, we could go back, but we'll have to go without air either way." What a choice! "Hot as hell outside and either way we point the car we have an hour's drive?" I questioned him angrily. "Do you have any better ideas?" John looked at me expectantly. "The man should be sainted for his patience," I thought. "No, no. OK. Sorry. I'm not mad at you. Let's just go forward. We may as well hike and the temperature should be cooler tonight on the way back anyway." "That's what I was thinking too," John said, ignoring my momentary outburst. We opened the windows, refilled our water bottle, and resumed the journey.

Predictably, a few miles down the road the temperature gauge was still inching itself into the hot zone. We both cursed this time as we pulled onto the road's shoulder. "I know this sounds crazy," John said while I waited for the punch line, "but I've got to turn the heater on to bleed off the engine temperature or pretty soon we'll be going nowhere." "What? Can't we just stop?" "Sure," he replied, this time with far less patience. "You want to sit by the side of the road for a couple hours while the car cools down?" I believed he was actually giving me the option. "No." I answered slowly. He was right. There were no trees and no shade to be found anywhere along the side of the road. We turned on the heater and pulled back onto the highway. The stifling hot air blasted us inside the car but the engine finally stabilized at a reasonable temperature.

We were exhausted and drenched with sweat by the time we pulled into the dirt parking lot near the trailhead forty-five minutes later. Hungrily, we devoured our picnic lunches in the cool shade of an ancient juniper tree. The wind had started rustling overhead and the steady hum of grasshoppers and locusts was hypnotic. I leaned back against the tree trunk and shut my eyes. The creek gurgled happily in the distance, offering a promise of cool water that was more tempting than a glimpse into paradise. I got the strange sensation that I was part of the landscape. Something awaited me at the end of this journey. There was a reason we had persisted in spite of so many obstacles. I furrowed my brow, opened my eyes, and kept my thoughts to myself. Sated finally, and somewhat cooler if only because the hot breeze had dried our sweat, we set out along the trail.

If I had expected relief from the heat, I was sadly disappointed. For the first two miles John and I traipsed along a hot and dusty cattle path, teased every now and then by a glimpse of the creek off to our right and far below the trail. The heat was becoming unbearable. "Are we crazy," I asked John? My heart was pounding like an incessant hammer. "You all right?" he replied. We stopped under a mesquite tree for a rare bit of shade and drank some more water. "Yeah," I breathed out. I wiped the sweat off my forehead with the bottom of my t-shirt. We walked on, stopping every ten minutes or so to rest. "This is the mythical journey through hell," I thought, wondering why on earth we were here. I thought about the shamans I had been reading about in my new books. They were forced to face all sorts of trials as part of their training. Hot and dusty trails, long hikes, and days without food or water pushed the human mind past its perceived limits... or killed you. I was no shaman's apprentice, just a crazy white woman walking in heat that she hadn't been trained to endure. Still, I wondered if this hike was a call for me to push past my own limitations. I stopped complaining, took deep breaths, and concentrated on taking slow even steps to calm my heart rate. The strategy seemed to work. I became more comfortable as soon as I stopped pushing myself and started to walk in tune with the rhythms of my body.

At the two-mile marker, we reached a fork in the path. Checking our notes, we veered to the left. The narrow rocky trail that we had chosen meandered high up along a rock ledge on the canyon wall. Far below to the right, the creek snaked back and forth, twisting among the ancient trees, and pooling occasionally in inviting swimming holes that would have offered us cool respite had we taken the easier path. "My life is like this hike," I thought, "one surprise after another, up and down, arduous at times and rewarding at others." I hadn't taken the easier path at work. What awaited me at the end of my journey?

At long last, the trail started to dip down toward the creek and within two hundred yards we reached our destination. The spot was a Mecca in the midst of the dry desert. A crystal clear blue-green swimming hole had been formed where the canyon walls narrowed and squeezed the creek between them. Ledges along the walls offered varying heights from which to dive into the pool. Fifteen feet below the surface of the water we could see the boulders and gravel shimmering at the bottom. A few fish swam in the peaceful depths, oblivious to the kids who had hiked in earlier and were busy daring each other to jump off the ledges. John and I carefully made our way to a spot where the rocks eased into the water. We sat on our heels while we splashed the dust off our sun-baked faces then quickly stripped off our sweat-drenched clothing to reveal the swimsuits underneath. Together we walked into the icy refreshing water. Heaven couldn't have felt more wonderful.

After an invigorating dip we laid on our towels on the red rock ledge and dried quickly in the heat of the early afternoon sun, looking like the lizards that were sunning themselves on the faces of the cliff side behind us. Lazily, I watched the kids jumping off the ledge into creek. They were having a terrific time. I thought of something I had learned in the course of my reading, "Are you going to watch life go by, or participate?" Without hesitation, I scaled the twelve-foot ledge, screamed with delight, and plunged over the edge. My stomach lurched then I was hitting the water with a loud splash and the bubbles were tickling all around me. Exhilarating! I popped to the surface, sputtering, and floated on my back while I watched some guys standing on the twenty-five-foot ledge. The only way to reach that height was to jump off the lower cliff as I had done, swim across the pool, and pull yourself up via a precarious set of rock hand-holds onto a slim rock ledge. From there you could scramble easily to the top.

A young guy who had been standing far above me for ten minutes finally leapt. His screams echoed off the rock walls and his arms flailed wildly before he tucked them close at the last minute as he hit the surface of the water. "That looks like so much fun. Ooh." I dared myself to jump. "It must be safe enough," I reasoned. I felt goose bumps forming on my arms. *"Spectator or participant? Which do you want to be?"* From another plane of existence, my thoughts showed me the parallel between the insignificant jump and the direction my life would be taking. This jump was the reason for our hike. This leap. Would I walk past my fears here, while I had the opportunity to do so in a very physical way, or would I leave as the same person, always regretting the things in life I dared not try. Would I turn down the wild passion of living for a few moments of safety? One jump. A small thing in the physical world, but a large leap in the world of my mind and my spirit. I sensed the whispers that I couldn't quite hear.

Cradled by the waters, I rocked back and forth while I floated in a waking dream. No longer sure about what was real, I looked up at the sky and the cliffs towering above me. Splash. Another boy jumped. *"Children aren't afraid to live; when did you become fearful?"* Like dragonflies, the thoughts from an unknown source flitted through my mind, dancing from one topic to the next. I was part of the landscape again, perfectly centered between the solid earth and the brilliant sky. The water below me was the same substance that filled and nourished my cells and the air above coursed through my lungs, mixing with the breezes upon each exhalation. *I slip into the eternal "now." There is no distinction between human and nature. The buzzing of the locusts is a loud unceasing hum in my head that lulls me deeper into awareness of the dream we call life. The winds whisper to me, hinting at the joyful freedom of flight. The thought-voices become more persistent, reminding me why I am here.* "Reach out and touch the turquoise sky. Leap or live safe. Pretend or play. Live or be dead! Choose. Choose!" There's an urgency in the thoughts. "Act now. Now!" Without thinking, I swam to the base of the taller cliff, and gripping the wet slippery rocks, hauled myself out of the chilly water.

Snap! I was out of my reverie, standing on a narrow moss-covered ledge and shivering. I looked above me. Was I really going to do this? I wasn't usually afraid of heights but suddenly I was gripped by a fear that I couldn't comprehend. What on earth was I thinking? I pulled myself up onto the next ledge, shaking fearfully. What if I slipped? Hands holding rocks like vice clamps,

I carefully inched up the cliff side. Surely jumping must be easier than climbing up this rock. Determination forced me to the top. I looked over the edge.

"Oh no." I groaned and gripped my stomach. "What have I gotten myself into?" I chastised myself. "The heat must have short-circuited my brain!" Whereas the twenty-five-foot jump looked reasonable, although frightening, from below, the leap seemed crazy from this perspective. What looked like a wide pool at ground level was only a sliver of water far below. Worse yet, the rock ledge on the opposite side of the creek was way too close for comfort. I took several steps backwards and sat on a flat rock while my heart pounded erratically.

"You gonna jump?" The voice startled me. I hadn't even noticed that there were five younger guys standing on the ledge with me. "Have you done it?" I asked, not wanting an answer. "Nope, but he has," they said pointing to the brave one who was contemplating his second fall. The young man's toes were curled around the edge of the cliff as he stood shivering wet with his arms wrapped protectively around his midsection. He stared down into the waters while I considered my options. I had really gotten myself into a predicament this time. The only way down, other than jumping, was to climb backwards along the rock face from which I came. Neither choice was attractive. "This is insane," I spoke to my fears as if they were real. I stood behind the young man as he jumped and watched him plunge under the water then pop up like a rocket, shaking his hair and yelling at his friends. "C'mon!" The voice echoed on the rock walls. His friends followed in quick succession. I was alone at the top.

"Shoot." I was shaking again, petrified and feeling foolish. "Forget this mythical jump business," I wanted to cry. "If I know this is safe, then why am I so frightened?" I questioned myself and demanded an answer. Kids could jump. What was my problem? The fear was intense now, a huge knot in my stomach and tight balls of my fists hanging by my side. I was angry with myself for being afraid. "This is ridiculous!" I was talking to myself right before the unidentified voices in my mind spoke again. *"You aren't afraid of jumping off a cliff. You're afraid of dying before you've lived."* "That's right," I thought vehemently. My mind might be stupid enough to believe that throwing my body off a cliff into a narrow pool was safe but my body was smarter. I shivered again as cloud started to cover the sun. "C'mon!" one of the guys treading water at the bottom yelled. "You gonna fish me out if I sink?" I retorted, both joking and serious. "Oh boy, what if he says yes?" I thought. "Sure," he replied. "You can do it."

I looked over the edge again. Since the cloud had passed overhead, I could no longer see the bottom of the pool. Instead, the creek looked black and foreboding, and I couldn't see where the water ran deep even though I remembered. A few raindrops began to fall creating concentric circles as they hit the obsidian surface of the water. *"Black void. Womb of mother earth. Surrender yourself. Give up your fear. Jump and I'll catch you."* The thoughts came again from nowhere as I transitioned into that strange state of awareness between waking life and the dream. *"Trust the earth, trust the waters. Leap and know you'll be caught. Take the leap of faith. Now!"* I thrust myself over the edge... Falling, falling, falling forever...splash! Under water, cool, wet, slippery, I plunge deeper and deeper. My feet hit the bottom. Up I go. Air! Ah, air has never tasted so sweet. I'm alive! I did it! Salty tears of relief mix with the earth's waters and washed down the stream. My life would never be the same. John woke up from his nap and looked at me groggily. "You have a new wife," I wanted to tell him.

The mythical moment was over but I couldn't shake the feeling that I had just left some unknown fears behind.

I jumped several more times that day. Each time I named one of my fears and symbolically left the fear behind me as I plunged over the edge. I practiced shifting my attitude quickly and easily from terror to courage, so I could take action. My body taught me so much more effectively what my mind had taken years to learn. I learned that day that mind, body, spirit were all facets of the same diamond of self. Teach one and the others learn as well. I would need the lessons this day offered in the very near future.

The trek back to the car seemed quick and easy compared to our earlier hike. We walked along the precipice as a hawk flew below us following the creek downstream and piercing the brilliant stillness of nature after a rain with her shrill cries. The rain showers had cooled the hot and dusty trail and the sunset was turning the clouds into brilliant puffs of oranges, fuchsia, and purples. Night overtook us on the drive home and with the cooler air, the car behaved well. I watched the stars sparkling brilliantly in the umbrella of the night sky and felt a strange peace, knowing somehow that the hike, followed by the refreshing waters and then the leap of faith, mirrored my own spiritual journey. I wondered when and where my next real leap of faith would occur.

The days before the mind/body/spirit conference seemed to go by on fast-forward. I was still busy at work but having a mini-vacation on the horizon gave me occasion to stay calm and happy in spite of the ups and downs of engineering life. In this peaceful state of mind,

I noticed that Spirit was whispering to me with increasing frequency, not only in my nighttime dreams, but in the reflections of the natural world as well. As a child with a "vivid imagination," I had talked to the trees as if they were my playmates and conversed with clouds as if I could command them to dance. Adulthood and maturity forbade such seeming foolishness until on my hike through a veritable hell, I was reminded that the road to heaven might be found as easily in a forest or a desert as in the solemn splendor of a cathedral. Earth seemed to pardon my years of ignorance and began to offer me a constant source of inspiration and education. I started tuning in to the signs and symbols that she offered:

> Dear Journal – A storm is brewing outside. Earth waits anxiously for the rain, ready to taste the healing waters. The clouds swirl and the sky is getting darker by the minute. The stillness is broken now by a hiss, and then I hear a freight train sound, "whoosh," as the winds come. The trees dance in wild anticipation of the water and the flowers send their harbinger petals on the wind to announce their joy. The earth watches and waits for her lover. She's parched and thirsty after a dry July.
>
> While talking to a friend at work today, I found myself explaining that this life is truly a dance between polarities: attraction and repulsion, light and dark, good and evil, calm and storm, death and life. Where did I get that notion? "Neither of the polarities is bad," I heard myself continue. One tries to pull us apart while the other calls us together. Without the polarity of darkness and of separation, would our spirits

merge into one? Would we know the boundary between ourselves and others, or would we simply become elements of a larger organism and work for the good of the whole race? Wouldn't we be like drops of water seeping into the big ocean of consciousness?

I wonder if there is a way for me to have a separate identity and still know myself as part of the larger whole. Is this what God is like—a big ocean? Maybe we're the raindrops that evaporate from this ocean of God and then fall to earth, to return eventually via the various winding pathways of the rivers and streams of our lives. I wonder...

Now the thunder rolls and interrupts my thoughts. I guess I should shut off the computer. How can I consider the nature of consciousness during a storm when the lightning threatens to come through the outlet and eat my words? Looks like this is going to be a wild one... Rebirth and change. The storm's apparent destruction creates new life...

"Rebirth and change." The storm raged outside while I watched in silence. Huge forks of lightning plunged out of the sky. Death. Charges from the ground reaching up and, pulling the power from the black swirling dervish skies, the white light heat from heaven wreaked death and destruction to the desert, often starting huge grass fires that would sometimes burn for days. New life. The rains ran off the cracked hard earth, flooding the ravines and turning dry desert washes into raging rivers for a day or so. Thirsty plants would spring up reaching for the skies with their tender green shoots soon after a rain, and then a few weeks later the cycle would repeat. Tumbleweed would grow quickly—green spiny balls of bush that would turn brown within months, uproot, and then race across the desert in the storm's winds before decaying back into the soil. Rebirth and change. Nature reminded me that life is a cycle of endless deaths and births.

I had died to one way of life recently when I realized that I had been assuming I was never good enough. I was struggling to birth myself into a new life where I lived from the assumption that I was fine. I had died to my helpless whining and complaining at work and was rebirthing myself as a leader. I had died to some unknown fear on the cliff side and was waiting now, like an expectant mother in her time of quickening for the birth of a new awareness that I could sense but not yet name. I wondered what my new life would be like. I wondered about my new identity. I found myself looking within, searching my soul, asking myself questions about who I was and where I was going. Once a desperate search for anything that would ease the pain of my living, my questions, musings, and dreams now took on the character of a mythic journey through the labyrinth paths of my psyche.

Dear Journal - Last night I dreamt I was hiking through the fields of a snowy landscape. I reached a creek that bordered the forest. Along the banks of the creek, piles of branches were nestled closely together in huge mounds. I peered into one of the mounds and realized I was staring into a den of wolves. I've been seeing them frequently in my dreams these days. Their curious eyes gazed back at me, loving and wise. This morning, poetic images come to mind:

The power of the dream calls me to look within. I see myself reflected in the deep womb of the earth mother as I ask permission to retreat into the den.

Peering out I watch the endless snows scour the landscape with dazzling, blinding, white. Only when I look inside, against the dark background, do I know light. Otherwise, the brilliance blinds me.

Mother wolf peers from her den. Fiercely loyal, she protects her cubs from the barren winter. There is no barrenness here; there is great warmth, love, and sharing within.

Their eyes peer out at me. They stare and wonder how one so bold dare come up to their family hold, and beg to come inside.

Mother wolf, teach me, I beg. Allow me to look inside and embrace all I find.

Enable me to see the glistening white light against the backdrop of the endless void.

Two weeks before the conference, metaphors from nature were penetrating my sleep, creating strong symbolic images in my dreaming mind. Inside of myself, I knew there was a place where the answers to my questions could be found. To me, the creek symbolized the streams of consciousness that flowed through my being. Look within. Look inside, the dream told me. Trust your instinctual nature. My instincts told me that I would soon find a key, a missing link without which my life couldn't move forward. Anxiously I awaited the conference, knowing somehow without being able to explain why that the convention would forever change my life. The omens would prove to be true.

— § —

The first day of the conference was a typical hot and sunny September day in Phoenix, Arizona. I rolled out of bed, uncharacteristically energetic and happy for a weekday. What a treat to wake up and not go to work! While my friends were downing their two cups of coffee, I was embarking on an adventure. Over breakfast, I examined the conference literature one last time. The flyer describing the seminars read like a vacation travel brochure. "Try yoga in the morning, Tai Chi, or meditation." Explore the leading edge therapies of psychodrama, movement therapy, Rubenfeld Synergy Method®, humor therapy, play therapy, or Reiki. I might as well have been paging through a leaflet describing activities in another language. Therapy was, for me (forget-emotions-give-me-logic), a fairly foreign culture.

I read the description of the Reiki seminar one more time. Reiki was described as a "transformational tool," a method of healing with the universal life force and human energy fields. This was one of the seminars that originally captivated my attention. For the past several months I had been reading about healers who moved and balanced the human energies to bring about healing where traditional medicine had failed. I couldn't believe I was actually going to meet someone who could do this. I danced around in anticipation, hastily picked up the dishes, and headed out the door.

I parked in the north lot of a plush Scottsdale resort and walked up the drive, feeling like a kid playing hooky from school. "Wow!" I couldn't help exclaiming aloud when I reached the courtyard. Usually, on a Wednesday, I was walking into a building with few windows and scores of fluorescent lights glaring in the otherwise dull cubicles. Work was a sterile environment designed, I supposed, to keep us glued to our computers. But today, what a difference! Here I was walking across a tiled terrace that was artfully landscaped with gurgling fountains and pink bougainvillea flowers spilling out of their containers. The great conference hall was filled with natural light that poured in through the glass panes in the massive wooden doorways. Crystal prisms on the huge chandeliers cast a thousand rainbows on the ceiling. Opulence and beauty were everywhere. Even the restrooms were elegant, I noticed, with wooden doors on the stalls and faux marble countertops. What a relief to be in an environment that felt alive!

After registering, I sat outside under the scant shade of a Palo Verde tree and planned my activities for the next four days. I circled the seminars in my brochure that I planned to attend and then went back inside in search of new friends. Like a puppy exploring a new park, I couldn't sit still for long. Most of the participants, I discovered, were therapists, counselors, nurses, or doctors—all people who were interested in expanding their professional knowledge and picking up continuing education credits along the way. Except for one other woman I met who was also an engineer (coincidentally working for Boeing on 777 airplane parts in Texas) I was the outsider in this crowd. I discovered for the first time in my life, the freedom of *not* belonging. I loved being able to move easily among a crowd without having to look good or impress any of my peers. I savored the unusual luxury of not having anyone depending on me or looking to me for answers.

The conference brochure indicated that mini-massages were available in the hall so I went to take my place in line. "Oh my gosh!" My heart skipped a beat when I saw that one of the women would be doing free Reiki mini-treatments. She was about 5'9" tall and dressed in a loose and comfortable ethnic print. She had beautiful curly auburn hair and a gorgeous complexion. I don't know why I reacted so dramatically, but I stopped her as she walked to her chair. Was she the one I had come to meet? "What exactly is Reiki?" I asked, wanting to know more.

The woman looked at me briefly as if she were weighing her choices for a response. I didn't understand at the time the difficulty one has in trying to explain Reiki with a quick reply. Seconds passed, then the woman's expression betrayed the fact that she had made a decision. As I waited for her answer, she smiled instead and placed her right hand on my left shoulder. I felt a jolt as if something had shocked me, but surprisingly there was no pain. Instead, a tingle and a warm sensation rushed out of the woman's hand and into my shoulder. The feeling trailed through the entire left side of my body and seemed to leap into the floor like a spark. I looked at her with my eyes wide open and my mouth slightly ajar. She grinned, knowing I felt the energy. A warm feeling still permeated my entire body and I was instantly relaxed. What was this? I wanted more.

Later, I would learn that the person receiving Reiki draws the energy through the practitioner much like a vacuum will pull in the surrounding air. At the time, I knew nothing of the sort. I stood in line, both agitated and excited, staring at the strange woman who now felt like a friend. I had the bizarre sensation that the power and warmth I had just experienced was somehow familiar. Something else stirred my memory— unconditional love, as if I had been touched by the brilliance of an angel's smile. I shook my head. This was beyond explanation. "Are you Jessica?" I asked, wondering if she was the one I had read about in the brochure. "No," the woman answered, "I'm a massage therapist. I learned Reiki to enhance my practice." The strange feeling came over me again—butterflies in my stomach. "You mean anyone can learn this? Anyone?" I questioned eagerly. "Yes," she replied. A different future flashed quickly before my eyes.

The conference workshops passed by in a happy blur. I laughed, I cried, and I played as I learned all sorts of ways to treat my mind, body, and spirit to healing modalities that I hadn't even thought necessary before I attended the seminars. I filled my journal with my thoughts and with techniques that I would use over and over during the upcoming months. On Friday I was barely able to contain my anticipation as I searched for and found the room where the Reiki seminar was about to begin. Jessica, an elegant woman with a soft and yet powerful voice, stood in the front. She talked about Reiki as if hands-on-healing were as common as the corner grocery store and as easily fit into everyday life as brushing your teeth. I was impressed by her professional and intelligent manner, as well as her articulate speaking. She seemed so... normal! I laughed. What had I been expecting? She explained that no special gift or talent was required; anyone could learn this healing practice. When she asked if anyone wanted a mini-treatment I rushed to the front of the room and sat in front of one of her helpers.

The woman who worked on me was tiny. Slightly graying hair and wrinkles betrayed her years, but the sparkle in her eyes and glow under her skin told me that age hadn't claimed her spirit. She put her hands over my eyes and I tried to relax, waiting for the electric-shock feeling of the previous day. Instead, waves of calm rushed up and down my body as if a mild sedative was gradually taking effect. Slipping into a soothing blackness, I saw rings of purple and yellow moving past my closed eyelids. The woman's hands were pouring a numbing warmth into my head and I soon forgot any self-consciousness as I let my head slump forward in front of the conference room full of people. The short treatment was over before I realized that I had slipped into an altered state of consciousness. I felt like I was floating when the woman tapped me gently on the shoulder and asked me if I would like to take my seat. I smiled and looked at her happily. "No." I got up from the chair and felt my legs waver as if I had been at sea or at least very drunk. Smiling, I managed to find my seat and drop into the chair.

"Mm. Peace. Relaxation. Not a care in the world." I wanted to hum. Light and happy as a spring breeze, I felt a warm fuzzy feeling enveloping me as if I was rolling in soft cotton. I swayed from side to side just slightly and swung my legs back and forth—graceful fluid movement. When had I been this relaxed? "Once," I answered myself daydreaming, "when I was about twelve, picking blueberries." Lazy summer days from times gone by drifted through my mind—sweet memories that came and went like wisps of perfume on a night wind. "Oh," I remembered my surroundings and tried to focus on the discussion. The fog in my head started to clear and my thoughts were like a beam pointing at the speaker. Super-relaxed and yet hyper-alert, I heard the words being spoken while I watched in wonder as sparkling golden lights came into focus around the heads of the people giving the Reiki treatments. "I've become Alice in Wonderland," I thought to myself. Nothing surprised me except for a burning thirst that I couldn't ignore. I was parched.

"Drink lots of water," the woman in the front said as I wondered about my condition. "OK," I answered agreeably as if she were talking directly to me. I threaded my way to the back of the room where chilled glasses and pitchers wet with the dew of condensation offered some relief. I had never been so thirsty. One glass slid down my throat easily, then another. Four glasses later, I began to feel a little odd. I drank more of the icy elixir then started to quiver. Jolts of something akin to electricity were running up and down my spine. My back started to spasm and jerk as I did sometimes just when I was about to fall asleep. My hands shook and my teeth quivered violently, but I wasn't at all cold. I looked around the room to see if anyone else was having strange reactions to the treatments, but so far no one seemed to be experiencing any ill effects. I shook more, feeling waves of fear wash over me. "What am I afraid of? Why am I shaking?" I started to become concerned. I raised my hand to ask the question and even my fingers in the air waved as if battered by a gusty wind. The seminar was almost over by this time and most of the people had left the room, smiling and relaxed. The few of us remaining seemed to be the ones that felt the treatment most strongly. "I'm shaking," I said dumbly to the gentle and beautiful woman still standing in the front, and I held out my hand to show her. She touched my arm. I felt warmth flow from her hand and as quickly as the spasms had begun, they stopped.

I looked at her in shock and in that instant her eyes and her touch spoke volumes to me. I quivered inwardly as the hand on my arm somehow communicated to me secrets I had once forgotten. "This is your life," the touch told me. "You've come home. You remember. You're back. Welcome!" I didn't hear any of those things, but I knew them all at once as if a thought that had been germinating in my mind since the day I was born suddenly exploded into being. I didn't know who was speaking these thoughts into my mind. I didn't understand the sensations or the feelings of déjà vu. I only knew I was burning with physical thirst and I had a burning desire to learn more about Reiki.

"Why was I shaking?" I asked Jessica. She smiled knowingly and replied slowly. "It's just fear." She smiled, and again I had the strange sensation that she knew everything about me. "Your entire life is about to change." I looked at her, eyes wide with wonder and thought to myself, "Yes. Yes, I know. I've been preparing for this my whole life."

"How do you describe magic?" I wrote later in my diary.

> "How do you describe a peace, an inner knowing, and a feeling of coming home? How do you explain shaking uncontrollably with fears you can't name, only to be calmed when a woman lightly touches your arm? This is what I've been waiting for. The simplicity of Reiki appeals to me. Truth and beauty lie not in our

vast reservoirs of knowledge but rather in what's right in front of us at times. I can't explain the feelings I'm having right now but at some level I know I've reached a turning point in my life. I will learn this work and I will heal."

Never before had a decision point in my life been so clearly marked. As I had done on the hike, I chose my path and never once looked back. I took my leap of faith and registered for the Reiki training, not quite understanding how the simple energetic initiations that would allow me to help others heal would also alter my future. As the omens had predicted, I had chosen, albeit unwittingly, death to an old way of life and birth into a new one. I told a friend the next day that I felt for the first time as if someone had just placed a signpost in front of me that read, "Yes, you are here, on the right path, the roadway to heaven, and the highway to the life of your dreams."

— § —

Three nights later I sat in the courtyard of a small shopping plaza next to a Mexican-style fountain. Beyond the courtyard to my right, I could see the sun setting over a nearby pond while the ducks made a huge ruckus. Behind me, the sounds of music and soft conversation from a nearby restaurant floated on the night wind, while to my left the bright lights of a jewelry store glistened off the gold and gems inside. In front of me Jessica's tiny eclectic art gallery, which doubled as her Reiki classroom, waited in the dark. I looked at my watch and realized I was fifteen minutes early. Just a few days ago, I had experienced Reiki for the first time and now, drawn to the practice as if an invisible magnet had me caught in its force, I was going to learn this technique for myself! I couldn't have been more excited. What had once been on my list of things to do "someday, maybe" would soon be a reality. Jessica arrived five minutes before class, and informed me that I would be the only student that night. "You just never know," she said smiling.

We went inside and sat on bright cushions on the floor. Amidst paintings with colors and shapes that would transport me into alternate worlds just by the viewing, and surrounded by crystals and gemstones of every color of the rainbow, I learned more about the mystical force that animates life. "Reiki," Jessica told me, "is Japanese for universal life force." I smiled in recognition. I had read about the "chi" energies that flow through the body, the ones that are manipulated in the Chinese disciplines such as acupuncture and martial arts. I knew that the force was called "prana" in India. Native American healers use "Spirit" or "medicine." Some say the force is God, while others say the force comes from God. I gathered that Reiki practitioners did not need to make such distinctions.

Universal life force—at the time I accepted the simple definition with utter knowingness. Beyond the words was an energy coming into my heart and my mind that spoke to me of mysteries that were beyond description. Later I would tell friends and co-workers about Reiki and find myself struggling to translate the simple concept, so easily felt, into a complex system of language. "While the Big Bang theory of the universe says everything should be going toward maximum disorder," I would tell my friends, "life is always tending to bring itself into greater balance and order." Modern chaos and fractal theories have begun to show intricate underlying patterns in all of nature. "What is the force, the mind, the heart, the soul, the Spirit that creates the order?" we ask. Reiki is simply one way to describe that force of life.

Reiki practitioners, Jessica explained to me, do not "do" much. They simply place their hands on a person, plant, or animal and the energy flows in accordance with the needs of the receiver. The practitioners make no diagnosis or decisions concerning the "healing" of their client. Instead, they act as a "drinking straw" for the life force, allowing the client to sip the forces of life through them. I laughed at the analogy. So much for being an all-powerful healer. My first lesson in humility had begun and I didn't even notice.

When the time came for the first attunement, I sat in a chair and listened to the music playing in the background while Jessica did her work in my energy field. Within seconds I entered the blissful state of consciousness I remembered from my Reiki treatment in the seminar and then I began to dream. The chair seemed to rise above the ground and then float high above the trees in a virgin forest. Curiously, at the same time, some part of my awareness remained conscious of all that was still going on in the gallery; I could even hear the ducks quacking outside of the office. When Jessica indicated that she was finished, I was surprised, as if I had fallen asleep and was suddenly being awakened.

I slowly sat down on my cushion and stared at Jessica in silence. I saw energy around her head again, a halo-like aura glowing brightly in a golden yellow color. I felt light and peaceful. My muscles were relaxed, and my breathing deep and full. "All my life," I thought, still in a blissful stupor, "I've waited for this all my life. So simple, yet so profound." "All my life I've heard, and read, and studied about being in a state of grace, but until this moment," I thought, "I never knew."

This moment I knew grace. This moment, I knew beauty. This moment, I felt truth and the love of God shining through the woman's hands and into my heart. I stared at Jessica again and she smiled broadly as if she had just witnessed this miraculous process for the first time. I would later learn that each attunement is different. Each one is like the first of its kind. Each brings different experiences to both the Reiki master and the student. Reaching into a mystical grab bag of experiences, the student unconsciously pulls the ones they need and want to guide them on their path. Every one of my four attunements was different. I dreamt again during the second, felt like I was floating for the third, and simply knew a deep peace in a comforting blackness during the fourth. Since then, I've witnessed dozens of other attunements with other people and have constantly been amazed at their diversity.

In between the attunements, while my system adjusted to the influx of new energy, Jessica recounted the history of Reiki. This method of natural healing was rediscovered in the late 1800s by a Japanese Christian professor teaching in a boy's school near Kyoto. When asked by his students if he knew how Christ healed, he realized that his entire life was based on faith rather than knowledge, and he wanted to know more. He left his position and went on an educational quest to learn about healing. Ten years later, after studying Christianity, Buddhism, and the ancient Chinese and Sanskrit Buddhist texts, Dr. Usui received the vision he had been waiting for. Near the end of a twenty-one-day meditation, he came to understand the meanings of some of the ancient texts and remembered how using the healing energies had once been the birthright of humanity.

I sat entranced as Jessica continued with the story. Surrounded by stores bustling with modern living, I sat in a quiet shop while a wise woman recounted the history of her trade in a time-honored tradition of the ancient storytellers. I was overwhelmed by a feeling of being intricately connected to a tradition immersed in the past, and one that would play an integral role in my future. Anchored as such, between past and future, I sat fully present while I listened and learned. Dr. Usui taught Reiki to a retired Japanese Navy admiral, Dr. Hayashi. Dr. Hayashi in turn taught Hawayo Takata, a Hawaiian woman of Japanese descent who later brought Reiki back to the United States. When Jessica showed me pictures of Dr. Usui, Dr. Hayashi, and Mrs. Takata, the breath froze in my throat and I stared in silence. Mrs. Takata looked exactly like the Hawaiian "aunt" who had appeared in my dream only a few months prior asking me if I was willing to give up life as I knew it. The moment I saw her picture, I re-experienced the immense love I had known in the dream. Already dizzy with emotion that felt like it would consume me as easily as a fire consumes its fuel, I felt as if my heart was going to burst.

Two days later, my training was complete. Four times I sat in a chair while Jessica did her work in my energy field that looked to me to be simply the air around my body. Four times I found myself in altered states of consciousness while still being aware of the physical room and the sounds around me. Four times I felt deep gratitude and a sense of homecoming. Four times I wondered if the initiations were working. I learned how to give myself a Reiki treatment and learned how I could work on another person. Still wondering if this ability was real, I put my hands on my head at work the next day and felt them burning with the same healing energy that I originally felt in the massage therapist's hands. In awe of myself for the first time in my life and overwhelmed by a feeling of being reunited with a part of my soul that I barely remembered, I thanked God/Spirit/life force—the source, creator, and sustainer of everything—for the remembering.

I didn't understand scientifically how the attunements worked. I was wont to explain how my hands would heat up when I placed them on my body. I found myself groping for words every time I tried to explain what I was doing to a friend. Yet, deep down, I had knowing. Where science failed me, mysticism did not. The healing power in my hands felt as old and familiar as a childhood stuffed toy, as if I had known, loved, worked, and healed with this energy once before but had long since forgotten the ancient knowledge. The energy taught me, via experience as I worked on myself, friends, and family, how to practice my new art. Where my mind failed me, my heart took its place. I watched people who were completely stressed become blissful after only twenty minutes under my hands. I felt only gratitude, knowing the healing power was coming through me, rather than from me. I was, for the first time since early childhood, wide-open, trusting, and thankful for my wonderful life. The week after the attunements, I felt as if I could finally rest and bask in the warmth of love and good feelings that permeated my being. The energy soon taught me that the only constant in my life was change.

— § —

Dear Journal - Today at work I was so frustrated I could barely keep quiet. I had a very difficult day. I'm trying my best to support the entire department, but the people we depend on are not on schedule and we're falling behind as well. No one is really to blame. The deadlines are nearly impossible, and the people are trying their best. But why, why, why do I feel like I am the only one who will stand in front of our customers and tell them all "Yes, we can meet this deadline," with the disclaimer, "if everything goes perfectly?" I feel they know this, yet everyone ignores the disclaimer, the fine print. Everyone knows that nothing goes perfectly and we will likely fall behind schedule. But they ignore all that and instead say, "Well, you told us we could make it." Sure, "if this and this and that happens," I say. Oh, what to do? I've done my best. I feel the people in the department are doing their best. Perhaps there are things I can do better.

My thoughts were in a swirl driving home. Again, I wondered about my future. Even if my career is going incredibly well, this is not what I really want to do for the rest of my life. Earlier, I prayed for guidance and direction. At that moment, sitting on a post near the road I saw a jet-black crow. His head turned and he watched me as I drove by, following my car with those haunting black-mirror eyes. There was something different about that bird. He had a surreal quality. I'm having a difficult time putting my finger on the feeling. I've never seen a crow in the Phoenix area before, and I've been here six years. Is he lost? Maybe I've just received a visit from one of those shape-shifter spirit guides that I've read about.

"What am I writing?" I wanted to censor myself as I wrote in my own diary but I had promised myself I wouldn't do that. Did I really believe in spirit guides, signs, and omens? "Yes, I do believe," I answered myself quietly. "Why?" The scientific part of me still desperately sought an explanation for phenomena I couldn't explain. Nonetheless, my instinctual feelings were starting to overpower the limited knowingness of my computer-like mind.

I was beginning to suspect that my instinct was the key to some of the answers I had been seeking. Feelings and intuition taught me to recognize the signs that nature provided. Intellect helped me understand them. I never knew whether the appearance of animals or phenomena at particularly significant times in my life was a natural occurrence or not. What mattered more was that the things brought to my attention called me to seek truths and answers in all forms, and to learn how much knowledge is inherently contained in the wisdom of the universe. Crow, I learned when I looked up the symbol in one of my books, was often viewed as an omen of change. I've not seen a crow in the Phoenix area since.

The hawks were starting to appear in my life as well. Although they were native to the area, they seemed to show up at the oddest times. Just when I was considering a question and had arrived at my own answer, I would look up and see a hawk circling overhead. Hawks fly high and see the big picture, but aren't afraid to dive low to glimpse the details. I was a hawk woman at work. I would grasp a concept quickly and learn the details when I needed them. Hawk became one of my personal allies, an animal that connected me with my own innate nature. Some days the magnificent birds flew just twenty feet to the left of my car window, as if they were escorting me on my way.

Other days, they flew in front of my car. Too many hawks found and followed me in too small a time-period for me to believe the occurrence mere chance. I felt the presence of an unseen guide telling me I was headed in the direction I had asked to travel. Tentatively, I asked my unseen guide to help me recognize each step along my journey. My prayer was soon answered.

— § —

On a Friday night in late summer as the sun dipped low near the horizon, a girlfriend and I hiked quickly through the desert just behind one of Arizona's plush conference resorts. We climbed surreptitiously into a sandy ravine, under the umbrella of an age-old mesquite tree, where we quietly unpacked the varied contents of our backpacks: bundles of herbs, cornmeal, our notebooks, and the bone-white masks of our faces that we had created only a few weeks before. In answer to an unspoken prayer, I had recently found a book[1] on mask making and ceremony that prompted the evening's exercise. Making the masks in my bathroom at home the week before had been an unsettling exercise. As the strips of plaster-impregnated gauze hardened on my face, I experienced an eerie sense of how I felt being spirit immersed in the shell I call my body.

Now, looking up at me like some horrific face out of a cheap thrill movie, my mask was the first three-dimensional representation I had ever seen of my own countenance. The face was visibly different than the flat image I saw every day in the mirror. The sunset cast long shadows on the mask, reminding me that we had to

---

[1] Andrews, Lynn, The Mask of Power. San Francisco, CA: HarperSanFrancisco, 1992.

hurry. My friend and I finished arranging our belongings and gathered four stones to represent the four directions: east where the sun rises, the place of illumination and insight; south where the sun travels in the height of the day's activity, the place of innocence and trust, and the place where you carry your work out into the world; west, the place where the sun sets, the darkness of the void from whence all life springs, and the place of introspection and dreaming; north, the home of the elders, and the place of wisdom where you go to share the teachings you have gathered in the other directions. Next, we collected a handful of smaller rocks that represented the problems, worries, and fears that we wished to leave behind.

As we walked through the "doorway" of our crude medicine wheel, the sun began to sink into the horizon. A lone hawk flew just twenty feet over our heads and settled into the black branches of a nearby tree that had been deadened by lightning. She turned her head and peered straight into my eyes as if waiting for me to begin. I fought back tears. Her black silhouette, sitting in the gnarled branches against the backdrop of the blazing orange sunset gave the setting a dreamlike quality. My friend and I exchanged glances and then quietly placed our masks in the small "graves" we had dug for them in the desert floor. Staring up out of the earth, our masks seemed to watch us while we took turns throwing the pebbles we had collected out of the circle. With each pebble, we "gave away" an attitude that no longer empowered us. "I give away any remaining thoughts of not being good enough. I give away my judgments, assessments, and evaluations of people. I give away relying on others to make me happy. I give away whatever prevents me from knowing who I really am and what I am capable of doing and being in this life." We spoke slowly and deliberately, each time reclaiming our personal power by symbolically releasing the attitudes that disempowered us.

The sun melted into the ground while the sky above turned a deep periwinkle blue and the first stars twinkled brightly overhead. The mesquite tree danced slightly in the gentle wind. The hawk that was perched in the ancient tree kept watch while we completed our ceremony. We buried our masks and the small mounds reminded us of blank faces looking up out of the floor of the earth. We stood up as the sun stole the last bits of light. The desert hummed with the sounds of night insects and the winds tickled the brush. The earth began to absorb the coolness of the evening air. We walked back to the car in silence, lost in thought. I was awed by the simple power of praying aloud in a natural setting. I had never done that before. I had only prayed in a church, using words that other people taught me. Here, I could feel the energy and the life force of the place like water flowing gently around me and a faint electric tingling that surrounded my body. I had never prayed so sincerely. I felt odd also for conducting a ceremony that contained elements far removed from my own tradition, and awkward because we were within earshot of people living and staying in the resort community nearby who would likely think us crazy if they only knew what we were doing. I was thankful for the small ravine and the cover of the desert trees.

That night I awoke in the middle of a sound sleep. In one of those dreams you have in a half-conscious waking in the night, I saw the stars in a blackened sweet cool desert sky. The leaves of a mesquite tree above me were lit by a silver moon, and the stars danced behind them, twinkling in time with the beating of my heart. Even in my dream state I knew the vision was one from the perspective of the mask I left buried in the earth. I felt as if I was part of the earth itself in this dream, synchronized with the cosmic dance of the stars.

I awoke early the next morning and drank my herbal tea on the patio before the sun rose. Everything I saw was outlined in a thin electric blue color but strangely, that didn't seem strange. I went back inside, gave myself a short Reiki treatment, and slipped into a few more hours of sweet slumber. Around 10:30 a.m., my friend and I went back into the desert to complete our ceremony. The masks were still there but the face of the desert looked completely different in the bright morning sun.

We prayed this morning facing each of the four directions, asking for help in our lives. In the east, I requested spiritual illumination. "Tell me how to make my entire life a prayer to the one Spirit and life force," I prayed. In the North, I asked for the wisdom to make clear decisions and know the direction my life was taking. From the south, I asked for the innocence and playfulness of a child and for the ability to trust that life presents itself to us joyfully and abundantly. Finally, in the West, I asked that I always be aware that true power is to be found within. I prayed aloud, sincerely, feeling my prayers were indeed being heard.

My friend and I entered our circle of stones then took turns telling the desert winds what we wanted in life and what our "new faces" would enable us to have. I asked for success in my career and in all my relationships. I asked for direction in my life. I asked that I be able to fulfill my life's purpose. We didn't petition, but rather said aloud with conviction, "I want..." whatever it was. We asked for love, joy, and great abundance in our lives. With gratitude, we thanked Spirit for prayers that were already heard and fulfilled in the future.

As our gift back to the world, we stated powerfully who we were committed to becoming. "I am one who shows people that it is possible to be energetic, enthusiastic and in love with life; to celebrate the vast diversity of all creation; to awaken our consciousness; to know our true nature; and to see beyond our limitations to know what is possible. This is the new face I wish to create." Then, using our hands to brush away the dirt, we gently unearthed our masks, smoothed the earth's surface, and packed our bags. For a few hours we hiked around the desert, gathering objects with which to decorate our new faces. Here a coyote had left a few feathers from his last evening meal. There the grasses grew strong and dry. A few twigs and quartz stones agreed to come with us. We scattered our cornmeal and herbs as a symbol of giving back to the earth, then left with our bags and our hearts full of the things we had seen and prayed for.

After lunch we decorated our masks, using only intuition and the colors and symbols that attracted us: a splash of paint, a bead, a feather, an animal, some rose petals. My friend glued broken glass she found in the desert above the eyes and painted horses on her mask. Works of art were taking shape under our hands as we labored, and yet none of our decisions were made consciously. At the end of the day I was amazed. What had been earlier a blank white face, nothing but a canvas upon which I was to create, was now a thing of beauty. The form of my own face was a work of art that stared back at me.

The left side of my mask was a deep forest green; the right was painted bright white. I realized later that the colors were ripe with meaning, symbolizing the various polarities that influenced my life. The mask reminded me of my light and dark side, the parts of myself that I showed others and the parts I hid. The green represented nature and humanity, fecund, earthy, feminine energies, and the native cultures that honored the earth as their mother. Paradoxically, the white reminded me both of spirit and of our white society that, for the most part, seems to have forgotten our need to live in balance. Light and dark symbolized both the dark and the light. I hadn't considered any of these meanings when I reached for the paint jars.

The other symbology was easily understood once I silenced my busy mind and let the thoughts flow unimpeded. As I stared at the blue-green globe that I had painted on the chin I heard the voices in my head once again, *"You are of the earth, and the voice of the earth. Speak her truth."* I considered the small jagged streak of flames that snaked along the left jaw-line. *"Burn away the anger that you hold in the tension of your jaw,"* the mask told me. Fire converts objects into pure energy and light. *"Transmute your pain."* The flames reminded me that I was in the process of transforming my materialistic view on life into a more spiritual perspective.

On the right side of the mask, I painted a blue lizard decorated with stars and was surprised to learn that lizard is a symbol associated with dreaming and the night. A spiral danced along one side of my mask—a mirror of the unfolding evolution of our spiritual selves. At the top of the mask, a crown of feathers spread in every direction, much like the energy that flows through the crown center at the top of our heads and fans out like a fountain flowing over us. The placement of a peacock feather glued just between the eyes was also no accident. These feathers, I read, were symbolic of the third-eye, the energy center located in the middle of the forehead that is associated with inner sight and psychic vision. Rose petals along the green side of my face told me that I would soon be learning to honor the more delicate and beautiful aspects of my feminine nature.

I sat holding my mask in my hands, and for the first time, truly comprehended Carl Jung's concept of the collective unconscious—a vast pool of symbolic knowledge from which we all draw inspiration for our dreams and our art. I had taken a dip in the pool. The symbols I chose were rich with meaning when considered within the context of my life. As the mask so vividly pointed out, I was involved in a balancing act between all of my different polarities. "Reiki balances and aligns," Jessica once told me. I was working to face my own dark side and to heal myself with the light. I was trying to be more intuitive, feminine, and gentle in appropriate situations, while still maintaining my reason and ability get things done quickly and aggressively. I was exploring earthy spiritualities, trying to reconcile them with what my white society had taught me and to integrate the two into a worldview and way of life that was sacred, holy, and meaningful to me. I was honoring my dreams, traveling along my spiral path, and awakening my own vision. The mask was a physical representation of all that was going on in the world of my mind and my spirit.

In the months following the simple ceremony, the prayers I prayed aloud in the desert would be answered, slowly but surely.

Dear Journal -

Late at night and I can't sleep.

I rock back and forth.

The energy carries me in landscapes

and oceans deep,

in rocky crags and murky depths within my soul.

Light my way.

I am merging spirit with humanity,

at last, becoming whole.

— § —

As the weeks after my Reiki attunements and mask ceremony passed, I found that my enthusiasm for Reiki grew even stronger. Never before had I felt so drawn to any type of work or play and I longed to learn more. "Remember" might have been a more accurate word than "learn." I still had the uncanny sensation that I had done energetic healing before. When? I knew no way of answering the question.

I called Jessica and asked her if there were any more classes available. She had already told me that Level I was all I would ever need for self-healing, but I knew I needed more. More what? I wondered. I couldn't say exactly, but when she told me there was a Level II available, I had that strange, nagging feeling that told me this was the next step in my spiritual journey. We arranged a date and a time for the training.

En route to her shop a few days later, I was deeply lost in thought when I stopped my car at a red light. A sudden sleepiness overcame me and caused me to turn my attention inward until I was focusing completely on a vision whose scenery made me forget all about my actual surroundings. In my mind's eye I saw a Native American dancer dressed in colorful yellow and tan buckskins. He looked at me with a piercing gaze and then bent over, and with two fingers, traced a symbol in the sand beneath him. He stood up again, looming over me and looked into my eyes. I was taken aback by the deep kindness and compassion reflected in his gaze. He seemed to be imploring me to understand some sort of unspoken communication. For a moment, I didn't understand, and then all of a sudden I knew he wanted me to look at the symbol.

I turned my inner eyes toward the image in the sand and felt a shock of recognition fly through me, like a large dose of electric current. The scene branded itself in my memory. I looked back at the man wanting to know more and to understand why the symbol felt so familiar. Instead of answering those questions, he spoke directly into my mind, telling me that he was giving me a sacred and valuable gift—"a key to my soul" were the words ringing through my mind—whose meaning would unfold at some later date and time. The scene faded as quickly as the vision had formed, and I looked up with a start, surprised to see that I was still sitting in traffic with the stoplight just turning green. I put my car in gear and drove to class, still shaken by the sudden and unexpected nature of the vision, and still wondering about the meaning of the symbol.

I should have known that there are no ill-timed visions, or chance coincidences. I was only mildly surprised when Jessica told me that level II involved learning about symbols. "You might be seeing them in dreams or visions," she said. "They're the key to your soul." Overwhelmed by the reality of the vision, and immersed in a feeling of intense gratitude for a gift I couldn't quite comprehend, I said a simple prayer of thanks and recorded the symbol in my notebook for future reference.

Grudgingly, I began to admit that I was being gifted with signs, visions, and dreams that were guiding me on my life's path, and symbols that reflected the hidden qualities of my soul. Nonetheless, the voices of doubt and logical skepticism tried their best to dissuade me from believing these events to be anything out of the ordinary. One moment I was sure that I was receiving messages from Spirit, while in the very next, I tried to convince myself that these occurrences were mere coincidence. A hike was just a hike. A leap from a cliff was just a leap. A storm was simply a storm. A vision was just a daydream—wasn't it? Trained to approach life from a logical, scientific perspective, I worried that I was making up the rest. At times, I wondered if I was going crazy. *"Then why,"* the inner voice countered, *"are these meaningless events occurring at meaningful times?"* The subtle voices in my mind suggested that there was more to reality than meets the eye and much that science has yet to discover.

At long last, I conceded that there were different ways of perceiving reality and knowing "truth." One way was based on logic, rational thought, known facts, and accepted belief systems. The other was based on intuition, metaphor, and personal experience. Neither one need necessarily invalidate the other. All my life, however, I had been trained to believe that knowledge comes from learning established fact, and that truth is what you can prove. Now I was learning that wisdom is bred by experience and truth is a malleable construct.

I began to interpret my surroundings in two ways: at face value as I had always done, and also *as if* they were symbols bringing me messages from Spirit. In doing so, I found that there were unseen layers of reality superimposed on the world in which I was accustomed to living. As I started "listening" to the secret language of the soul, I began living my life on two levels—one foot firmly anchored in the physical world and another in the world of spirit. I didn't doubt that the colors, animals, and other objects that attracted me were natural occurrences that I noticed because of my conditioning and interests, yet their appearance conveyed far more meaning than I could attribute to chance. A hawk was still a hawk, just a bird flying high in the sky, but the timing of his flight over my head just as I was considering a situation from a higher perspective, made me suspect that all of life dances in some beautifully orchestrated synchronicity. Questions were answered. Choices were made more easily.

We all have signposts and symbols to guide us. Anything that captures our attention can be understood as a message from our soul or a reflection of our inner state of being. Watch for the colors that attract you. They speak to you of emotions and issues in your life. Notice the animals that cross your path. They might be messengers that herald your current life lessons. How do you decorate your house? What books do you read? What texture feels wonderful against your skin? What music do you listen to? What attracts you in nature— storms, the seashore, a snowy forest, a peaceful rain, a hot summer's day? Ask yourself what these things mean to you. Before you seek outside sources of information, ask your inner voices and wait for the answers to come. Use free association. Trust your gut instinct. Then use reference books. You're likely to find that you already know the meaning of the symbols in your life. Play with them with a childlike sense of adventure and discover a treasure chest full of hidden wisdom. I did.

The whispers of Spirit are so subtle at times that they are easily missed. I always thought that an experience of the divine would be something like Moses hearing the voices from the burning bush. I wanted a clear message coming from on high, impossible to misinterpret or discount as anything but the voice of God. I now know otherwise. Spirit may have spoken dramatically to the prophets in ancient times, but in most people's lives the whispers are so cloaked in normalcy that we hesitate to believe them anything but circumstance. We explain away an unlikely coincidence. We say we had a "lucky accident." We tell people we "just guessed" when we know something we have no logical reason to know. In order to acknowledge the whispers in my life, I had to take a leap of faith and believe first that there was a message, and second that I was worthy of receiving the communication. Then, like a radio receiver, I had to clear the static in my mind and tune in to the twenty-four hour broadcast of Spirit's voice.

Through symbol and ceremony, my work with Reiki, and my continuous exploration for truth, I started to understand my connection with the world and the people who surrounded me. I began to understand the force of life as part of my being, not simply something that flowed through me, but something that *was* me as well. I sensed this force carrying me toward an incredible future in which all of my life's dreams would be realized. The signs and symbols were pointing my way. I was beginning to learn the language of soul.

Chapter 4
The Masks in the Mirror

Shortly after dinner, after reading the day's mail and cleaning up the kitchen table, I snuck into the bathroom unnoticed. John was reading contentedly on the couch and the dogs were sleeping quietly at either end of the family room. I knew I would have at least half an hour before anyone began to question my whereabouts, or my sanity. I shut the door and took a few deep, metered breaths then began my nightly ritual of staring into the mirror. With enough patience, I hoped that I would learn to see my own energies. The tantalizing glimpse of the golden glowing lights around Jessica's head during the Reiki classes was all the incentive I needed to practice regularly.

Life was becoming increasingly strange after my second level Reiki classes. Even when I wanted to, I could no longer deny the reality of the invisible energies that flowed through my body and out of my hands. Like a wave rushing through me, or sometimes a whirlpool or a gentle stream massaging me from the inside out, I felt the energies' ebb and flow. At times my hands became inordinately hot while in other cases I felt a bone-chilling cold. In some spots just a few inches away from the body, I perceived a tingling, like static electricity, while in other places I sensed an effervescent fizzing as if I had placed my hands in a bubble bath. Sometimes the energy felt light and refined; other times I felt a subtle resistance as if my hands were running through thick tar or Jell-O. The sensations were as tangible to me as touching any physical object, but I had been raised and trained in a culture where we generally agree that things you can't see or measure don't exist. I wanted to use my sight to validate the perceptions of my touch.

As I watched my image in the mirror, the thoughts passing through my mind were like familiar guests who had long overstayed their welcome—comfortable but annoying. "My nose is too big. My makeup looks tired. My hair is dry. I really need a trim. Look at the bags under my eyes." I waited for the mind chatter to be still. "I should get more sleep. Wonder if I'll see anything tonight."

"Let the thoughts go." I concentrated on my breathing and continued to stare. Suddenly and unexpectedly, the voices of judgment and criticism ceased their chatter. Standing, staring, I felt myself shifting into a light trance. My breathing buoyed me up and down as I floated in a sea of unfamiliar consciousness. As if I was seeing myself for the first time, I gazed into the eyes of a face that appeared totally foreign to me. The face was better looking than I had supposed and deeply thoughtful. The eyes of my double in the glass stared back into my own as if she too was contemplating the nature of the spirit that animated her flesh.

"I've really never seen myself before," I thought. I was amazed that I could watch the face in front of me as if I was looking at someone else. Stripped of the masks that I had superimposed with my thoughts and critiques, I barely recognized myself. Did others see me this way, or did their judgments color their perceptions as mine had done? I studied the face objectively. The lights in my eyes glimmered and for a second I knew that there was an entire universe behind them—one where a spirit called "soul" peered through these tiny windows into the world of physical form. Who was I really—the body, the spirit, or both?

"Breathe," I told myself. I focused on the rise and fall of my chest and let the thoughts drift away. I gazed loosely at a spot three inches above my head and leaned back against the door to steady myself. My legs were starting to feel strange and wobbly, and my head was starting to spin. One. Two. Three. I counted slowly and deliberately as the air filled my lungs. One. Two. Three. I counted as I exhaled. In. Out. In. Out. Breath rushing down my abdomen to the base of my lungs and then coursing back in an endless cycle. In. Out. Eyes unfocused, almost crossing. Lights starting to shimmer under my skin. Eyes heavy, closing, can't keep them open. Can't think. Can't stay awake... Jerk! My chin hit my chest shortly before my eyes flew open. I looked around, surprised that I had nearly fallen asleep on my feet. What was that I had just seen? *"Breathe, Ann, breathe now!"* The thought-voice commanded me back into the altered state. *"Watch carefully."* The face in the mirror wavered in front of me as if a heat wave passed between me and the image I was watching. From beneath the skin, I could see an ethereal light beginning to glow that had a kind of yellowish-white luminescent tint. I focused my attention on the rhythm of my breath and continued to stare loosely. A few moments passed. A golden-colored light began to sparkle and shimmer around my form, splashed in places with an aqua green color reminiscent of the color of a shallow sea on a sunny day. "I'm doing it! I'm seeing my aura!" The lights faded with the thought. I took a few long deep breaths and relaxed my eyesight once again. The lights came back into focus. "John. John! John!!" I yelled as if I were being attacked, not stopping to consider the fact that he had no idea what I was doing. I wanted to share the wonder. "I'm glowing!"

Excitement was a one-way ticket out of the strange dimension. The instant I opened my mouth, the lights disappeared and the face in the mirror was simply mine—flesh and blood, blue-green eyes, and wavy brown hair. "Are you alright?" John asked, alarmed because of the urgency in my voice. He was off the couch now, trying to find me as I popped out of the bathroom. "Yes!" He looked at me strangely. "I just saw my aura!" I squealed with delight. He looked at me again, waiting for more of an explanation. "I was glowing. Green and yellow. All around my head and down my arms, and when I held my hands together, the light was between them too, and I almost couldn't stand up because I was getting really dizzy." I stopped to breathe again and grinned like an idiot. "Really?" he asked, not quite sure what to think of my rambling. I tried to tell him all I had been sensing but the words weren't adequate. Energy was a good metaphor, but how could I describe life's mysteries? I could only offer analogies and examples.

I walked back into the bathroom and stared into the mirror once again. The lights were gone for the night, still dancing in some dimension, I was sure, but invisible to my regular eyesight. Instead, I studied the woman who stared back at me. Who was she? The masks that I had seen in the mirror over the past few years were slowly fading. The faces of doubt and self-criticism were being replaced by the tentative and vulnerable face of a woman who was just learning to love herself in this life. As I stared into my own eyes, I realized that the woman I used to be was slowly vanishing. The harried, hurried woman who never considered herself "good enough" was being transformed, step by step, into a woman who knew herself as an integral part of a much larger world. Over the years, the sparkle and life in her eyes had grown dim, but now I saw the veils being lifted and the life force returning. "I'm a survivor," I thought and then corrected myself quickly, "No. I want more than survival. I want a life that I absolutely love." That no longer seemed too much to ask. I flipped off the light and left the masks in the mirror, wondering about the face that was beginning to emerge from beneath them.

The symbol I had copied into my notebook during the Reiki class was beginning to haunt me. In my mind's eye, I saw the glyph as I walked from my desk to my meetings at work. Circles, double lines, and zigzag patterns seemed to stand out wherever I looked. The persistent reminders were signs telling me the time had come to unravel the meaning of my vision.

I sat down on my living room floor late one Saturday afternoon surrounded by reference dictionaries. In front of me I placed a single white piece of paper with my symbol drawn in crisp black ink. I focused on the image for a moment then shut my eyes and asked for understanding. Immediately, the original vision began to replay in my mind's eye. "What are you trying to tell me?" I asked the Native American dancer who had traced the shape in the sand. "This is who you are," he replied and looked at me in a manner that told me he could look beyond any masks I might wear and know the true nature of my heart and soul. "Tell me what you mean," I pleaded, but the scene faded quickly into obscurity and soon the vision was only a memory. I stared at the image on the paper in front of me and waited for the insights that weren't long in coming.

The circle, I knew, was a symbol for wholeness, for the soul, and for all that exists in creation. The vertical line according to some traditions symbolized the spiritual plane of existence. It represented a type of Jacob's ladder to the heavens. The horizontal line could be interpreted to represent the earth or the physical plane of existence. In other traditions, the roles were reversed. How fitting, I thought, that the two lines should section off the northeast quadrant of the circle. I was born—spirit immersed in flesh—in the northeast, in the first quarter of the year. How fitting also were the interpretations of the medicine wheel: north for wisdom and east for spiritual illumination. This was consistent with my penchant for exploring knowledge and spirituality. Perhaps the circle represented the soul, and the quadrant sectioned off was the personality I called "Ann."

The double line, I realized suddenly, was a bridge connecting the world of spirit with the physical world. "I journey that bridge often," I thought, slowly beginning to understand the symbol's meaning. From the world of spirit—from dreams, symbols, and the signs in nature—I gathered insight and understanding that I could take across the bridge for use in my life and in my work. From the ordinary world I took regular experiences, and crossing the bridge, understood these to be valuable spiritual lessons. A new thought bubbled up from the depths of my unconscious mind. "I *am* the bridge."

Perhaps part of my life purpose was to help people merge spirituality with the practical concerns of every day living.

I became almost dizzy as the unseen energies began to swirl around me. The meaning of the symbol continued to unfold effortlessly. The zigzag line was a bolt of lightning, a symbol according to my books that represented a storm or a catalyst for change and new growth. Lightning also represented "enlightenment" or "shamanic initiation." I *was* the catalyst for change at work, striking swiftly with new ideas and moving with force to initiate their institution. No wonder I loved storms so much! The raw power and force of nature enlivened me. Lightning, I understood suddenly, was also a power that bridged earth and sky—a bridge, coincidentally, comprised of pure energy and light. Lightning occurs when a charge on the ground reaches upward to draw down power from the heavens. I understood that I was also a bridge between heaven and earth, sharing not only wisdom and information from the heavens, but also reaching upwards to connect with the force of Spirit's love, and to allow this power flow through me into others who were willing to receive.

"This is who you are." I heard the powerful voice of the dancer who spoke to me in my vision, and suddenly, I understood that I had opened up the record books of my soul and was being allowed to glimpse the meaning and purpose of my life. I sat in shocked and awed silence with the books scattered around me and the paper and pens strewn about. For months, I had been praying for some guidance in my life, and for months, I had been getting the guidance in bits and pieces, but here in front of me on a single sheet of paper was a symbol that confirmed the nature of my existence. Here was a representation of the energies of the woman who lived behind all the masks—the one who would bring spiritual concepts to people in logical terms; the one who would later learn to connect people with the truth of their nature and their spiritual guides; the one who acted in her career as a catalyst for change; and the woman who was ever striving to bring greater consciousness, awareness, and understanding into every situation in which she found herself. Here was a clear and clean mirror into which I could gaze and see the depths of my life purpose.

I stared at the symbol and held the paper close to my heart. I closed my eyes and took a deep breath, still thinking of the spirit-man who had gifted me with the vision. All of a sudden, although I didn't see him, I was overcome by a feeling so intense I could barely contain the emotion. If the feeling could have been translated into words, I would have heard the most incredibly tender voice telling me I was loved and deeply cherished. If the feeling could have been translated into music, the notes would have swept me away in ecstatic waves of sound. If the feeling could have been pictured, I would have seen the velvety soft petals of a perfect red rose. Instead, the feeling transcended all of these sensations, and I knew for the first time that I had never ever been alone.

By the time I opened my eyes, the tears of gratitude that were flowing freely had smeared the ink on my paper. I didn't care. The essence of the symbol's form was branded into the very core of my being. I felt the unseen presence that had given me this rare and precious gift, and in that moment I knew the nature of unconditional love.

— § —

Mirrors, mirrors on the walls

of my house, and in the halls;

at work, at play,

at night in dreams,

and still all day,

I see myself in everyone,

and every situation,

knowing that we're all the same,

just simply permutations

of the One

who wrote this game.

After unraveling the meaning of my symbol, I found that the mirrors in my life—those situations that revealed more about my nature and personality—were not limited to extraordinary or mystical experiences. All my external surroundings, including the people in my life and the situations in which I found myself, were also reflections of my inner triumphs and struggles. At work, I was coordinating the people in my department while juggling complex, ever-changing assignments. At the same time, I was managing an inner reality comprised of emotions, attitudes, and beliefs that were also in a state of wild flux. I noticed that the people who seemed to irritate me the most were simply mirroring some aspect of my personality that I refused to acknowledge or were triggering some emotions and issues from my past that needed healing. Similarly, the people I admired reflected positive qualities in myself that I had not yet seen.

My job was becoming increasingly visible, as I managed to accomplish the impossible while maintaining a genuinely good attitude about my work. I changed my hairstyle and clothing to become more feminine and caught people who had known me for years staring and wondering about the shift in both my attitude and appearance. At the pinnacle of my career, I accepted once and for all the inner knowing that I wouldn't remain in engineering for the rest of my life. I would forget this many times over the upcoming months, only to remember the insight again and again. John and I analyzed our budget and I began to save the money I would need to support our desired lifestyle on a smaller income. As I drove to and from work, the hawks continued to chase my car or fly across my path at the exact moment I received an insight or new thought about the future I was creating. These majestic birds mirrored the flight of my own spirit toward freedom.

As well, insights about my life and behaviors were revealed to me almost as quickly as I requested them.

— § —

Dear Journal - As promised, Reiki II is bringing numerous mental and emotional issues to the surface. I feel I'm on the verge of freedom again—freedom from the constraints placed on me by society, from the emotional burdens I've accepted, and from having to bear the sadness of some of the deepest separations within my own psyche.

Today, I have my period so I did Reiki on myself and asked that Spirit help bring to the surface of my consciousness whatever thoughts or attitudes lie at the root of the cramps. While I lay on the couch, hunched over, I realized that I've always joked that Mom thought I was a pain in the side from the day I was conceived. She thought she had appendicitis, when in reality she was pregnant. Without warning, I was flooded by a torrent of emotion. My whole life I've resisted being "feminine." I hide my feelings from people because I equate vulnerability with weakness. I've seen too many men trivialize women's opinions because they're conveyed with emotion. I was a tomboy during childhood, determined to fit in with the boys, to be strong, and to avoid behaving like a "stupid girl."

In college when I finally accepted myself as a woman, guys mistook my friendliness for flirting so I shut myself down again. I wanted to be accepted and to fit in. I didn't want to stand out. I didn't want any special attention, sexual or otherwise, for being female.

Then I went to work and found more of the same. Men and women are equal at work, as long as women behave like men. God forbid, we should be different. I overheard a manager at work the other day making a comment about a pregnant woman—"should've kept her at work later," or something to that effect, "Ha ha." I fumed in silence. I could have had him reprimanded, but to what avail? He wasn't malicious. He was simply ignorant. The workplace, no matter how enlightened it tries to be, still sees pregnancy as an interruption rather than a joyful part of the flow of life. I've never been a feminist because I hate extremes, but these imbalances do need to be rectified. Men and women have much in common, but there are some fundamental differences. We should stop fighting the notion.

Suddenly I realize that the cramps I feel are like the pain you feel when you're separated from someone you love. This deep heart-achy pain makes me feel as if my body is crying. Oh goodness. My body *is* crying, and has cried month after month, year after year, because I'm separated from an important part of myself and that keeps me from being whole and balanced. I have completely denied, ridiculed, and stifled my femininity. I have refused to allow myself to be vulnerable. I've suppressed my feelings. I won't let people contribute to me or take care of me. I have tried to murder a precious part of my soul.

The good news is she's awakening. In my dreams, the wolf appears as a symbol of the strong feminine nature. This fiercely loyal being guards her children in the dark of her womblike den and carries a quiet feminine power. She's coming to life inside of me. She's been buried for a very long time. I will have to observe myself carefully, and when I would otherwise stifle her, I will try to allow her expression. She is kind, caring, and beautiful. She's a joyful spirit who longs to love freely and accept love with innocence and abandon. This is a part of me, long lost, but now found. I mourn the years she's been buried, and I celebrate her return. Suddenly, I notice my cramps are gone.

I am sitting out by the pool tonight as I write. The air is cool and damp and the moon is just peeking over the neighbor's rooftop. This is a very beautiful night. A time to be reborn. I feel good right now.

— § —

Balance seemed to be a key word in my spiritual curriculum. Each of us contains a blend of the masculine and feminine energies, regardless of our gender. The Chinese yin/yang symbol represents the constant dance of the two forces as black and white halves that make up a perfect circle. The masculine energies are our drive to go out into the world and produce, to achieve results, to be aggressive with our goals, and to be forthright in our speaking. The feminine energies represent our ability to be still and listen, to honor our intuition and inner wisdom, and to tune into the source of our inspiration. In a perfect marriage of the energies of our spirit, we receive guidance from our intuition, use our logic to apply the guidance to our lives, and then act appropriately. When we're off balance, we act without honoring our inner guidance, or conversely we dream too much without acting. Without the proper "give and take," we find ourselves too aggressive or overly passive.

All my life, I realized, I had been comfortable with the masculine energies. I was always happy to be in motion and glad to be producing results. I was an aggressive career woman who was more likely than not to be called "one of the guys." On the other hand, I had never been comfortable with the feminine energies. To me, being still meant wasting time. Listening was a chore and being gentle indicative of weakness. The pain of my monthly cycle was a call to examine these beliefs and bring my spirit back into balance. As I awakened the dormant feminine energies, I learned to be a woman who acted like a powerful woman, rather than a woman who acted like a powerful man. I learned to honor my intuition or "gut instinct" without having to prove and justify my every decision with logic. I started to listen more carefully to people and their concerns. I took time to talk to the engineers about topics other than work, and I tried to leave each conversation on an uplifting note. I finally decided to allow myself to rest on the days of my cycle when my body demanded that I slow down.

Once I stopped fighting my own nature, I became much more effective. In meetings and in crises, I resisted my urge to draw a quick conclusion. Instead, I watched silently as the dramas unfolded and listened carefully to the differing opinions. Then, having ferreted out fact from fiction and personal interests from program goals, I spoke with greater wisdom. I became more adept at discerning the important issues, listening to my inner guidance and making decisions that were appropriate for each situation.

I attempted to practice scrupulous honesty with myself and exacting self-discipline. I stumbled often—at times reacting too quickly, offering advice before anyone had asked, and frequently speaking before I had all the facts. Nonetheless, I was able to see the consequences of these actions more clearly, and judge them far less then ever before. I observed my moods constantly, and when I was anything less than satisfied with a situation, I made myself examine the ways in which I had created or contributed to the outcome. Given this perspective, I could adjust my behavior accordingly.

As I slowly and laboriously stripped away the masks of stoic self-confidence, self-reliance, and arrogance, the face of a woman I barely recognized continue to emerge. She was strong, if not yet sure of herself. She was genuinely concerned with bettering the lives of those around her rather than simply achieving success and she was just beginning to awaken to her own worth. On days when I forgot who I was becoming, I went home and stared at my symbol or watched myself in the mirror until the lights around my form came into focus and reminded me that part of my soul's task was to bring more light, more joy, and more laughter into the world, and to help others see this light in themselves. Reiki continued to increase my self-awareness until I was no longer able to ignore the situations in my life that weren't healthy or in line with my life's goals.

— § —

Thanksgiving was just around the corner but there was precious little time to dream about turkey and stuffing this year. Seventy to eighty hour workweeks had given way to ninety hours, and I expected no respite in the near future.

Most of the engineers on the 777 program at Honeywell were working similarly long hours in the hopes of meeting a pivotal program milestone. The schedule had already slipped, and instead of delivering the software program to Boeing in mid-December according to the original plan, the program managers had committed us to a delivery the first week in January. My chance of a Christmas vacation was practically non-existent since I would be required to work during the final phases of testing our software. This year, more than ever before, I needed some time off over Thanksgiving to clear my mind and to prepare for the intense work I would be doing in December.

Long hours, fear of layoffs, resignation, and simple exhaustion were putting even the most stable individuals among us on edge. Somehow, I gradually allowed myself to be sucked into the frenzied state of desperation that permeated the work environment. Every day I attended meetings from 8:00 a.m. until noon, dashed off for a quick lunch, and then ran around until late at night attempting to help resolve the engineers' concerns and keep the lines of communication open. I worked like a woman possessed, personally trying to remove obstacles for people as quickly as they were brought to my attention. In addition, I was still actively involved in the management team and was working with one of my own department's smaller teams to help them set up procedures for testing the display software. During my "spare" time, I found myself a veritable "Dear Abby" for people who were concerned about the impending layoffs.

Making matters more difficult, I was becoming increasingly sensitive to the unseen energy flows that surrounded me. On days when I was tired and off-balance, I felt physically as if I were walking through a dark and murky pool of swirling emotional debris. I listened to one frustration after another until I was convinced I could no longer bear the complaining, whining, and desperation that surrounded me. I was exhausted. In mid-November, my patience snapped. I wanted out.

I decided on a course of action that seemed most reasonable. I wanted to write, but I wasn't willing to give up the financial security of a regular job. Considering my options, I decided that Reiki was the only thing I knew besides engineering that might be converted to a regular income. I fantasized about getting a job at one of the local resort's elegant spas. I envisioned myself walking through plush lobbies into my dimly lit private room, sweetly scented with some aromatherapy formula. I dreamt of hotel guests leaving my treatments feeling the deep relaxation and well being that result from the energy work. I calculated that I might make a lot less money than I was accustomed to making at first, but over time I would gradually build up a practice with regular clientele.

At night after I arrived home from work, I flipped through the yellow pages and canvassed the want ads in the Sunday paper. I studied the various resorts in town and on a few Saturdays, I left work early to read through the local magazines in the library, looking for ads for the well-known spas. I couldn't fathom leaving a prestigious job for anything less glamorous. I targeted my first choice—a beautiful resort in Scottsdale, Arizona—and decided that I would take at least a few days of vacation around Thanksgiving to secure a job interview with them. "Now or never," I told myself, wondering how much more of the negative atmosphere around me I could bear before I slipped back into complaining and desperation myself. On Tuesday night, before I left work for a brief Thanksgiving break I was a nervous wreck.

I woke up early the first day of my vacation and spent hours re-working my resume, wondering how to translate all the skills I had acquired in leadership and engineering into skills that would appear valuable to a spa director. Finally, at long last, I picked up the phone and dialed the resort. I was terrified and thrilled at the same time. "Hello," the voice shook me out of my reverie, "How can I help you." "Hello," I responded. "Could you please forward me to the director of your spa?" I used my most pleasant and professional voice. "The spa is closed for the holiday, ma'am," replied the hotel operator. "Oh, OK. Then could you give me his name and number," I asked? "One moment," the lady replied. "Oh here it is. Joe." "Thank you," I responded. I would have to wait until Friday to make the call.

On Thursday night, I slept fitfully, rehearsing what I would say to Joe. I imagined he would be at least as open-minded as the men at work. They surprised me with their interest in energetic healing. Of course, they never admitted to this in public, but in private we had some great conversations. I convinced myself that Joe would be the same. I tossed and turned in bed with my thoughts whirling in circles until I fell asleep shortly before dawn. I woke up, paced around the house, nibbled at my breakfast, and waited until around 9:15 a.m. when I decided enough time had expired for Joe to drink his morning coffee and take care of the morning emergencies. I called the resort once more. "Could you forward me to the director of your spa?" I inquired for the second time. "Yes, certainly." Ring. Ring. Darn it. My hands were clammy and my breath was short. "Your future career rests on this call. Get your act together," I commanded myself. "This is the opportunity I've been waiting for." I inhaled and took few slow, deep breaths.

"Hello, this is Jill," the voice on the other end said. She didn't sound too pleasant for a receptionist. In fact, she sounded as if I were interrupting her work. "Yes, hello," I said a bit impatiently. "Could you please forward me to Joe, the spa director." "This is Jill and I am the spa director," she said with a bit of an edge to her voice. "Can I help you?" "Ohmygod. I feel like an idiot!" I thought in a split second. "Um, uh, I'm sorry, the lady at the front desk told me your name was Joe," I said, thinking to myself at the same time, "That was so dumb. Why did you say that?" "People make assumptions all the time and generally don't listen well," she replied. "I'm sure the woman at the front desk knows my name." Oh no. This was going just awful. My heart sank.

"I'm sorry," I said, hoping to recover some semblance of dignity. "My name is Ann Albers. I do a form of energy work called Reiki, and I was wondering if you would be interested in talking to me about working in your spa." Oh brother. No introduction there, no lead in. I just blurted out everything I meant to say during the entire conversation. "Shoot!" Inside I was flaming mad at myself. "I'm sorry," she replied. "We just had our spa brochures printed up for the next year. I've spoken with another woman about Reiki, and we're not interested right now. However," and I detected a professional courtesy in her voice, "if you would like to send us your resume, we'll keep you on file." "OK," I answered weakly and stared at the phone in my hand as I heard the click at the other end.

In less than two seconds I was giving myself a litany of criticism. "You idiot! Bad enough you got her name wrong and assumed she was the receptionist, but then you tried to make up an excuse for your mistake. Worse yet, you go blurting out some unprofessional 'please hire me' sounding statement that is more than enough to leave anyone with a rotten impression! Ugh!" In an instant, I was beside myself, looking into my own mind, watching the wheels turn and the sparks fly. I realized how crazy I had become over the past two weeks and how I had foolishly bet my entire future on a single career path and single phone call. Now that I had failed to secure an interview, I was making this mean that my entire future was doomed. I started to laugh, feeling awkward and foolish, and then, still holding the phone, I rolled on the floor laughing until I shook. Relief from the nervous tension that had been building up for weeks spread through me like cool water on a hot day. I laughed until I cried, and then I cried until the tension was completely gone.

I put the phone receiver back in the cradle and dried my eyes. Somehow, I had the presence of mind to look for the lesson in my folly. I thought back over the last few weeks and realized that I had allowed myself to lose my mind. The more I changed my identity from being "not good enough" and a "victim of circumstance," the more responsible I felt for making my life work according to my own design. I had extrapolated this idea to mean that I was responsible for making everyone else's life work too. At some point, I concluded that I should be able to help people around me be happy and satisfied with their jobs... whether or not they shared the same goal. I now saw how absurd and arrogant this was.

In addition, the more responsibility I assumed for making my life work, the more some stubborn disempowering aspect of my character tried to reassert a firm grasp on my mind. The clearer I was in my conviction that I would leave engineering some day, the more I became paralyzed with fears of losing the financial security and success that came with my position. I had allowed my fears to grow wildly out of proportion until Coyote, the trickster energy according to some native legends, taught me a valuable lesson.

Coyote is the archetypal stinker—the one who takes human folly and holds up our weakness for all to see. He's the one that makes you lose your keys when you're in a hurry, or stress out and over-prepare for a presentation only to have few people show up. Coyote makes you spill your coffee on an outfit when you're overly concerned about your looks, or say something stupid on a first date. Coyote is the one who led me to call Jill "Joe." Coyote is a clown to be sure, but a sacred one. When I met Coyote during the phone call, he taught me that life isn't so serious. I learned that if I chased my own tail I would simply run in circles and soon fall down.

Still sitting by the phone, I gave up the notion of securing a job interview. I abandoned my plans for calling other spas in the area. I set the newly updated resumes aside and decided instead that what I really needed was some rest and relaxation to clear the cobwebs from my mind. I drove to my favorite mountain in the center of town and climbed to the top, sweating out the chemicals that stress had left frozen in my body. As I looked down at the tiny streets below, Coyote continued to teach me. In my mind, I heard his wisdom clearly. *"You think your career and your house and your car are so big, and so important,"* the thoughts flooded my mind. *"Look how tiny they are from up here."* I had to grin. *"When you're on a road, do you really think that's the only way to your destination?"* From my lofty perch on the mountaintop I saw the giant gridwork of Phoenix streets and knew that there were a number of different paths to reach almost any destination. So too, I realized, there were different paths that would allow me to follow my dreams of becoming a healer, a teacher, and a writer. If the road was blocked in front of me now, maybe I was supposed to sit back and wait for a new direction. My fears had done nothing except make me miserable.

I still didn't know what I would do for employment after I left engineering some day, but sitting there on the mountaintop the idea occurred to me that perhaps the right option would present itself to me at the right time. For the first time, I seriously considered the option of leaving engineering without having some other job lined up and waiting for me. I said a short prayer and then thanked the Coyote energies for teaching me to laugh at myself. I felt a huge burden lift from my shoulders and I knew that somewhere, in some other dimension I had a great deal of help. All I needed to do was ask and pray for direction and clarity. Then, when higher power decided the timing was right, I knew I would receive the information I needed to change my life.

Following that day, I began to work diligently with intentions. I started to envision and write about my ideal life. I made lists of the activities that made me happy and found the underlying themes. I focused less on the things I wanted and more on the qualities that would enrich my life. I wanted to be energetic and enthusiastic about life. I wanted to have time to enjoy home-cooked meals, and I wanted to spend time with friends. I wanted a career that I loved that would leave me uplifted at the end of the day, and one that would contribute to others as well. I wanted the security of knowing I had adequate money in my life to live well and be surrounded by beauty, and I wanted the freedom to take time off from my work to play. As I became clear on the qualities I wanted in my life—peace, joy, love, abundance, beauty, energy, and enthusiasm—honesty forced me to acknowledge that I had everything I needed to bring these qualities into my current life situation.

Every major change begins with a single step

in the direction of your desired future.

Even if I wasn't willing to make a major life change yet, I was willing to make a thousand smaller alterations. I resolved to enjoy the simple pleasures that life offered. Since I was practically living at work, I personalized my barren office area with plants and fresh flowers. I hung my favorite blessing on the wall, put some crystals on my desk, and framed pictures of people dear to me so I could see them smiling at me every day. I posted a family photo by my computer along with some gorgeous scenes from my vacation in Hawaii. These small changes did wonders for my mood. Every time I sat down at my desk, I was surrounded by objects that made me happy and reminded me that there was indeed a world outside of work.

Every day, I noticed in some small way how much my attitudes and beliefs colored my experience. The more I treated myself with the healing energies, the less I could stand to wallow in sympathy for myself over a situation I had created. "We're all self-employed," I thought. "We can all move on if we don't like our present situation." In good times and difficult ones, I reminded myself that I always had options.

Life continued to be my mirror. In early December, a friend and I bought Christmas decorations for our department at work in an attempt to make the grim atmosphere a little more cheerful. "Don't worry about the money," I told John when I mentioned that I had spent fifty dollars out of my own pocket. "Everything you give with unconditional love comes back ten-fold." A few weeks later I received a surprise bonus of five hundred dollars from the management team with whom I had been working. My words and new beliefs were starting to reflect back to me in the most beautiful ways.

During the most difficult December of my young adult life I learned that the real magic and spirit of the season could be found whenever I opened my heart to those around me. This year, when I had no time to cook regular meals, let alone bake the traditional sweets, a tin of cookies sent by a relative was a precious and thoughtful gift. During a time when I worked more hours than ever before and spent less time at home than during any Christmas past, I was learning invaluable lessons about owning my choices, and taking responsibility for my own happiness.

The holidays came and went as always but unlike other years, the resolutions I made didn't pass as quickly. I was determined to incorporate more of the things I loved into my life, even if I wasn't yet making drastic changes. I loved writing so I wrote as often as possible in my work and at home. I filled pages of my journal with prose and poetry, allowing my mind to wander all over the page. I reaffirmed my life's purpose and started to find ways to bring more light and laughter into people's lives, even in the strained atmosphere at work. I constantly practiced observing my own thoughts and behaviors and tried to act with impeccable integrity. I realized that I could always change my attitude, even if I couldn't change my circumstances. The more I cleaned up my internal act the more things fell into place around me. By some miraculous twist of fate and some not so miraculous compromises with the customer, we came up with a software delivery schedule that we could meet which would also satisfy the program's overall needs.

I thought of the words of wisdom Jessica shared with me in the Reiki classes. "You have to heal yourself before you can help anyone else heal," she taught me. I took time to eat three meals a day, and to take walks or do a few stretches each morning. When I was tired, I stole a few minutes away from everyone else to catch my breath, even if that meant hiding in a restroom stall for five minutes of deep breathing and meditation. As I started treating myself with more respect, I found that I was more able to heal others with my words and my actions. People who were irate left my office feeling calmer. People who had complaints left with some course of action to resolve the problem. People who just needed to vent their frustrations left feeling as if their load had been lightened and, for once, I didn't take on their problems as my own.

The "negative" people and chronic complainers no longer wanted to spend time with me because I would always ask them what we could do to resolve their complaints. Meanwhile, in the most unlikely circumstances, I was meeting people who uplifted and inspired me. I joked that my life lessons used to come in the form of angry people who screamed at me or harassed me. Now, people I wanted to call my friends were the ones bringing the messages into my life. "I must be doing something right." I smiled at the thought.

— § —

The software delivery to Boeing occurred in spite of the fact that all the electricity in the plant went out on Saturday after a maintenance worker pulled the wrong breaker in the central computer room. Luckily, I missed the excitement. After working all day Friday and then throughout the following night testing software on the cockpit simulator, I went home and slept for eight hours then woke up in time to enjoy a relaxed dinner.

On Wednesday and Thursday of the following week, there were surprisingly few crises and I was able to escape from work by 6:00 p.m. in time to attend a Reiki class that Jessica had invited me to audit. I sat in my teacher's gallery and was bathed with the energy of the attunements. I felt, as I had during my own initiations, as if I had come home to a home I barely remembered— a place in my heart where there was peace and quiet and love. The energy felt like great ocean waves crashing over my head and through my heart.

During one of the student's attunements, I slipped easily into an unexpected vision in which I saw Christ. In this altered state, he wasn't the mythical larger-than-life man-God I learned about during my Catholic schooling, but rather a beautiful spirit-man, dressed in flowing white robes. His heart pulsated with a blue-white light of love that flamed out in all directions. The glow was brighter than the sun, and His gentle smile felt like soft rain touching parched earth. He told me I was loved and cherished and then He held out his hand and clasped my own. I felt His energy running through me like white-hot lightning, and in that split second, I knew there was no difference between any of us and all of life. In that moment, I became pure love and felt His light pour into my heart until I thought my heart would burst. Instead, I walked with Him in the midst of the stars, and then, together, we stepped through a doorway of translucent blue-white light into the unknown. It was at this point that I lost consciousness.

The next thing I remember was Jessica's voice, gently requesting that we return our focus to the present time and space. I felt so sleepy that I could barely open my eyes. Slowly, I took a deep breath, and then peered around the room, feeling certain that this was the dream, while the other dimension was my true reality. I kept the vision to myself, feeling too overwhelmed with emotion to admit what I had seen. At home, I got on my knees and wept with gratitude.

Again, I felt satisfied with my life, my relationships, and my work. Again, I felt comfortable about where my life appeared to be heading. Again, I received a portent of change. I knew now that whenever I walked through a doorway in the sacred landscape of the dream, changes were sure to follow in my waking life. Soon after the vision, I noticed a shift in my attitude toward the people around me; I started sensing the spark of light I had seen in the heart of Christ in everyone who came into my life. No matter what our differences, I realized our essence was the same. I found that even the most difficult people were simply crying out for someone to throw them a lifeline and help them find the way out of their own dark labyrinths. I wrote in my journal:

You're a reflection,

of perfection.

You're a mirror of my soul.

As I watch you,

how must I see you?

Are you fragmented or whole?

When you struggle, do I see me

in the depths within your pain?

Or do I watch you from the outside,

judging you, while thinking I am sane?

I know better now

I've learned

the mirror never lies.

You're a reflection of perfection

of the light within my soul.

Our struggles are illusions

and I know we both are whole.

There are rich lessons to be learned from looking in the sacred mirrors that life offers. Our previously hidden hopes and longings, fears and frustrations, dreams and inhibitions are all reflected in the situations that life deals us. The people who are part of our daily routines, both the ones that bring us joy and the ones that cause us grief, unwittingly mirror the masks we still wear.

If someone annoys or angers us, we need to handle the situation appropriately and then look inside of ourselves to see why we still allow ourselves to be triggered by his or her tumultuous emotions. If we admire someone, we need consider the possibility that the qualities we admire are reflections of hidden strengths that we never knew we possessed. Mirrors never lie.

Likewise, the greatest gift we can give to a friend in need is the gift of being a clean mirror. I learned to listen rather than to offer quick advice. I learned to ask questions and allow the people in my life to come to their own conclusions. I found that most of my friends would answer their own questions if given the opportunity to simply "talk through" a problem. I learned to stay silent when people simply needed to vent their emotions. I found that when I allowed others to be angry or sad or frustrated without judging them or trying to fix their situation, they moved through their emotions much more quickly than when I attempted to "help." I learned that when others were able to see themselves in the clear mirror I presented them, when they were left with only my silence and their own words, they found the wisdom to handle their own problems and the courage to meet their own needs.

Life is like a great hall of mirrors. Everywhere we turn there's a chance to see something more about who we are and where our lives are going. I had learned well how to look outside of myself for wisdom. The mirrors of my life—the reflections that showed me who I was and who I was growing to be—were becoming ever clearer. Next, I would learn that there is even greater wisdom to be found when you go within and discover the source of the reflections.

Chapter 5
Past Lives, Present Mysteries, &
Conversations with an Angel

I never intended to buy a book on angels. In fact, angels were the farthest thing from my mind on a Saturday night date with John in old town Tempe, Arizona. After finishing a scrumptious dinner, we sat in the local coffee house where conversations flowed as easily as the steaming hot cups of cappuccino. People of every race, age, and character milled about on Mill Avenue, giving us pause to comment on the street's name. The university atmosphere was contagious. John and I instinctively linked hands and leaned on each other as we strolled out into the night and walked down the busy street past one quaint shop after the next. A warm glow reflecting off the wooden interior of one of the stores caught our attention. To my great delight, the local bookstore was still open, keeping late hours to attract the late night crowds. We ducked inside and I quickly lost myself among the used books while John wandered off to find texts in areas of his own interest.

After browsing awhile, I found an old flight of wooden stairs that led to the second floor balcony. The perimeter of the balcony was lined with new books on timeworn wooden shelves, while just across from these a wooden railing allowed you to peer over the edge onto the first floor. Turning around, I found myself face to face with a small collection of books about angels.

I scanned the titles, as if the subject really didn't interest me too much. Angels had only recently caught America's attention, and I felt strange about admitting interest in the topic. Did anyone really believe they could communicate with the winged messengers? Nonchalantly, I picked up one of the books and leafed through the pages before returning the text to the shelf. I had taken only a few steps toward the stairway when I began to feel a tugging sensation in my solar plexus. *"Buy the book,"* the thought crossed my mind. "No way," I thought in response. "I already own too many books that I haven't read yet. I took a few more steps toward the stairs. The feeling was insistent now, nagging me. *"Buy the book."* I walked back and admired the beautiful picture on the cover. "I don't need this." I turned to put the book back on the shelf and then stumbled. Instinctively I reached out and grabbed some pages just before the book hit the floor. My eyes widened when I saw the words on the page that had randomly flipped open. The text recommended that I ask my angels about "...security issues relating to your job, your living situation, your finances[2]..."

I was more than mildly interested now and irritated at the same time as if some part of me—some part that was smarter than my conscious mind—could sense the guidance that drew me to this section, this book, and these specific words. "Three hundred fifty pages and I find the sentence on jobs and security," I thought, grimacing. John found me at the checkout counter. "What are you getting?" he inquired. "Don't ask," I replied. I told him the story and he simply shook his head. Two days later I finished my reading and was

---

[2] Daniel, Wyllie, and Ramer, Ask Your Angels. New York, NY: Ballantine Books, 1992, p. 231.

ready to try some of the exercises that the book promised would allow me to talk to my own angels. I wondered if I was capable of succeeding.

On a chilly winter's night, I shut the door to my guest room and settled comfortably into the antique rocking chair that I had recently refinished. This was my favorite room, filled with found treasures. To my left the old desk that I had picked up at a yard sale displayed an eclectic collection of simple things that were dear to me—my crystal collection, seashells, and the rocks and feathers I had collected over the years. To the right, a kerosene lantern and a few candles sat on a wooden dresser that had once been caked with ugly white paint until I had chipped away at the stuff long enough to reveal a gorgeous grain underneath. The bed was covered with an antique-looking quilt that I stitched the weekend before my parents visited last year. "What better place to connect with my angels?" I thought, satisfied with the arrangement. The room and the flickering lights were already lulling me into a dreamy state of being.

I closed my eyes and breathed deeply, allowing the muscles in my body to systematically relax. I pictured cords of light reaching up from my head into the sky. Feeling slightly dizzy and certainly drowsy, I asked my guardian angel to give me a message and waited in anxious anticipation. Fifteen minutes passed and still nothing happened. A bit less patiently, I took several more deep breaths and waited a few minutes longer. No longer able to sit in silence, I opened my eyes and wondered if the exercise was futile. Frustrated, because I really did want to connect with these beings that were reputed to bring light, love, and clarity into our lives, I began to judge and criticize the whole endeavor. "I guess I just can't do this. Maybe they're not here. Maybe I need some special talent. Maybe I should take a workshop. Maybe I should just forget the whole stupid idea." I looked at the angel book sitting on the bed and as if the angel portrayed on the cover had gently chided me, admitted that "maybe I just needed more practice."

My interest in contacting the angels waned considerably after several unsuccessful attempts to communicate with them. Each time I did the exercises I felt very peaceful and filled with a sense of well being, but I told myself that could be easily explained by the fact that I had been in a deep meditation. During the weeks I was doing the exercises, I did have a few strange experiences but for the most part, I just ignored them— they didn't fit in my logical definition of life. Typing in my journal one day, I found myself writing down a name—Arian Angeles—that had popped into my mind without warning. The next day someone recommended a book to me, written by an author whose name was Angeles Arien. I felt incredibly strange about the coincidence but didn't feel comfortable mentioning the incident to anyone but a few very close friends.

Occasionally when I was writing in my journal, I noticed that my fingers seemed to take on a life of their own and type words that hadn't even been edited by my conscious mind. I didn't pay much attention to the phenomena until one night the desire to shut my eyes and type became so strong that I could barely stay awake and alert at the keyboard. I gave in to the insistent urge, closed my eyes, and typed the words as quickly as they popped into my mind. Making a game of the situation, I typed in a question and allowed my fingers to type the answers as they poured into my head.

To my utter and complete amazement I found myself having a real conversation with the voice in my mind that identified itself simply as "Ariel:"

Ariel: You are getting closer to the truth you are seeking. There is always more to learn, but be satisfied that you are at long last stepping into the mystery. This will be a grand adventure for you.

Ann: Yes, but how do I get past my fears? I find new layers of fear when I least expect them.

Ariel: Step into your fears in order to step past them. Remember in your Reiki dream how Christ held out his hand and you stepped through the plane of light into nothingness? Beyond fear is nothingness. The void. There is nothing in existence there. Only thoughts and possibilities.

Ann: I am seeing a picture in my mind's eye of me stepping into space. By the way, are you my angel, or my higher self that I'm talking to?

Ariel: I'm your angel, Ann, but we're all made of the same stuff. We're all One.

Ann: I have a picture in my mind now—I see a beautiful woman in a white flowing robe. Her shoulders are bare. She has auburn hair tucked behind her with wisps falling softly around her ears. She looks like an angel. Oh my goodness! This is you Ariel, taking a shape I can relate to. She looks at me and smiles.

Now I see a very realistic vision of Kauai. Ariel is there—she's a beautiful woman bathing in the stream, baptizing herself with the waters of life. She has transformed into a dove now, flying into the sun. She's a rose petal floating downstream. She's the wind in the trees on a balmy day, and the current on the azure water's waves. I'm falling asleep now.

My chin had dropped to my chest. With my eyes closed, I felt as if I had floated up above my body with my arms stretched out beneath me so I could still reach the keyboard. I was almost surprised to find myself still seated on the chair when my head jerked back up and I opened my eyes. I was confused. What was that? Was I talking to myself? Was I letting my higher wisdom flow? I didn't usually get pictures like that in my head when I was typing. "How weird," I thought. I wondered what I was doing. Ariel. Airy-Ann. Somewhere at the corner of my mind, I thought I heard a tinkling sound of delicate laughter.

I didn't think much about the experience for a few days. I guess I was avoiding a truth that I could no longer escape. Higher wisdom did exist. It/they/he/she was talking to me. I ignored the fact at first, preferring to live in the reality to which I was accustomed. In spite of my resistance, I did notice that strange coincidences were occurring around me with ever-increasing frequency. They were little things at first—simple but joyful surprises. Silly angel games. I barely even noticed them until they were too obvious to ignore.

I didn't think twice the day I told a friend that I had always been interested in rocks and minerals and would like to understand more about how they were used in various healing traditions. The statement was a simple part of a passing conversation—small talk over lunch. I forgot all about the discussion until two days later when a humorous synchronicity in my office area, of all places, reminded me once again that there were forces at work in my life that defied definition.

I was standing in the hallway talking to one of my "neighbors" at work while drinking a thirty-two ounce cola. Shivering a little from the ice and the air-conditioning, I barely noticed the man coming up behind me. "You cold?" he inquired solicitously. "A little," I replied and went on with my conversation. "Here," he said, and before I knew what he was doing, the man started moving his hands around me about six inches away from my body. I felt the heat and the now-familiar sensation of energy beginning to flow around me. Within seconds, my goose bumps were gone. I whipped around to face the stranger. "You're a healer?" I accused him, questioning eagerly and a bit too loudly for the office environment. "You were moving my energy field!" "Yes. Yes!" His eyes widened and he grinned sheepishly as if he were surprised to find someone who knew what he was doing. "Hi, I'm Ed." We laughed and shook hands and we talked. Ed had been doing energy work for years. He was a self-taught healer, and he had tried just about every different modality that he could practice on his own. He worked for our company now maintaining the Xerox machines and the shared printers. He had had a "real job" before, he told me, but he no longer needed the stress. I was reminded once again never to judge a person by appearances—my teachers were coming to me in all different guises.

The next day, Ed showed up at my desk with a workshop listing from a local bookstore. "Here, I thought you would be interested in this," he told me. "Thanks," I replied and tossed the brochure on my desk. One of the headlines immediately caught my attention: "Native American Rock Healing—Wednesday night." I picked up the flyer again and reread the line, shaking my head in disbelief. "No way," I thought. "No way. This is too creepy. No way." I had just told my friend a few days ago that I was interested in the subject. "Totally by accident I find out that the printer maintenance man is a healer, and then he leads me to a seminar on the topic I said I wanted to study. No way." I stared at the brochure again while I argued with myself about the probability of this happening. No, I wasn't hallucinating. I read the title correctly. I called the bookstore and told them to expect me at the workshop.

Wednesday night, I sat with others in a circle on the floor of the small bookstore while Arlene, a woman who smiled easily and talked without a trace of hurry in her voice, explained to us the healing traditions of her people. I learned a great deal in that simple workshop. I began to have a sense of how things that we considered "inanimate" did indeed have a life force or an organizing principle of their own. Lasers, with their crystal-focused light, are used in leading edge surgical techniques. I could almost hear Coyote laughing. Perhaps we aren't so smart after all. Perhaps the "new" knowledge of the present is simply a rediscovering of the old knowledge of the past. I considered the proposition. Native healers using crystals and modern surgeons using their lasers both rely on ordered structures from nature to focus and direct their healing energies: light in the case of the surgeon, and some to-be-defined-by-science type of energy in the case of the healer.

I wondered after the workshop if my angels had anything to do with the "coincidence" that led me there and caused me to see the tenuous ties between science and healing. I decided to try typing in the altered state once again. Still feeling self-conscious about the venture, I sat down at the keyboard and closed my eyes:

Ann: Hi Ariel, are you there?

Ariel: Of course I am. I've been tugging at the corners of your consciousness for the past few days. I'm glad you have created time to talk again. Difficult to type? Stick with the exercise and you'll soon have no trouble. You are coming into a larger awareness here and merging with the consciousness I carry. You are recognizing yourself as a being of light. You asked to anchor the higher frequencies in this world, and you are starting to do so. Never doubt. Remember the times you feel the energy in your feet pouring into the floor? You are helping the earth, for you are connected with her, very much so. Do you have any questions?

Ann: Yes. You said you had a message for me. Why have you been prompting me to talk with you for the past few days?

Ariel: I have this to tell you. You carry the life force within you and the river that runs through your being flows in all of creation. You are a tree budding in the spring and your challenge is to find the connection you have to all of life. Walk with us in beauty. Dance with us in joy. (I see a picture of a hawk, then a hummingbird). Live with us in perfect abundance.

The pictures lingered in my mind long after I stopped typing. My logical mind was having a terrible time trying to explain the whole phenomena. I couldn't fathom how words and images that were poetic and beautiful would simply drop into my mind and flow so quickly that I could barely type fast enough to keep up with them. I continued to wonder if I was making up the experience, and yet I realized that I rarely wrote with such grace and ease. I never felt as if I were floating when I sat by myself at the keyboard, and certainly never before had I been guided to explore so many new concepts. As I argued with myself, an image formed in my mind. I saw myself as a tiny bubble of light, where Ariel was a giant globe. "Maybe with all the seminars she's leading me to attend she's trying to stretch my consciousness so her globe could fit better inside of my bubble." The thought was just another one popping into my mind. "Globes and bubbles," I chuckled, settling down for the night. "I must be crazy."

— § —

Ed stopped by my desk with another flyer. This one advertised a seminar on past life regression hypnosis. I bit my lip and looked around nervously, wondering if any of my engineering peers could overhear our conversation.

What would they think? I didn't want to jeopardize my good reputation by advertising my atypical interests.

I lowered my voice and asked a few more questions. I always had a difficult time considering the notion of past lives.

An astute Catholic priest who taught at my high school once told me that time is a human construct and that God existed outside of time and space, everywhere and all at once. "When we die, aren't we also outside of time?" I asked myself. What do we do—jump back into time every now and then? Hang out in the heavenly ethers for several hundred years or so and then decide, "Hey, this era looks like fun." I doubted that was the case. According to my upbringing, things were even simpler. We got one life. "Yeah, count 'em," I joked with myself, "one life, one chance, heaven or hell at the end of the road, better not blow your opportunity." That didn't seem right to me either. "What the heck, the seminar is only fifteen dollars," I told myself, avoiding any further confusion caused by this line of thinking. Maybe firsthand experience would resolve my questions. I called the bookstore and registered for the class.

Thursday night came quickly. Coyote, the trickster, greeted me again at the bookstore. Imagine my surprise when I found the man leading the seminar was one I met through a friend several months prior. Back then, I had listened to his stories and with professional arrogance and dignity, decided he was a little wacky. Now I was asking him to teach me. "Be careful who you judge and criticize." I heard the advice I had given to others so many times coming back to haunt me. I told myself I had received a fifteen-dollar lesson before the seminar even began.

"I'm going to lead you through a visualization to relax you. Then I'll give you cues, but I won't tell you what you're going to see. You'll experience this as if you are watching a dream," the hypnotist told us. "I don't want you to get too involved in the experience or feel your emotions too strongly. I only suggest that in one-on-one sessions when I'm equipped to handle the emotions that come up. I can't do that with fifteen people," he quipped. We all laughed a little nervously. In spite of the fact that everyone was here for the same reason, I saw that the other people in the room were as anxious as I was to remain anonymous. Being discovered at a past-life regression seminar would be the equivalent of running into someone from work at the hairdresser's when you're under the dryer in rollers, I mused. I spread my blanket out on the floor and lay down.

"OK now, find a comfortable position and relax," the man said. The voice continued in a slightly sing song hypnotic tone as he spoke to us. When he suggested that we were becoming soft as wax, I did feel as if I was melting into the floor. I started to feel the same fuzzy, floating sensation that I was beginning to equate with an altered state of consciousness. "Picture yourself at age eight," the man told us. In my mind, I saw a young Native American girl with long dark braids. She wore a pair of simple brown moccasins with beadwork in the form of red arrows near the toes. She was standing in a desert area with grass and rocks. Then she shifted into a scene from modern times, and stood staring at some ruins John and I had recently visited. In shock, I saw "her" looking at "me" that day in the not too distant past, as if two different time periods had been superimposed. I was puzzled.

"Imagine your home," the man told us. I saw a teepee made of thick hide. The girl went inside to eat her dinner which looked like some sort of jerky. There was a white furry robe on the floor where she slept and some other furs and herbs hanging from the ceiling. I knew, in that way you know things in dreams, that she wasn't lonely. This was "part of her training," a voice in my mind told me.

"See yourself at age twenty," the man said. I saw a young woman riding bareback on a horse across a grassy plain with mountains in the backdrop. For an instant, I was no longer watching the dream but rather playing the main character. I felt the wind on my face and the power of the horse with its sleek black coat glistening in the sun. The horse and I became one spirit riding with the wind. "What is the year?" the man interrupted and I was simply dreaming again. I struggled to find an answer, but got none... something about "the year of the good harvest..." no dates.

The scene changed and I saw the woman preparing for ceremony. In a dirt clearing she used a twig broom to clean the area, and then arranged rocks in a circular pattern. The dream shifted again and the woman was now older, a mid-wife attending to a woman about half her age who was in labor. I saw the younger woman heave a sigh of relief and smile as her newborn child emerged glistening with the blood of birth. Mother and child glowed with electric blue lines and clouds of energy that surrounded them crackling and sparking. As the baby was delivered, I saw her lines of energy emerge from deep within a vortex in the mother's energy field. I watched in awe, realizing that I was witnessing a soul's incarnation. Just before the vision faded, I saw that the older woman wore a beaded pendant with a red thunderbird design centered on a blue background.

"See your death," the hypnotist's voice commanded gently. I saw an old woman in bed, with full medicine pouches and necklaces of various materials draped around her neck. A golden white light glowed softly behind her head, and as she said her final prayers, her spirit moved into the brilliant light gently and quickly.

She appeared to have been blessed with a beautiful, natural, and easy transition.

Soon after, the instructor guided us out of the hypnosis. We sat up and rubbed our eyes sleepily, then traded stories. A fair-skinned woman reported a life in Ireland. A robust looking man talked about seeing a Viking. I didn't know what to think. The scenes had come so easily, just as if they were a dream. I hadn't felt a real connection with the woman except when she was riding horseback and then again in the scene where she helped direct the energies coursing through the mother and child. Could I possibly have lived another life with a tradition so deeply connected to the earth? Could that explain why now, almost thirty years old, I was awakening to the feeling that I had done this energy work before? Richer in experience, but still poor in my ability to answer my own questions, I left the workshop and entertained John with my stories.

The notion of other lives continued to haunt me. A few days after the workshop, I asked my "higher self" (whomever or whatever that might be) to show me why I sometimes expected other people to betray me. Immediately a vision of a woman being dragged away as a witch by townspeople who gripped her roughly by the wrists, popped into my mind. "No. No!" My body shocked me, reacting fearfully to this vision and tensing up as my arms flew instinctively into a protective position. I began to sob violently without warning. "What's wrong?" John asked, wondering what had happened to me in a mere two minutes since we had been laughing and joking. "Just hold me," I pleaded uncharacteristically, still terrified by the vivid pictures in my head. The scenes were too real. "They don't understand. They don't know I'm innocent." I was writhing, still immersed in the vision. "Oh God. Oh No. No! Oh!" In an instant, I snapped out of the scene, frightened to the core. "What just happened to me?" I demanded, asking no one in particular. Why was I crying? Why was my body tense? John looked at me, not knowing what to make of the situation, but clearly concerned. I tried to explain. I was frightening him, I knew. I couldn't even understand what was going on. Could the vision be true? I didn't know what to think. Looking for answers, I decided to ask my invisible friend.

Ann: Ariel, are you there?

Ariel: Hello Ann. You've been going through quite an intense period of growth, I see.

Ann: Tell me about this past life stuff. I was feeling wonderful and then all of the sudden, bizarre scenes are flooding my mind.

Ariel: Perhaps you weren't feeling so wonderful before you began. You were over worked and not taking time for yourself to experience those things that bring life back to your body and mind. You are feeling the effects of being somewhat out of balance.

Ann: And what about these dreams of other lives? Are they real?

Ariel: What is reality, dear one? You ask if these visions are real, and yet you know already that your mind carries you to a time and place where things happen that affect how you feel now.

You are all beings of light. You are souls that exist beyond time and space. You are filled with the wisdom of the ages, as yet untapped. You ask me for answers, yet you are doing no more than asking a higher aspect of yourself to communicate with you that which it already knows.

Ann: So Ariel, are you me? Are you an aspect of me, or some other entity? Or an angel?

Ariel: Does that distinction matter?

Ann: Slightly. I think I have a limiting belief that someone outside of me would be wiser.

Ariel: Ah, and therein you err little one, but your misconceptions are not unique. We all look outside of ourselves for wisdom. We all refuse to look within. That seems too easy, after all. Ah good, you see pictures of the big island of Hawaii. The lava flows and recreates life. So too, your thoughts, your hopes and your dreams create the life that flows from the volcanic depths of your being. You disrupt the old ideas, you burn them away, and the new ones burst forth to bring new life. Listen in the silence and witness your own recreation.

You struggle to find yourself. You buy books, you look to the skies, but the tools you need, the riches you desire are all to be found within. Look inside. In the dim lit light of the room with your crystals, fall into a dreamy slumber and ask for the knowledge that you seek. Do not look for answers from an entity outside of yourself, but rather look within. Balance your every day world and the one behind the curtains of illusion for an optimum experience.

Ann: Ariel, I think sometimes I am making up these words, rather than receiving them from you.

Ariel: What is the difference? By now, you realize that I am not apart from you, but rather a larger part *of* you. Even more accurately, you are a part *of* me. We are all a part of something much greater. We are all part of One.

You sit here in this chair as Ann—a woman beginning to shed the confines of her own ego, and you yearn to dance in the light. Continue to converse with me so we may integrate, find the lost aspects of yourself, and bring them back home. Go now. Sit by your fire, and for a little while cease the struggle between what you know and what you think you should.

Ariel was slowly teaching me about the nature of a soul. Over and over she would repeat that we were part of one another. I began to understand that we were both part of something much larger—a small portion of awareness I called "God" that was beyond my comprehension. In any case, I found that my conversations with Ariel continued to enrich my life and encouraged me to tap into the wisdom that we all carry deep inside.

Dear Journal - Today is another one of those days when, cloaked in the veil of illusion of the mundane world, you would swear you had an awful day. Yet beneath the surface, dancing around the edges of my consciousness are great teachings waiting to find a place within my heart to rest. These words I'm typing don't even seem to come from my own mind but rather from a source of greater being. As I stop to wordsmith here and there, they loose their potency. As I just type, they unfold with a grace and beauty of their own.

I awoke this morning ready to go to work for the twenty-first day in a row. I believe this is part of my lesson on "focus," on what can be achieved by projecting one's energy in a narrowly directed space over a timeless time. I have been working so hard. My friends think I'm crazy. My co-workers think I'm overly dedicated. Why am I doing this? The dedication is a lesson to me and a teaching to those around. If I'm working this hard and long by choice rather than from a sense of duty, and if I can choose an attitude of power, of "can-do," of joy, even in this situation, then I begin to show others what is possible with only a slight shift in perception. Maybe our thoughts and perceptions truly can create realities.

On my way to work, the hawk, who has done the same thing three times this week now, flew off a telephone pole near the road and soared beside the driver's side window of my car. My heart danced with joy because her presence always signifies that I've integrated a new teaching. On another lamppost, her counterpart sat perched, watching me as well. No other cars were on the road so I slowed down, opened my window and shouted a greeting. The male hawk turned his head and with his deep dark eyes stared right through me. I drove to work ecstatic.

I am feeling so much emotion these days. The music in the background tonight raises my vibration to one of ecstatic love of life and a clear understanding of the struggle and the triumph of the human condition. I feel like dancing for the sheer joy and the beauty of being alive.

Oh my, I'm starting to dream at the keyboard again. I am flying through a tunnel, going very fast. I see light at the end and I burst forth into nothingness—sheer white light. I am blinded and at the same time bathed in radiant beauty. As I understand that I am made of this light, I see a woman dressed in white robes with long hair flowing behind her. "I am your light body," she says, "your higher self." Me? We merge into one being and float up into the heavens where we can see the earth as a small blue orb spinning below. An emerald green patch of earth catches our attention, and we zoom down into the rainforest where we merge with the tropical vegetation. I feel my life force in everything around me. As I focus on a leaf, I merge with each tiny cell and experience photosynthesis, singing in harmony with the sun and all of creation.   The sun dips behind a cloud and a gentle rain begins to fall.   I am falling, falling, falling, back into my body.

As so often happened after sitting in this altered state, I fell asleep at the keyboard and woke up to read the words I had put on the paper as if they were echoes from a distant dream.   The beautiful visions offered me solace during the days when my work was becoming more difficult than ever before.

— § —

Dear Journal - Today was a tough day at work. Some of the department managers decided to get involved in the delivery decisions today for the first time in weeks and were questioning why I was doing things the way I am right in the morning meeting in front of the whole group.   I stood behind my decisions because I think they're the right things to do, but I was ready to cry.   I felt like they were criticizing my efforts after abandoning me to an impossible task.   Later I learned that they're feeling badly about not being more involved in the management of the people and were just trying to help.   Wow.   I can hardly believe that I'm the one who decided she has to pull this whole thing off.   There's so much to be done. This isn't personal. I don't care about rewards and acclaim.   I'm focusing all my energy on getting this huge job done.   I want the program to succeed.   I want the people in my department who are working so hard to know the taste of success.   I want to grow and learn in the process.   I think I'll talk with Ariel now...

Ann: Why was I so stressed out today?

Ariel: You succumbed to feeling human. Someone implied that you weren't good enough and you bought the story. Then you started thinking about the things that you need to do to in order to look like you have your act together when Boeing comes down. If you didn't care so much, you wouldn't be so stressed. The key here is to remain committed, without attaching your worth to the result. Stop guessing about other people's perceptions and create whatever you want. Create a different perception of their reactions. Create a different perception of their opinions of you. See every situation in a positive light. Then, you cannot fail.

Dear Journal - Another rough day at work. I feel like I can hardly do all I need to do, yet I need to rest more than any thing and reconnect with the magic in my soul. Yesterday in the bookstore, I got the sudden impression that I should be writing a book about my own life, my journey, and my experiences with Reiki—a journal of my journey through consciousness. I sure didn't ask for that thought. I don't want to write about my life. Who would want to read that? I'm praying now and asking my guides for help. If I am really supposed to write this book then inspire me, motivate me, and help me. First though, help my job become easier. Help the miracles start to occur for us in the 777 Displays department. And help me always have faith in the light inside of myself and the wonderful magic this life has to offer. I need to remember who I am. I need to remember what I am capable of doing.

On days like these, I just want to give up and ask some god outside of myself to take care of me. I want to come home and beg John to hold me and take care of me and tell me he'll make everything better. I whine that I would like to feel more loved. But whom am I kidding? I have to love myself. When I long for someone else to give me strength, isn't that simply a means of escaping my task? On days like this I feel that there's no way I can find the strength within myself. I have to give so much up. I have to give up the suffering and the victimization that I really feel. I have to give up the pain and the ego. I have to give up my attachment to responding to situations the way the world expects me to respond. So much to give up, and yet so much to be gained.

I asked Ariel for some help and she showed me an image of a vast, translucent plane of lights and colors that existed several feet above the cubicles at work, much like a bank of clouds might exist above the landscape. In the vision, just over my head, a vortex formed in this plane and colors spun down like a wide tornado that seemed to connect with colors that swirled already near the top of my head.

I understand the image now. The lights are our collective thought forms. We suck the thoughts we choose out of the great planes of human consciousness and they become our reality. I also see that if one person emits strong thoughts back up into this plane of human consciousness, the currents of light and possibility for all are altered forever.

The scene changes. I see a tree that is surrounded by a luminescent green glow that seems to reach out and touch my mind with the words I am now hearing...

Watch me Ann. Remember, "I am the vine and you are the branches." Consider this leaf. (I see the leaf up close.) The leaf takes her life force through the stem. She is whole, complete, and distinct as a leaf, and yet she is part of something so much more. So too, you are the leaf and the energy of God flows through your veins. Do not hesitate to draw upon this energy; a leaf that attempts to hold itself together without the stem cannot live. Remember, all is calm, all is forgiven, and all is well upon the earth plane.

More visions fly before my eyes. The scenes change almost faster than I can enter them in my journal.

I see a soldier eating outdoors at an army base and then I see a plane above him. A hawk cries as she flies toward the sun. I am the hawk now. The ground disappears below me and I soar in ever widening circles, spiraling up on the currents. "Awk," I cry, celebrating life, and the universe shivers in joy.

—— § ——

Ariel, whom I now considered my guardian angel, worked with me unceasingly. Night after night when I was tired or discouraged from work, when I felt that I had given my all and my all wasn't enough, she would encourage me and help me to see the humor in a situation. When I called upon her, she taught me to distance myself from the problems and negative emotions of others. She repeatedly urged me to create my desired future with positive thinking and intention. Ariel taught me to look inside of myself and to see how far I had come from the days in which I felt hopeless and desperate about my life situation. I wasn't by any means finished with my spiritual exploration—I probably never would be—but I felt I was well on my way. She constantly reminded me that we were all part of one greater reality. She guided me into visions and experiences in other dimensions, where she taught me that I could merge my awareness with any aspect of creation for the sake of my own education.

On the roughest days at work when my co-workers and I struggled through the night and again until the next evening, I could feel her presence. One night another woman and I worked so hard to meet a deadline that we were near exhaustion when an error occurred in our computer system and destroyed the entire evening's work. We cried together and shared all the fears that we felt but didn't want to admit to the people we were leading. We went to breakfast at some unforgivable hour and then went back to work. The next day, as if the heavens were trying to tell me "keep going, don't give up, you're doing well," I received more compliments than I had in the previous six months.

Broken down from lack of sleep and emotionally drained, I felt Spirit working to rebuild me again. I knew that I wasn't going to ensure the success of the program alone. I had to surrender to a higher power, then trust and intend for miraculous turns of good luck on this incredible airplane program. I began to believe I was strong enough (spiritually) to hold my intention in the roughest times despite the momentum around me that carried the engineering population to despair and the fears that said we would never succeed. I held my breath at times, but I continued to pour my energy into my work. John, who was also working long hours on a different aspect of the same 777 program, listened to my trials and tribulations with great patience.

Dear Journal - What magic these times are bringing. Under the seething surface of a choppy sea of emotion, a strange calm wells up waiting to make its presence known. I dream of the surge. I feel the energy flowing through me, and I know the sense of urgency. The energy on earth is changing. I can no longer choose pain. I do sometimes, but my lack of integrity becomes increasingly obvious. All the information says the same thing—from the hummingbird that hovered in front of my face on Camelback Mountain last week, to the flowers who showed me their yellow auras in the courtyard at lunch—choose joy, and choose now. The forks in the road between joy and pain become wider.

Driving home from work today, I saw one of the hawks near the right side of the road. She was flying low and as I put my arm out the car window in greeting, she flew in front of my car as if she were leading me somewhere. I followed in wonder and awe feeling honored, but once again not able to explain why. Then as if to acknowledge the feelings bubbling up inside me, she dove down and flew just in front of my windshield. I was scared to death that I was going to hit her. Luckily, she veered off to the left, leaving me with a feeling that I've been visited again by one of my guides.

Later I climbed up Camelback Mountain right before sunset. In front of me, dark storm clouds reached over the land. Showers fell on either side. The afternoon was cold but beautiful. As the sun dipped low, the light peeked below the cloud cover behind me and appeared trapped between earth and sky. The land turned into a million sparkles awash with the sun's brilliance—a gleaming city dotted with trees that sparkled in greens and golds. What a surrealistic picture. I felt as if I were in some altered state of consciousness like a lucid dream because the images were all so sharp and clear and so beautiful. A pack of coyotes near the base of the mountain serenaded us with their yapping and howling, sounding as if they were singing for sheer joy of the beauty of the landscape. I wanted to give nature something in exchange for the sacred moment. The only gift I could offer was a simple prayer requesting a blessing for the land and the people below.

Tonight I am at home. I don't want to go to work tomorrow, and I wonder how to deal with some of the folks in the office and their recent biting moods. I picked up a book and read about the division between those who choose love and those who choose fear and wonder if this is all part of the lesson I am learning. My job is to heal those who want healing and to live with love and acceptance for those who do not. This is a difficult lesson because my first reaction is to take all the fear-based comments personally as if I should be working harder to make everyone happy. The second reason is that I really would like to see the people I care about choose the joyful path... but some won't. We sure live in exciting times. I am honored to be of service as Spirit becomes more manifest within human history. I feel small, but no longer insignificant.

— § —

I felt as if the pieces of the puzzle of my life were coming together. Issues that had haunted me for years were coming to closure with each new day. As I became more at ease with who I was, I had an easier time allowing others to be themselves. I no longer reacted strongly when angry people yelled at me at work. I didn't feel bad when someone criticized the program. I knew we were all doing our absolute best. When someone spoke highly of me, I learned also not to take that too personally because in the long run over a hundred other engineers supported every bit of good I was able to accomplish. I gave credit where credit was due, and in turn, I received even more acclaim. As always, my outer life reflected my inner one.

In early May I took a business trip to attend meetings with Boeing in Seattle, Washington. Before the meetings began, a Boeing friend took me out to the tarmac on Boeing Field to see the very first 777 airplane.

A team of workers was readying the engines to be powered up for the first time, and since they were busy, we were able to duck into the cockpit unnoticed. Seated in the captain's chair I saw the six flat panel displays that represented over a year and a half of my life, and years worth of effort from hundreds of other people around the world. I had never seen them in the airplane before this. I looked out the cockpit windows and envisioned the plane lifting off the runway while the displays came to life. "We did this," I thought. For an instant I forgot my exhaustion and had the fleeting sensation of being part of something so much larger than me.

Already emotional after seeing the results of our department's labor for the first time and bone-weary from lack of sleep, I left the aircraft and stood back for a final glance. I wasn't prepared for what I saw next. Painted on the nose of the beautiful airplane were the words, "Working Together." I asked why they were there and my friend told me that this was the motto for the entire worldwide 777 airplane program. I hadn't known. In a flash of memory, my awareness moved back in time. I saw myself standing in front of a class a year and a half before, stating with conviction, "My vision is that people communicate, cooperate, and *work together* to create great things."

The scene in front of my eyes had the quality of a dream. I watched the men working on the huge engines. The belly of the great plane loomed over me, big as a barn and painted the blue color of the evening sky. White paint on the top half of the jet glistened in the sunlight. *Working together.* More than just an airplane, this machine represented communication and cooperation on a global scale. My life over the last eighteen months flashed before my eyes. I saw the reason for my obsession. I understood my passion for making my piece of the program work. I felt a choking sensation in my throat as I held back sudden tears of overwhelming joy. I felt the energy, the force of life rush up my spine and whirl through my heart and in the back of my mind a tiny voice, whispered like a barely perceptible breeze, *"See you really do create your own reality."*

I closed my eyes for a second, barely a blink, and said a prayer of thanksgiving for the whispers of the Spirit that led me here to see my own vision unfold before my eyes. We weren't just building an airplane, I knew now—we were affecting the way global business was conducted. We weren't just writing software—we were ensuring safe flight. Who knows whom this plane would carry someday—perhaps a world leader on the way to some conference that would change the fate of world affairs, or maybe just ordinary travelers like me who don't want worry about their mode of transportation. "Look what we've done," I thought. "So much more than a job."

That night in my hotel room, after going to a baseball game and then a local restaurant with the engineers from Honeywell and Boeing, I got on my knees in the quiet suite and wept with gratitude. I thanked Spirit for allowing me to be a small part of something so huge. I prayed, aware now that my entire life was always operating within the context of a force and an intent much larger than my own. I was privileged and honored to be a part of the changes that were subtly restructuring the way some of America's large corporations did business.

The whispers of the Spirit spoke to me that night from the depths of my own being. *"Remember, remember, who you are,"* they told me. *"Regardless of your circumstances or your occupation, you can offer the world communication and cooperation.*" In my mind's eye, my symbol spoke to me. "*Be a bridge. Connect differing viewpoints and bring them together for a common purpose. Take this feeling back to work, share with people and let them know they're part of something so much more. Connect them with their souls.*"

I knew more clearly than ever before that my work at Honeywell was nearing completion. My work with Ariel was changing too, as I started to really understand what she had been saying about being a "higher" part of the "One." I saw her now as an angelic being who, unlike me, had never forgotten the power of living within the sacred circle of life. In one sense, I felt a loss as I realized her wisdom was in some way not new, but something that had always been buried deep within me. The feeling of loss was soon replaced by a sense of homecoming as I realized I had regained conscious access to the wisdom of my soul. I had discovered, at long last, the whispers from within.

Chapter 6
Secrets of the Flesh

Everything looked different in the office Monday after I returned from my trip. The hustle and bustle of the hectic program schedule seemed to be like hurricane winds whipping around my calm center. Outwardly nothing had changed. We had serious problems, but they no longer seemed catastrophic. We appeared no closer to meeting our deadlines than we had before I left town, but in spite of the "facts" and the statistics that projected our failure, I now knew that the program would succeed. I knew the Federal Aviation Administration would find our software certifiable and that the plane would fly. I knew that the 777 would stand in aviation history as a symbol of corporate communication and cooperation, demonstrating what can be accomplished when people in companies all over the world work together. While eating lunch at my desk, I quietly typed an e-mail message to the entire department and told the people I worked with how I felt as I stood under the airplane. I struggled with the words that seemed inadequate to convey my feelings. I wanted the people who were working so hard on this program to see the bigger picture and to know they were part of something much larger than a complex software design. I bared my heart and my soul and hit the "send" key on the computer, worrying that people would think my message just another ploy to get them to work harder. *"That's not your worry,"* the thought drifted through my mind, *"you've done what you needed to do."*

I finished my lunch as another person came into my office with the next crisis of the day.

The days that followed flew by quickly. I felt I was living in a dream, moving through life calmly as if I was play-acting but no longer part of the reality of the drama that surrounded me. Without the stress, I was more effective. I knew my work wasn't finished, but I finally felt fulfilled and satisfied with what I had accomplished. "If I died tomorrow," I thought driving into the sunset on my way home one day, "I would know I made a difference." A warm feeling ran up and down my spine with the thought, and I drifted into a reverie while wondering about my future. I knew that I no longer needed to stay with the program to see its completion. Everyone around me would have argued otherwise, but I had what you might call a vision, an instinct, or simply a simple faith in the impossible—I saw the program succeeding in the future, with or without my continued presence at the company. In the unseen dimensions of reality, my task was complete.

Practically speaking, however, I was still torn between the differing options for my future as success and happiness played tug-of-war games with my mind. Success teased me like one of the mythical Sirens that lured unwary sailors to their ultimate destruction. If I stayed in engineering I would have a glamorous career with travel, abundant cash flow, and more than adequate recognition. Happiness beckoned quietly, suggesting that the attractive glimmer of money and glamour would fade over the years if I weren't living a life consistent with my dearest desires. Deep down I knew I would opt for happiness in the long run, but some fear I still couldn't name, some insecurity I couldn't pinpoint, was still holding me back from making the final decision to leave engineering. In a quiet state of meditation one night, I intended that I find a way to expose and confront my hidden fears. Within days, the phone rang and I received a surprise call from a friend who offered to guide me through the next phase of my spiritual journey.

—— § ——

Dear Journal - What strange twists of fate life has to offer. Earlier this week, "out of the blue," a woman I've studied with called me. She offered to work with me, using hypnosis and visualization to help focus my energy. She's going to practice her skills and I'm going to learn what can be achieved in this altered state of awareness. Amazing. When the student is ready, the teacher really does appear.

My first session with hypnosis exceeded all of my expectations. My friend guided me through a sequence of suggestions that left me limp as a rag doll and as worry-free as a passing cloud. She then had me envision my energy expanding to fill the entire room. In my mind's eye I saw a golden yellow field wavering inside my physical form. Then as if the light was water seeping beyond the matrix of my body's boundaries the glow expanded in all directions forming a huge bubble. In the center of the bubble, I floated in absolute weightlessness, buoyed by the light and breathing in the brilliance that seemed to cleanse my spirit. As I brought the light back into my body, gravity seemed to pull me tenderly back onto the chair. I opened my eyes and stared at the woman opposite me. Her eyes were as wide as my own. When I was expanding the bubble, she told me she felt a force so strong pressing down on her hands that she had barely been able to move them. The experience was too real for both of us. Unsettled, but still intrigued, we scheduled another appointment.

In subsequent sessions, I learned the power of focused concentration. My friend guided me in visualizations where I practiced sending energy to various areas in my body for healing or relaxation. I would imagine myself breathing in energy of a certain color and breathing out all my tension with every exhalation. In no time, a headache, or the tension in my neck and shoulders would disappear. I learned to focus my thoughts and eliminate distractions. Slowly I gained control over my never-ending mind chatter. I began to delight in the experience of silence and inner peace. The exercises I practiced during the hypnosis spilled over into my waking life and enabled me to direct my attention fully to a given project. I completed my tasks at work more easily than ever before, which gave me more time for our sessions together. I loved my new lessons and felt as if I was learning and playing at the same time.

I didn't realize during the first few sessions that playtime was about to end and more serious work soon to begin. After a few weeks of experimenting with focus and concentration, we decided to use hypnosis as a tool to release some old emotional patterns that were no longer empowering to me. "Maybe this is just what I need to move past my fear of leaving engineering," I told my friend. She smiled. I had no concept of the adventure that lay ahead.

Throughout my adult life I had been somewhat of a secret intellectual snob. I prided myself on how quickly I could grasp and apply new concepts. Even my spiritual growth had been primarily a mental exercise. The seminars I attended and the books I read introduced me to the concepts that I had been using for over a year now to understand and analyze my limitations and then overcome them. I allowed myself to feel joyful when I talked to my angels or when I received sudden bursts of intuition, but I refused to face the dark side of my emotions, preferring instead to keep the beast locked away in the murky depths of some distant memories.

However, hypnosis, combined with my energy work, would soon force me to feel. "Be silent," I commanded my busy mind and to my surprise, the chatter would suddenly disappear. Left with an empty feeling in my psyche, I allowed the darker emotions to bubble up from the depths. As if a frozen ice cube was suddenly placed on a hot stove, sputtering and hissing as the heat dissolved its rigid form, my frozen emotions thawed in violent and sudden outbursts. Soon after each session, I relived childhood traumas in my mind, feeling for the first time the anger and sadness I had repressed for so many years. I felt like I had entered the proverbial "dark night of the soul."

Hi Journal - Things have indeed been interesting since I started emotional work in the hypnosis. The first week I sure let out a lot of that repressed anger. I was mad at everyone, even if they didn't deserve my anger, and I was extremely short-tempered at home. Of course, I did my best to conceal the rage. The second week my jaws were so tight they were almost painful. Now they're loosening up, and I think things in my emotional state are looking better but I'm so tired that I just want to sleep all the time. This week I made the mistake of saying I was "burnt out" on Thursday and lo and behold, I went home and was really burnt out—101.5 degrees to be exact. I used Reiki to bring the temperature down and went back to work on Friday, but I sure received a good lesson on how the body listens to the mind.

At first, the experience of going back in time to review memories of age-old pains left me emotionally and physically exhausted. I felt as if I was fighting to hold the lid on a boiling pot that wanted to explode. Usually a social creature, I hid from family and friends, screening my phone calls and declining invitations. I needed the quiet time to be alone and to contemplate the events that had shaped my life. I needed time by myself to experience the wealth of emotions that flooded me—time to cry, time to rage, and time to mourn the years I spent withholding love from the people I cared most about in my life. I slept far more hours than usual, and the dark circles under my eyes belied the weariness I felt inside. Some days, I was perfectly sane and pleased with the progress I was making. Other days I felt as if I was dancing near the edge of a frightening mania. The crying wouldn't stop. The anger wouldn't release its hold. The energy along my skin crawled as if a thousand little pinpricks were dancing on my arms, and I felt stalked by a thick cloud of dark fear that I refused to face. Confused and tortured at times, I turned to Ariel, my angel, for comfort and guidance.

Dear Journal - I actually took a Saturday off from work so John and I could escape to Sedona for some much-needed relaxation together. For kicks I went and got a psychic reading. All accurate, but nothing new. The interesting part occurred when the lady told me that there was a blob of dark gunk (my words not hers) in my energy field. When she pointed to the location of this blob I was suitably impressed. This is the exact spot where I've had a lot of pain and stiffness lately.

After the "reading," John and I rested in a gorgeous spot along the creek and then hiked back into one of the canyons. The day was beautiful and the forest should have soothed my soul, but this emotional release process I'm going through is difficult and the emotional gunk I'm dealing with is dark and heavy. I should feel happier and closer to John, instead I feel very much alone. I'm the one isolating myself. The dark energy clouds my perception, dulls my brain, and hurts my side. I feel like that damn "not good enough" fear of mine is literally hanging on to me for dear life while everything else in me tries to let go of the insecurity and pain. I guess I have to be patient and allow the old program to leave gradually. This is darn difficult. I think I'll have a talk with Ariel.

Ann: Ariel, Hi, this is me, Ann. What's going on with me lately?

Ariel: You say you don't know, but really you do know what is going on. You've channeled enormous amounts of energy through yourself during the hypnosis sessions, and this is shaking loose some old emotional baggage. Humans do hang on to their old programs for dear life. You want to keep them. To maintain your current identity you must cling to all that causes you pain.

Ann: I guess I do know that, in theory, but what are my issues—the ones I need to release?

Ariel: For starters you can trust your intuitions about people—all people—and that includes men and women. You have to give up the fear of being hurt, dominated by men, abandoned by women and criticized by both. These are your themes. As you've figured out, the issues weren't born in this life, but the mini-dramas that you perform now are centered on these themes. You have to give up the notion that people won't like you for who you are. You have to give up the fear of being considered flaky for your beliefs and you have to own what you know. You weaken yourself when you downplay your wisdom. You leak energy like a sieve when you apologize for your behavior.

Rest now. Slip into the unknown and let the primal waters heal you. Comfort yourself. Treat yourself well. Do small things that indulge you. Perfume your bath or your hair. Give yourself a manicure or a pedicure. Put tea bags under your eyes. Read with a candle lit next to you that has been perfumed with scented oils. Do things small and large that are near and dear to your heart. Be creative and surround yourself with beauty. Dry your herbs. Drink your herbal tea sweetened with honey. Go out for lunch. Do a thousand things that honor the bright spirit you are. Let go of that shell. Break out of the fears that entrap you. Let your light crumble them like the dust that a rock becomes in the light of the laser. This is the way out of your trap. This is the only way out of the dark depths that you feel weighing down your heart at these times. Honor yourself. Go within. Discover, and then bring that light out into the world to be a beacon to others. To do otherwise is to live life as a pale shadow of the true self. Go now, do something you enjoy...

Slowly I began to understand the information that Ariel was trying to impart. Pieces of our spirit remain trapped and inaccessible to us when we don't allow our emotions to flow. I was freeing those pieces of my soul's essence, allowing them to be felt and heard in my life now. Each theme in my life was a necklace with many beads of experience on the chain. Each experience left a mark in my body somewhere: tension in the neck and shoulders, tightness in the jaw line, swirling in my stomach. The "blob," as I called the dark energy in my system, manifested physically as stiffness along the left side of my body and tension that culminated in my left lower back. Energetically, when I put my fingers into the "blob," I felt a sensation that could only be described as a feeling you get when you drag your hands through wet concrete. The "blob" was an energetic mass of all my old emotional baggage. Using the hypnosis and Reiki, I continued to work with energy and intention in an attempt to move the disturbing tension out of my system.

Me again, journal. I dreamt last night—one of those dreams that have more power in the dreaming than you can ever recreate in the telling. In the dream, I saw a calm canal parallel to the ocean. The ocean became mighty and the waves spilled over into the canal, disrupting the stillness. I'm the canal. Water in my dreams always represents my energy, my life force. For a brief while, all was still in my heart and my mind, but now I'm doing hypnosis and the great ocean waves of Spirit's consciousness are spilling over into my banks, disrupting my stillness, and rocking the boat. What a dream that was.

Today, the "blob" is around my head, on my left side, down my left arm, and around my back left shoulder blade. The thing moves as if I have a tangible bubble scooting around my body. Sooner or later, the bubble is going to burst. The "blob" is about to disintegrate, blasted to pieces by the light that is much finer than the dense energy can handle. I am about to lose an old identity. I will lose the part of myself that must drive herself into the ground, work to be good enough all the time, slave and wish for approval. Oh boy, the "blob" doesn't like that—even as I write, my left side starts to throb. I feel my energy pulsating around my temples, and physically my head begins to hurt.

Can't I tell the fear that I—the me who is the crystal at the core of the geode—will be able to shine ever more brightly if the crust can be removed? I respectfully ask the dense thought forms that drift around my aura to depart. They have served their purpose, and now I no longer need them as my teachers. Like leaves, once useful to the tree but now dead, they are free to drift from my being.

The essence of my soul is emerging. She's the creative one, the one whose poetry flows forth without asking, without pushing, without reservations. She's the quiet one inside who I've been embarrassed to let out because people around me, although they don't judge, don't understand her. At long last, her voice will be heard in my life. Like the gentle spring rains, she'll wash away the tensions, the struggles, and all that I cling to so desperately that doesn't suit me.

God, and Ariel, my dear guardian angel, help me shed this stuff, this emotional baggage that I'm sorting through. Help me release my limitations and accept the full knowledge of the great being that I really am. Help me connect with my other selves, my other lives so we can use our intuition, our knowledge, and our connection with the earth mother to heal. Help us live as one being—just different cells, at different times, on the body called earth. Help us filter her air, breathe in her light, and sing with joy for being alive. Today, this is my prayer.

After each good cry or each bout of anger, no matter how difficult, I experienced a feeling of being more free, more powerful, and more in control of my life than ever before. My writing became more creative and my life more joyful. As I learned to let go of all the years of judgment and self-criticism, I found that the words and images flowed into my mind ever so freely. I would ask a question and type while I received the poetic answers. Ariel, my angelic companion, continued to speak to me of life's mysteries:

Hi Journal.

Hey Ariel, tell me about *time*, please.

Time breaks fast upon the shores of life's ocean.

Reality is malleable, a flexible, workable notion.

Spirals of light unfolding and bending,

weaving the web, your cycles unending.

You live and you love and you teach and you die.

You move on in the dream, and just now, you ask

"Why?"

Like a lover awakening from a long-deepened

sleep, you hover between worlds,

you long for the dream.

Your eyesight is clearer, your head full of light.

Awake in the sunshine, step out of the night.

I can barely type I am so relaxed. I am very excited to speak with the angels tonight. I see a vision of an angel who looks somewhat Victorian. He's wearing golden robes with some red. He has the most magnificent wings of soft but sturdy feathers. His hair is a mass of golden curls, and he is wearing sandals. He speaks to me:

I am an angel, I fly with the skies.

I see energies whirring,

spirals unfurling,

light exploding in all her days.

Creation unfolding,

the love lights the rays.

Dancing proclaiming, singing

heralding each new day.

We angels dance in anticipation

of the last of you who will someday awaken.

Dance with joy.

Let your heart be light.

Join us in splendor.

Take thee to flight.

Ann: Ariel where did that come from?

Ariel: You were just translating your vision of our light dancing. Stay with this one. Let the feelings overtake you.

Ann: I feel such love now, such warmth, and such a peaceful presence. I can almost hear you. I hear a ringing in my ears. Am I tuning in to your frequency? Maybe, someday soon I'll hear your voices.

Ariel:

Pay attention to your dreams,

to your teachers in the night.

Let your fantasies take you to flight,

and ride the starry skies of night.

Allow us to draw you ever closer to Source.

Watch us in our spiral dance.

Feel us in our flight.

Learn from our melding

in the soft lights of night.

Look for us in every source.

Watch for us in every corner.

Find us in each gleaming heart.

Shadows lurk but where we stand,

your life need never be so dark.

Ann: I had no ideas you guys were such poets.

Ariel: We are translating our vibration through your fancy. Let your fingers dance on the keyboard. See how joyfully they bounce from key to key. Listen to them as you type. They sing! Earth sings, the locusts sing, the trees and the wind sings. The ocean hums a deep baritone as her waves crash upon the shore, and the creek murmurs while the rain sings a mournful song to her lover earth. Listen. All of creation is singing; all of creation is dancing. Feel this. Hear this in your heart.

— § —

When my hypnotist friend became busy and we could no longer continue our sessions, I took time to rest and enjoy my feelings of newly found freedom. My seventh anniversary vacation with John was magical. We took a short trip to Sedona in Northern Arizona, and at my request we didn't make any plans. We booked the last available hotel room in town at an incredible price. We saw the largest shooting star we had ever seen the night before John gave me the anniversary card he had purchased weeks before—a card with a shooting star on the cover that told me I was bringing some new light into his life as well. We discovered a little out-of-the-way coffee house where an African Zulu-Reggae band played for the small close-knit crowd. I swam in the pure waters of the creek then allowed the sun's warmth to caress my skin and bake my cares away. As we hiked, I made each step a prayer to the earth proclaiming my gratitude for the scenery that surrounded us. Using intention, focus, and trust, we created a vacation filled with delightful surprises. I changed my attitudes so I was attractive and fun to be around once again, and as a result, I began to experience the magic life had to offer. I felt I had finally graduated from a class entitled "Self-Awareness and Right-Living 101."

Unfortunately, my work in clearing out the old emotions was by no means over. Just a few weeks after my anniversary, another friend called to ask if I would trade Reiki treatments for deep-tissue therapeutic massage. I agreed and scheduled my first appointment. Two days after the massage, I learned more about the mind-body connection first hand.

Well, journal, I don't know what I got myself into. The deep tissue work is stirring up so much. Old emotions, old garbage, old crap. My body reacts and emotions start streaming out. For example, right now my body is MAD, screaming mad. I don't know how to describe this sensation except I feel crawly and tense. I'm repressing the anger right now because if I let loose I'm afraid I would be kicking, screaming, and yelling, and I might break something. I have to get this out somehow, so I'm just going to let my brain dump whatever the hell it wants to, right here on the paper. One caveat before I cut loose. What comes out isn't new stuff; it isn't stuff I believe any more, but it sure reflects how I felt at one point in my life. I've got to let this out. Deep breath. OK, here goes....

I took a deep breath and let the feelings overtake me. I was twelve again, cowering in my room after an argument, sobbing, and wondering what I had done wrong. I was fifteen and I was rebelling against the explanations for the disagreements. In my mind's eye, in the swirling whirling sensation in my stomach, in the lines that pulled my face taught, there was no difference between past and present. As an adult, I grudgingly let the child speak through me for the first time...

I can't release these damn emotions in front of anyone. I can't let them see how they get to me. I won't let them hurt me. Can't they see? Can't they see what the hell they are doing to me? I hate the fighting. I hate it. I want them to just cut it out. Go AWAY. Stop your screaming. I am so mad. I am pounding the keyboard and want to break something. My arms are tense. My jaw is tense. I feel like I did when my parents were angry at each other, screaming at me, screaming, and explaining later. I didn't believe a word they said. They hurt me. They hurt each other. Let me be, just let me be. Go away.

STOP IT.

Leave me alone.

Both of you.

Can't you see what the hell you're doing to me?

UGH.

I can't even type anymore.
I'll break the keyboard.

I was frightening myself, pounding on the keyboard with a fury that spoke of a rage inside of me that was pounding and pounding and waiting to be expressed. I had enough presence of mind to get up from the computer and walk around the house. I realized with some last thread of sanity that I had just pulled the cork on years of emotions that had been bottled up inside of my body, and the volcano was ready to blow. I looked around for something to hit, or something to hurt that I wouldn't regret later. I remembered the scissors I had once thrown into the wall in a similar rage and knew I didn't want to feel foolish by leaving any incriminating marks around the house. I paced angrily like a caged cat, waiting to bare my claws and snarl. I found John reading in the living room and, breathing deeply, asked him if he would take the dogs for a walk. "Please go now," I begged, nearing tears of hysteria, "I'm going to blow. I need to go through with this. I need to get these emotions out and I don't want you to watch. Please." I pleaded with what little composure that remained.

John took one look at me, started to ask if there was anything he could do and changed his mind. He called the dogs, leashed them up, and said he would be back in half an hour. I felt I had reached the limits of my rational mind. Now, finally, the time was ripe for me to confront the beast that prowled the labyrinth of my psyche. I had waited and asked for this moment. I wanted so desperately to let go of the rage that smoldered like a seething cauldron in the depths of my black heart. I felt foolish and stupid and I didn't want to storm. Some little part of my mind reminded me I loved my parents now. "True, but this isn't about NOW," I told myself firmly. The time had arrived to call back my soul, to let the damn burst and the floodwaters of my tears flow.

I remembered a seminar on psychodrama that I had attended. "Act out your feelings," the instructor told us. Furious now, I grabbed a terry cloth rag and felt my fingers clench the cloth as if the rag was responsible for all the pain in my life. I beat the walls of my house silly, screaming all the ugly things I had ever wanted to say when I was younger, when I was getting yelled at, when there were arguments in my home. I was screaming louder and louder. I wondered if the neighbors would hear; what they would think. I clenched my teeth, snarled, and screamed some more. "Take that, and that, and that, and THAT! ARGGHHH." I growled like an injured beast. "Leave me alone!!!"

I took a breath. I felt horrible, stupid, mean, ugly, and ungrateful as I shouted out the obscenities. I wanted to stop, to retreat from the feeling, and find refuge in my thoughts. The shred of logic remaining in my mind said, "KEEP GOING. Get all of the anger out." In my mind I fought a battle that had been raging inside for years. "No one ever really meant to hurt me," I insisted. "So What?!" the snarling bitch inside cried out. "They Did." "Leave. Me. Alone." Whack. Whack. Whack. One last outburst of rage when I though surely I would drive my fist through the wall and then the flood gates burst and I heard myself screaming, as if my life depended on someone hearing my cry, "I LOVE YOU!" My voice turned into a whimper. "I love you."

I slumped to the floor and pulled my knees close to my chest and rocked back and forth while I sobbed the tears I had never allowed myself to cry for the emotions I had never allowed myself to feel. The anger at my parents that had masked the hurt born of misunderstanding had just been stripped away. The dark cloak had been flung off. Underneath the raw scar of emotion was revealed. I sobbed uncontrollably now, collapsing like a rag doll, holding the harmless terry cloth rag like a hurt child. The tears cleansed me, washing away the darkness I had stored for so long in my hardened heart. On the left side of my body, I felt a stirring, a bubbling in the energy surrounding me, and then I felt a "pop" as my muscles released their tension and a portion of the "blob" disintegrated. John came back just at the perfect time, and even though he didn't understand what I was going through, he let me cling to him and sob as the tears of relief washed the last remnants of anger from my soul. I wiped my bloodshot, tear-stained eyes, explained the ordeal as best I could and told him he looked like an angel.

— § —

Hi Journal. Boy did that massage last week stir up the hornet's nest in my soul. It's funny, I wasn't mad at the people my parents are now. I was mad, raging mad, at a situation that occurred many years ago. The people we were then don't even exist anymore, except as they lived, locked up in my body and my mind. I felt like I had a thousand pounds lifted off my shoulders after the last session. The two days following the outburst, I was very joyful. I felt lighter and less burdened. It's a tough thing to explain. I called home and told Mom and Dad that I loved them and for the first time I felt my own words. "I love you too," Mom said as she hung up. She said, "I love you"—three words I would have killed to hear so many years ago.

This week's treatment was quite different. I was feeling so emotionally beat up I didn't want any more deep tissue massage. Instead we did a great deal of energy work this time and some relaxing massage. The therapist's hands felt like hot metal on my skin. I wonder if this is what I feel like to others when I work on them.

Today, the sadness beneath the anger that we stirred up is attempting to surface. I feel the emotion physically. I touch my jaw where I was massaged and I want to cry but my stomach holds steadfastly on to those emotions. My chest is heavy with this cloud of sadness and my jaw quivers, but the next round of tears won't come yet. In due time they will. The very hard part is not mixing up these old feelings with my present life. I know this is hard on John. I know I'm not a "normal" wife anymore. Thank God, he still he sees me with compassion, if not understanding. I know that he knows that deep down, I'm a very bright spirit struggling to set herself free. I would do the same for him.

Through all of this, I just feel like I need time alone. I don't need the pressures of worrying about how I am affecting others. I don't want to hurt anyone else, but I have huge healing to do and my tendency is to make sure everyone else is OK and thereby ignore my own issues. I have to face this. I have to feel the sadness, the hurt, the anger, the pain, and the grief. I have to meet my demons and let them go free. This is very difficult to do.

I had no idea I would need such courage and focus to remember who I really am through all of this. It would be so easy to lose control and slip into the dark throes of insanity. A frightening thought, but I would never let that happen to myself. I know there is a very bright light at the end of this dark tunnel. I am just having a hard time maintaining a decent relationship with anyone while I confront myself. I wish so desperately that someone around me could really understand what I am going through and console me, but then again, perhaps if I had that type of support, I would never force myself to find my own strength. Throw in my ninety-hour workweeks, and I'm having a difficult time keeping my head above the water and staying positive at all.

Maybe if I just keep writing, I can get myself in touch with the feeling and the sadness. Oh good, I'm seeing pictures again... this time I see a child's story:

Locked away in a tiny cage with steel bars much thicker than necessary, the little bird sings. Her soft tuft ruffles as she dreams of the bright blue sky above. She's heard tales of this strange and wonderful land outside but here in her cage, cold gray steel and hard floors are all she knows.

Loneliness, terrible aching loneliness, is all she has ever known. She was locked away when she was very young. Her owners were afraid of giving her freedom. She might fly away and never come back. She might not love them. They showed her love in the only ways they knew how. They gave her shelter and fed her well. They talk to her and treat her like the pet she's become. They don't realize that they've killed her spirit, robbed her of her true nature.

"Let me free," she cries in song. She doesn't know what "free" means, but she has a faint glimmer, a dream, a longing. Her wings know the feeling of flight even though she's never soared. Her feathers dream of rustling through the breezes she's never known. "Set me free," she cries. Her

soul is anguished; still she feels no feeling. She is
numb.

I'm crying. I'm finally crying. I don't know
why. I don't even know what is causing my
sadness. However, I do feel like that caged
bird. My spirit knows what freedom is but in
this life, as this Ann-person, I've not
experienced freedom in the way I know I can.
I've been locked away. A great spirit living a
shadow life of the existence she is meant to
know. I mourn for the loss of my freedom...

The door opens. Some lucky accident. Some
person with great love has taken a risk to set the
little bird free. She fluffs her feathers and peeks
out the door. It's so big out there, so unknown.
What if the cat gets her as she flies to the window?
What if she tries to get out only to find the windows
of the house are closed and the door shut? To be
put back in her cage after a brief excursion would
hurt far worse than never to know the sunshine at
all. That would be heartbreaking. She stands at
the edge of her cage, looking back, feeling the
security of being a captive, and also the longing to
be free. She stands, uncertain and afraid, at the
edge and the end of everything she has ever
known.

This is me. Story is my therapy. I stand too, poised on the edge of everything I've ever known. I mourn the passing of my old life. This is my sadness. If I could only drop the veil, the curtain of illusion that obscures my vision, and see what lies ahead, my heart knows that I would be rejoicing instead. I am in a time of passage, transition. I would never have seen all this if I hadn't let myself write. Thank you angels. You come to me in many ways.

The next week when I went to see the massage therapist, he asked me how I was doing. "I got the impression that you had some emotion to release," he said. "You were like a caged bird." I stared at him in complete and total amazement. Was I really so transparent?

—— § ——

With each session, the emotional releases became less traumatic. I learned to transform my pains from the past into new creative energy. I filled the pages of my journal with writing, and at work I discovered I was even more relaxed, a little more joyful, and a lot more compassionate with people. I was able to think more clearly and take pleasure even in the most difficult of tasks. My sense of humor was returning too.

The bodywork taught me that we reach a point in our path when we must return to the past and clean out our spiritual closets. We can't travel any farther until we lighten our load. We've left pieces of our spirit behind, trapped in dark repressed emotions, lost in time and space until we have the courage to go back into the darkness and find them.

The stories of our lives—the unexpressed pains, the unfelt agonies, the tears not cried, and the repressed angers—store themselves in our muscles and etch their outlines in our living flesh. When we're angry, we clench our muscles tightly. When we're frightened, we forget to breathe. When we're sad, we slump. Over time, these postures become habitual; our bodies literally reflect life's inputs to our psyche.

Having no healthy outlet, these lost emotions simmer just beneath the surface of our personalities, waiting until they are triggered to erupt. As we silence the judgment of our intellectual adult selves and allow the feelings of our child-self to emerge, the rage, the sadness, and the despair dissipate in the light of consciousness. The whispers of the Spirit, ever present in even the most difficult of my life situations, helped me see the ecstasy to be gained once I moved through the agony.

Almost eerily, for the third year in a row, John and I scheduled a vacation to Kauai. I knew I was about to complete a major cycle in my life's history, but I had no idea how or when the end of the cycle would occur.

Chapter 7
Through Heaven and Hell

Hi there, journal. I had another vision today. I saw myself in spirit form standing at the top of a mountain ridge. An enormous hawk flew over my head. I held up my hands offering the bird huge black tar-like chunks of dense energy that represent all those attitudes and beliefs that hold me tethered to the ground. The hawk, my messenger, took the dark forms from my hands and dropped them into a deep green pool. The waterfall spilling over into the pool smashed them into harmless bits of earth that would nourish the nearby vegetation. Symbolically, my fears were being shattered and recycled to sustain new life.

— § —

"Flight 1061, you're cleared for takeoff." I could hear the voice from the control tower through my headphones that were tuned into the cockpit voice channel. The engines revved on the 737, and the plane raced down the runway at Phoenix Sky Harbor International Airport. The ground melted away beneath us as the sun rose in a burst of fiery orange on the eastern Phoenix skyline. My heart soared with the plane. John and I were headed to Kauai for the third year in a row. As if that weren't blessing enough, the airfare was free, courtesy of a promotional travel company whose presentation we had attended.

I left work late the night before after furiously rushing around to take care of last minute details. I made sure that people were lined up to attend all my meetings for me, to coordinate the daily status and problem reports with the customer, and to make sure the paperwork associated with each interim software delivery was complete. I was deeply grateful to my coworkers who were covering for me while I vacationed during a busy time. Nonetheless, after working ninety-hour weeks, I didn't feel the slightest twinge of guilt. The job was quickly forgotten.

The flight to our stopover in California was uneventful. We had a little more excitement en route to Honolulu when the pilot aborted takeoff soon after the airplane started to accelerate down the runway. A warning light came on in the cockpit telling the pilots there was a problem with their leading edge flaps. In the massive body of the packed 747, John and I, along with the rest of the passengers, heaved a collective sigh as we headed back toward the gate where we waited on the plane for an hour before being allowed to disembark.

"How different I've become," I noticed as we walked off the plane. Two years ago I would have been fuming about the delay and still worrying about the work I left behind. Now I was happily joking about what we had to go through to get a free lunch. The flight attendants handed out meal coupons to pacify the frazzled passengers, and we enjoyed an impromptu date in a crowded airport cafeteria. Within hours, the plane's brakes had been allowed to cool, the flap problem had been fixed, and we were back on the 747. Passengers clapped when the giant bird eased itself into the air. In Honolulu, we hopped planes and arrived in Kauai slightly before our luggage. No matter. We checked into our hotel and wandered around the grounds.

Already, Mother Nature was beginning to erase the ravages of Iniki that we had seen only last year. Many of the major resorts were still closed but the flowers were flourishing once again and new branches were growing back on the tops of the trees. The choppy surf pounded the coast, and in the distance, the chiseled cliffs of Na Pali on the north side of the island rose from the ocean like moss-covered pebbles.

A large lawn behind the hotel led down to the ocean. The beach was a wild one, not one of those filtered-sand tourist beaches, but a real beach littered with driftwood, shells, and seaweed. Being on the windy side of the island, the waves were always frothy, and the trees were permanently fixed in a slanted posture assumed by standing so many years in the never-ceasing blast of wind. John and I returned to the hotel for a quick dinner then meandered back to the beach for a long walk with our feet in the surf. We watched the sun that had risen in our Phoenix desert sink into a watery world over three thousand miles away.

Tired from traveling and stiff from my massage two days earlier, I sank down into the comfortable bed that night and silently thanked Spirit for sending me to heaven once again.

— § —

Dear Journal - What a day. John and I went on a beautiful hike. The walk into the jungle was easy. The journey into the depths of my heart was not. I should have known the massage three days ago would stir things up.

The guidebook promised that the ridge trail was a "breathtaking, razorback, winding, rolling trek into paradise." I could hardly contain my excitement. We left the hotel early, feasted on a breakfast of homemade papaya pancakes at one of the local diners, and then jumped in the car, ready for our adventure. The sky was somewhat cloudy and a soft rain was falling, but nothing, I thought, could daunt my high spirits.

The trail began up a muddy slope with a small rivulet cruising down along the center of the path. Mists shrouded the mountains ahead of us. Lost in the fog, their beauty and majesty was well hidden. Tall trees, purple orchids, and broad-leafed vines lined the trail. Wild berries grew in patches here and there, offering us their sweet fruits. The journey might have been an easy walk through a steamy jungle had I not been in the midst of an intense period of emotional clearing. Ten minutes into the hike, I began to feel the effects of the previous massage. With each step the familiar stirring in my solar plexus intensified. "No. Oh no. Not here. Not now," I begged, becoming irritated. "I'm on vacation," I mumbled to no one in particular. John glanced my way.

Switchbacks cut into the mountainside as the trail wound a sinuous path to the overlook. My anger was building as I climbed. "Damnit!" I swore inwardly, knowing I was about to erupt once again. "You're the one that asked for this," I reminded myself. "You should have known better than to have a deep tissue massage right before your vacation." I stomped harder and wondered if John would recognize the signs of an impending explosion. Thank God, I always maintained enough self-control to avoid taking out these emotions on him.

At the top of the ridge, I felt old rage straining at the outer layers of my aura, begging for release. An itchy, crawling feeling tingled all over my skin as if someone had smeared thick paste on me that was oozing slowly down my arms and legs. I had been through this so many times before, but each time I was shocked at how physical the sensations were that preceded the emotions. "You and that stupid second-shift work really hurt our marriage early on," I thought to myself, shocked at my own anger. Some part of me really wanted to lash out at John only seconds after I warned him that I was going to lose control. I kept my mouth shut and didn't say a thing. My anger wasn't his fault.

Each time I faced the "unspeakable" emotions from my past, I felt vulnerable and exposed. What if I said something hurtful and my horrible actions triggered John to step out of his role as my healing partner and into one of being the victim of a venomous wife? Frightened to the core each time I began to connect with and let go of the old feelings, I knew the task was necessary. The old baggage had to go.

Graciously, or perhaps out of a desire to avoid the onslaught of emotion that was about to occur, John offered to let me walk alone and I accepted. My body was mimicking all the hurt and the anger I felt years ago when I had realized that our fairy-tale marriage had drifted apart while we pursued careers that did not make us so wonderfully happy. I wanted to run back to John to escape the feeling I had run from so many times before. The voices inside my head commanded me, *"Go deeper."* "No!" I didn't cry aloud, but my body heaved a heavy breath as if I had. No, I didn't want to go deeper to face the feelings I had denied so many years ago. This was awful. I thought I was finished dealing with this pain.

A small path led off through waist high ferns. The view I was afforded of Mt. Wai'ale'ale in the distance was breathtaking, even though her peak was still hidden in the clouds. Waterfalls trickled tears down through the lush vegetation, as I went deeper into the jungle and deeper inside my own heart. I traveled back in time, searching for answers where I had run from them before. Why this hurt inside? Why this pain? I wanted to cry, but I held back the heart-wrenching sobs of long forgotten agony while the silent tears streamed down my face. *"Go deeper,"* the voices said. Once again, I cried inside, "No, I can't." I had been to this place in my heart before. I had been in this space where I felt rage turning into hurt, and hurt turning into unbearable self-loathing. I always stopped here, distracting myself, refusing to face the pain that lay buried in my psyche. I never had any great trauma or abuse, but still I felt the ache that came from being a child in the middle of my parents' arguments, and the agony of a young woman "deserted" by her husband while he worked odd shifts. I remembered feeling alone even when we were together. I had been through the anger. I had faced the sadness. Now I had reached the threshold of emotion that I never dared to cross. Would I be brave enough this time to confront my deepest, darkest fears? "This is the doorway," I thought. Go deeper.

I took a few more steps down the fern-lined path. "What have I done?" I cried out in anguish. "I don't understand," the voice of a little child wailed inside me, echoing my voice from the distant past. The scenery around me was quickly disappearing, and I was soon beyond reason. I whimpered aloud, "Why do they hate me? Why?" "My parents never meant to hurt me," my adult voice piped in, reprimanding me for feeling when I "knew" better. "John has always loved me." Hurtful scenes from the past flashed through my mind again. Then, the unspeakable emotions hit me like a freight train ramming through the barriers I had erected in my heart, bursting to broadcast all I had worked so hard to hide. Feelings I couldn't even voice because they were so ridiculous whirled around me as tangibly as if I was lost in a hurricane's grasp. Dizzy, I tried to steady myself. "I'm ugly, hateful, hurtful, flawed, defective, evil, a trouble-maker. I'm despicable, ungrateful, unworthy, unlovable... unlovable... unlovable. NO!" I cried aloud and the echo never came back from the faraway mountain.

Tears rained down my face, their salty waters dripping onto my tongue and mixing with the raindrops that still fell from the leaden skies. So, this was why I worked so hard, constantly trying to be the best I could be, but never feeling that what I did was enough. I had dealt with all these emotions but not at this level; now I had time to feel them deeply, heart and soul, body and mind, and then let them go. I sobbed loudly, choking for air and wanting to distract myself from the terrible pain. No matter that I knew these things were false; I felt them now at my very core. These were the lost and tarnished portions of my psyche—the dark bits of illusion that remained in the depths of my heart.

No wonder I felt unworthy of love; I didn't even love myself. No wonder I couldn't leave a "perfectly good job." Something deep within me didn't feel I deserved any better. My whole life flashed before me, structured around the assumptions that I was unworthy of all life had to offer, and based on the nasty little underlying belief that what I did was more valuable than who I was. I stroked the fern in front of me, wondering at its perfection and then in a flash of insight that struck like the sun just beginning to break through the clouds, I saw the truth.

My soul screamed out in anger, finally emerging from the dark labyrinth of false beliefs, clawing its way through the jungle of tangled emotions, proclaiming to the world, "I AM NOT BAD! I AM LOVABLE! I DESERVE A LIFE THAT I LOVE NOW!" My perspective shifted suddenly, and I saw myself in two dimensions—one through my own eyes and one through the eyes of my higher self—watching a thirty-year-old woman dripping wet and standing among the ferns in a misty jungle while going through the doorway of her own self-hatred into the light of her soul's never-ending love. *"How else could you feel your true perfection unless you know the lie within your pain?"* The voices in my mind whispered the rhetorical question with exquisite tenderness. I couldn't answer.

Mists swirled once more around the mountaintop in front of me, so much like the clouds of intense emotion that had been obscuring my own inner beauty. The sun peeking through them was a mirror for the light that was finally beginning to shine inside of me. I walked back along the trail with the tears drying on my face as the rain-drenched land began to dry in the warmth of the afternoon sun. I found John and thanked him for waiting then kissed him with the deep compassionate love of an old friend. An egret circled overhead reminding me of purity, wholeness, and perfection—the circle of life. I understood in that instant that my trip to the past had been necessary in order to complete the circle—or close the loop as we say in engineering—before I could move forward. I practically danced down the muddied trail. Drenched with rain, sweat, and tears, I felt like I had been washed clean. At long last, I had found, faced, and slayed my inner demon. Like the egret and the mythical Daedalus, I soared now above the labyrinth that was my life and saw the switchback pathways from a new perspective.

We traveled later that day to our favorite south shore beach, and I lay in the soft sand while the relentless sun baked away the remnants of the gut-wrenching experience I had just undergone. We feasted that night in a beachfront restaurant at one of the local resorts, and then back in our room, I fell into a deep and healing dreamless slumber.

The following morning John and I drove to the north side of the island to enjoy some lazy time on a pristine beach. Of all the sweet swimming spots and tropical paradise locations on Kauai, this was one of my favorites. Huge vines traversed even the tallest trees, and plants with leaves larger than my whole midsection were everywhere. Jungle flowers perfumed the warm, moist air and the sea was a sparkling palate of blues and greens colored by the various depths of the water, the submerged lava rocks, and coral reef. I didn't remember colors ever being this bright.

We hiked past the beach and up to the ruins of an ancient Hula temple that rested high on the cliff side overlooking the ocean. The path meandered along lava stones through the thick jungle then abruptly turned left through a dense fence of vegetation. We climbed quickly, winding our way up the trail to the ruins. Walls made from the same lava rock that lined the shore below created natural looking terraces. Grasses, soft as a baby's hair, grew in the uppermost terrace. The area was still enclosed by two-foot lava rock walls that were carefully pieced together. The place was obviously sacred so we entered in silent reverence.

Children from a local hula school were practicing in the grassy arena. We watched respectfully, feeling the peace and power of the place. I wondered what the drums must have sounded like hundreds of years ago when the first hula dancers paid their tribute to the island gods, in the times when dance was less of an art and more a form of worship. Did their bodies discover secrets in the ancient rhythms—secrets that our modern minds still long to grasp? Underneath the bright sky that arched over an endlessly undulating sea, I could feel the "mana," the life force of ancient Hawaii, in my bones. The children from the hula school left quietly when they finished their exercises, and I moved to sit on one of the old stone walls.

"Who had been here before me," I wondered? I felt myself a tiny speck on the face of the great mother earth. The cliff, carved by wind and storm and time rose abruptly behind us and to the left, while to the right we could see the other tourists gathering in tiny groupings below on the whitewashed beach. For a moment, I was lost in time. I slipped into a dreamlike state in which I merged with the energies of the earth and felt their pulsating rhythm in my own body. A pleasant tingling electrical sensation enveloped me and I lost track of the boundaries between myself and the landscape. Staring out over the ocean, I saw mother earth's curving horizon and imagined that I could see beyond the canopy of the sky into the depths of space. I soon began to sense her immensity and feel her motion. I became aware of her spinning on her axis, spinning around the sun, and traveling through the galaxy, which, in turn, cycled through the endless reaches of the universe. I felt myself to be part of that motion, and yet an individual as well. I came out of my reverie feeling both incredibly energized and at peace.

After making our way carefully back down the narrow trail, we drove along the winding road toward Lumahai beach. A hitchhiker caught our attention and, uncharacteristically, we decided to give him a ride. We would not have dreamt of doing so back home, but the island residents we had met so far on the north shore were friendly and good natured. He was a tan, sinewy fellow with unkempt long blond hair. He told me he "quit the mainland years ago, because it was a sinking ship." "Why not move here?" he asked me pointedly. "Why not, indeed," I wondered inwardly. "I would love to live here." "You don't even have to shop," he prodded me further as if reading my thoughts. "You can live off the land and bathe in natural spring waters. And you can be a caretaker of one of these estates, like me, so you don't even have to pay rent." I wondered who was the wiser: we with all our riches, or this man with a simple, beautiful life?

We dropped him off at his destination, shortly before we reached the cliff side parking for Lumahai beach. A steep trail wound downward through tenacious waist-high grasses. The beach was yet another gem in a series of north shore beauties. A gentle curve of sand ended in a small protected area where the water gently rose and fell. Farther down the beach, larger and more powerful waves crashed and pounded against the shore, carving those areas into steep sandy slopes.

Likewise, Spirit was relentlessly pounding away at the shores of any last reservations I might have about leaving behind the security of my job in engineering. While bobbing up and down in the protected waters, John and I met a gentleman from Toulouse, France, who lives here now. He gave up his former career in order to be a waiter in paradise. "Who's the wiser," I thought once again, contemplating my slowly changing notions of success. As if Spirit wanted to prove I wouldn't have to truly give anything up, in the long run, in order to have the life I wanted, we met another gentleman just a few minutes later—a man who bragged he had started his multi-million dollar business with only one hundred dollars many years ago. Now he and his wife travel most of the time. He told us he brought sixty of his best customers to the Princeville Resort for a week. "Small price to pay for their business," he told us. "How fortunate we are to be equals in the ocean," I mused. "How fortunate I am to be receiving these messages so kindly."

Dinner was a long stop at a south-shore restaurant with mahi mahi steaks that made our mouths water, and tropical drinks that made my head swim. After dinner, I talked John into taking a moonlit drive into the island's interior to see Wailua Falls, made famous in the opening scenes of the old television show, "Fantasy Island." I wondered what they would look like on this bright and beautiful night.

No one else was on the road that meandered between fields of sugar cane whose stalks rasped back and forth in the soft night breeze. We drove slowly, alerted to the presence of the bullfrogs on the road by their bright white underbellies. After dodging the frogs, we reached the overlook to the falls. In the moonlight the water shimmered and danced a ghost dance of silvery white light. The sound of the falls was deafening in the dark of night with no other hint of noise except for the dancing grasses and whispering cane fields swaying in the night wind. The silver water disappeared into a bottomless pit of jet-black void beneath us. We couldn't see the bottom. The depths were blacker than any black I've ever seen. The power in the air was palpable. I felt as if any moment the energy in the falls would reach out and throw me over the cliff too into the murky black nothingness below. The void, the pool that represented the feminine powers in my dreams, scared me. Who would I be if I went over the edge and surrendered myself to the powerful flow of life? I didn't miss the symbolism that continued to haunt me on this journey.

I moved farther back from the railing, still more comfortable with all that was safe and familiar. Spooked and awed, we got back in the car and drove out of the mythical scene into the safe and familiar setting of a semi-urban tropical hotel.

After a quick breakfast of Portuguese sweet bread and French toast, John and I headed to the Big Save grocery store to buy fish food. Snorkeling was on the agenda, and we wanted to make sure we would be popular with the local fish. I certainly didn't expect today's messenger from God to come in the form of the guy selling tours outside of the grocery store, but that's exactly what happened.

"Hey! Where you guys from?" He greeted us from the tiny booth that was loaded with brochures, discount coupons, and advertisements. "Arizona," I answered in a friendly tone. "Ever think of moving here?" he asked. I rolled my eyes and shrugged, wondering how many more people would ask the same question before I would seriously consider an answer. I was tempted. "I'm an unpublished author," he told me proudly. I couldn't believe my ears. "I want to write too," I told him, "but I'm afraid to leave the security of my current job." I couldn't believe I was spilling my soul to a total stranger. He responded with a kind look in his eyes. "Find something you love and write about that," he told me. "You'll earn money when you need to, here and there. Having a lot of money isn't so necessary when you're happy doing what you love." I started to buzz with that funny warmth I felt when the angels were around. "I'm into spirituality for example," he told me. He proceeded to share stories about his experiences with psychics and channels that were too real to doubt. In less than ten minutes, the man validated the past year of my life and made me feel as if it were possible to achieve my dreams. We booked a boat cruise and looked forward to another wonderful sunny adventure the following day.

As with many things in life, the cruise did not start out the way we planned. A tropical storm drenched us as we boarded the catamaran for our ride along the beautiful but mist-shrouded Na Pali coastline. Only a few years ago I would have been upset and demanded a refund. Lately, however, Spirit seemed intent on teaching me to expect the best and to trust that life would take care of all my needs and desires. So, I surrendered to the circumstances and chose to assume that there was something magical in store for us today.

In the sunlight, the Na Pali cliffs would have glistened like emeralds with all manner of green vegetation growing along their steep sides. Today the weatherworn shoreline had a different complexion—grey and gloomy. At least our companions were interesting. We sat down next to a well-to-do middle-aged couple and their fifteen-year-old daughter.

The daughter made it obvious to all that she would have preferred to be sleeping on a sunny beach catching up on her tan or watching the bronzed, steely muscled young men on their surfboards. I could tell she loved her parents, yet she wanted nothing to do with them at this age. I had a flashback.

In addition to two other couples, the captain was a rugged fellow and his mate was a lanky younger guy who looked like he had a good sense of humor. As the rain poured, we donned our yellow slickers, sat in chilly puddles on the seats of the boat, and headed out to sea. We couldn't resist joking about a "three-hour tour." What a different experience to be on the ocean in a rainstorm with the gray skies and clouds scudding overhead. The waves didn't look quite as friendly as they did when the water was see-through sea blue.

In spite of the downpour, we stopped a mile offshore from Haena Beach Park. "Look carefully," the captain told us. "A pod of dolphins frequents this area." Now I knew the treat that life had in store for us today! With my eyes skimming the glassy black surface of the water, I calmed my thoughts, and mentally projected a request, asking the dolphins to pay us a visit. Within seconds, two of them emerged from the depths with a joyous leap, followed by three more. They danced in a harmonious symphony of play, rocketing out of the water, gracefully arching, and then piercing the surface of the waves, only to spring up out of the water again and again. They seemed blissfully unaffected by the rain. A baby dolphin who was only two feet long swam beside his parents. He wriggled using all of his strength to jump. He looked so joyful and filled with life that none of us on the boat—not even the previously indifferent young lady—could resist joining in his delightful exuberance. The grey skies hadn't clouded his mood at all. I said a silent prayer of gratitude for these beautiful beings. They looked so happy and in love with life. I grinned inwardly. Even the dolphins were telling me to follow my bliss.

The group on the boat continued to take pictures until these mysterious and beautiful creatures disappeared once again into the depths. We had forgotten all about the rain.

— § —

Hello Journal! I'm writing from the Honolulu airport today as we start the first leg of our journey home. A woman complains loudly about the wait to check in, and while she does so, she neglects to see that an express line has become available for her flight. Goodness. We do indeed create our own realities.

John and I just walked to the gate, and then I returned for some of that wicked Lappert's Kauai Pie™ ice cream for breakfast! Coffee ice cream is mixed with chocolate fudge, toasted coconut, and macadamia nuts. If I am supposed to follow my bliss, this is a great way to start. What a trip this has been. What an incredible rediscovery of the soul. I can't even begin to count the number of people I met who were my teachers.

The hitchhiker we picked up on the road to Hanalei forced me to rethink my priorities. With his wide-toothed grin he bragged excitedly about the crystal clear spring that provides him with pure water, which, he pointed out, "is more valuable than gold." He nearly demanded that we embrace a more tangible definition of abundance, rather than placing our emphasis on the almighty dollar.

The woman who owned the metaphysical store in Hanalei shared her own stories and insights with me as well. "When I lived in Oregon," she told me, "I stocked my shop with things I thought people would buy. Now I buy what I love, and those things sell much better." I made a mental note to remain true to myself.

The man selling tours and activities next to the grocery store validated my desire to follow my dreams. "Find something you love and write about it," he urged me. "You'll find ways to make money here and there." His message was direct and to the point—stop worrying about money and write.

Then there was a woman at another activities desk, who, like the man near Big Save, finds odds jobs, and other joyful means of making a living. Two days a week, she works on the boats because she loves the dolphins. She was beautiful, confident, and graceful. She obviously honors her heart. Her message was conveyed simply by her presence—life is too short to do what you don't love. Live now.

Kauai has become my symbol of love, beauty, and incredible positive energy. I came here to drink in the atmosphere and to allow the sun, sand, and sea to purge my soul. I was not disappointed. The tropical vegetation breathed life back into my weary body and at night, the moon that shone like liquid crystal melting on the jet-black ocean reminded me that I had never truly been alone—not even in the darkest of times. The sound of the rustling palm trees dancing in the wind reminded me of the voices of Spirit that whisper in my own mind. I cried my tears as the rains poured from the heavens, and in the presence of the mystical dolphins, I once again remembered my own playful and innocent nature. In every moment during this trip, I was privileged to rediscover the magic and mystery that life has to offer. I feel as if I tapped into a timeless dimension of reality in which I can sense the eternal nature of my soul.

I felt like I was experiencing a time of quickening. My spirit was ripening like the fruits that grew wild in the jungles off the north shore, and I too was restoring a natural beauty to my own once-windswept life.

I left the island behind, but the lessons remained imprinted in my heart.

Chapter 8
A Dance with Death

Changes.

Breaking the patterns of the present now.

Curving off on a trailing path –

one that we've not seen

A fork in the road, a split in the canyon...

Why hadn't I noticed this way before?

"Welcome Back," the card read. I found the message in a small envelope lying on my desk next to a vase containing two of the most exquisite peach roses I had ever seen. I sat down and smiled, feeling happy to be working with such incredible people. The woman who left the flowers had become a sister to me. We had been through hell and back together, as we tried to get the software packages delivered on time. We had often worked through the night and encouraged each other when one of us was sure we were going to lose our minds. "She's another angel," I thought as I sat down to flip on my computer and read the e-mail that had accumulated during my vacation. "Two hundred and thirty-six messages?" I was incredulous. I smiled and joked with myself, "Surely I can't be that popular!" One by one, I read each note, stopping every now and then to enjoy the sweet scent of the roses.

The morning's meetings flew by quickly and easily. I had only been gone a week, but the respite felt like months. I was happy to see people who had become a second family to me and they seemed genuinely glad to see me as well. I floated through the next few days, feeling a joy that came from doing my job well after returning from a vacation that left me rested and at peace. After confronting my inner demons and facing the beast within me deep in the jungles of Kauai, I had a newfound love and respect for myself. I moved through the days following my return with a grace and ease that I had not felt before, even on the best of days. I worked long hours with many people to meet our ever-impossible deadlines, but the stress was gone. I Knew— Knew-with-a-capital-K—that the deadlines, however important at this time, were irrelevant in the larger scheme of my life. I worked to meet them and when I failed, I still smiled, knowing I had done my best. Life was to be found in the journey, I reminded myself, not only in the moments when we reach some arbitrary destination. I rejoiced, happy that I could immerse myself in the process of living rather than confining my celebration of life to those few moments when I could relish the results of my labors.

New guides and angels, distinct from the voice of Ariel, appeared to be celebrating this glorious outlook on life with increased communications.

> Dear Journal - It's only Wednesday night. Who would guess what would happen in the span of only two days? Amazing. Two nights ago I was in bed, sitting in a very relaxed state. I started getting words in my head as I do sometimes when I am typing, so I began to say them aloud. All of a sudden, I started dreaming

that I was floating in space, looking down above the earth. I felt immense and I could sense that I was filling the entire room with my energy. Then, as I started thinking less and talking more, the thought hit me: "My God, if I keep this up I'm going to start channeling!" I had NEVER, EVER entertained that notion before. So I tried a little exercise. I asked an angel to appear, and in my mind's eye, there he was—near the bed to my left—a young-looking guy in white robes with wings and curly light-colored hair. I wondered if the way he appeared was real and got some answer to the effect of "*we appear in ways that make you comfortable.*" Then he took his face off and became a being of white light that moved off in a spinning rainbow vortex! Whoa.

I don't know what possessed me to do this next exercise (no pun intended!), but I thought, "OK, let me feel your energy briefly." I sat and felt an energy and warmth settle around me and then a tingling sensation ran down my arms. I heard the name "Daniel," then I freaked out and got spooked by the whole thing. Ooooh. It's one thing to believe in guides and angels and energies in unseen dimensions but what a shock when they start visiting you!

As if that weren't enough, I couldn't sleep so I started looking at the mask I made a few months ago. Tonight, the globe I painted on the chin caught my attention. "What does this mean?" I asked myself, and as soon as I had the thought, words started to pour into my head:

*"I speak to you of a loving presence. My children, I
have carried you like possums on my back through
the millennia. I am awakening, awakening from a
long sleep of dulled pain. I stretch. I groan. I
shake, and you feel the tremors. I am awakening,
coming into my fullness, and still you sleep. Some
of you are awakening into the light of this new
dawn. Some of you rejoice with me. Others resist.*

*I, the earth, am a living being. My size is of
no consequence, for you with your 'smallness' are
just as great as me. Space, and time for that
matter, are illusions. You could fill my entire space
with a single thought. We are one. We are the
same. Yes, think of the vast oceans, with their
endless horizons in the distance.*

*We are one. We journey together. Rejoice
with me. We are turning into the light."*

I just can't believe how wonderful life is lately.
I know with great certainty that life will always
continue in cycles of bliss and challenge, but I
feel a shift finally—one toward joy. I don't know
what subtle shifts are going on in me behind the
scenes of my everyday life, but I know the
change is something really, really good. There's
a great purging going on in my soul, and the
shift is making room for more light and more joy
to come.

I love my journal.

— § —

On Thursday, I went for my regularly scheduled massage and was shocked to discover that after all the work I had been doing and despite the absolute bliss that was permeating my life after the vacation in Kauai, my treatment was still deeply painful. Afterward I felt as if I were on the verge of bursting into tears once again, not from physical pain, but from the whirl of emotions that were stirred up each time my muscles were massaged. Just under the surface, I felt there was one last packet of emotion ready to be unleashed. I wasn't quite ready to deal with the trauma. I ignored the feelings that night, breathed deeply, and went to sleep.

Friday came and went quickly. I felt as if time were spiraling faster and faster in my life. New experiences occurred for me and then, before I could figure them out and integrate them into my current beliefs, something else would occur to disrupt all I thought I knew.

On Saturday, I escaped from work for a few hours to attend a local alternative health fair. I signed up for a Reiki treatment, and wondered why. I knew I could do Reiki on myself just as easily, but something prompted me to allow someone else to nurture me for once. At the time, I didn't realize that I was breaking a pattern of stubborn self-sufficiency that I had embraced my entire life. I rarely asked for help in my personal life, and honestly didn't trust most people to take care of me better than I had learned to take care of myself. I sat in the practitioner's chair, shut my eyes, and surrendered.

After putting me into a deep state of relaxation, the Reiki practitioner turned to me. "I received a message from Spirit while I was working on you. Would you like to hear what my guides had to say?" she asked politely. "Of course!" I replied. She smiled and for a moment, I thought I saw a golden glow around her face. "You have reached a new level of spiritual awareness," she said. "Congratulations on your golden crown of achievement." I hugged the woman and went back to the office, feeling as if I were the one glowing now. I had worked so hard, for so long, to progress, to grow, to become more aware of myself, my thoughts, and my feelings, and to integrate my mind, body, and spirit. How inspiring that this woman brought me such a wonderful message. The rest of the workday went smoothly.

The same evening, John and I went to the movies with friends to see Tom Clancy's film, "Clear and Present Danger." Always the type to get totally sucked into the story, I was sobbing my heart out during a tearjerker scene of death and destruction when I heard the voices once again. Typically, they sounded like thoughts that popped into my mind. This time they were as clear and true as if they had been spoken outside of me. *"Now would be a good time to practice being centered and to allow your emotions to flow through you. Rise above this scene and see life from a higher perspective. Movies are a great time to practice the skills you'll soon be needing in real life."*

I glanced around the theater quickly to see if someone was playing a joke on me, but the voices came again, this time, clearly from inside my mind. *"Try to remain calm and centered."* "Please! Can't I even watch a movie in peace?" I quipped with the unseen presence. The voices became more insistent, *"Practice being centered."* "OK. OK," I told them, whoever "they" were. I took a deep breath and watched the terrible scene on the screen from a higher perspective. *"In the greater scheme of eternity, death really isn't so sad, is it?"* This thought popped into my mind quite unexpectedly. "No," I thought, "death really isn't a tragedy or a horrible disaster to the soul, but rather only a transition or a graduation of sorts—a means of moving onward into a new existence." I was amazed at how quickly and easily I could rise above the drama and see the scene with compassion and wisdom. I never did figure out which angels were talking to me. As the night wore on, the relentless lessons became stranger and more intense.

Dear Journal - Would you believe I had more emotional release tonight? I thought this was going to be just another typical weekend. John and I were listening to a tape after the movie. Then, something he said or did—I don't even know what—triggered the anger that the last massage stirred up. I felt blinding hatred "against those who hurt me," whatever that meant.

I excused myself and tried to figure out what was going on, but my mind wasn't the right tool for such an exercise. So, I chose instead to stand in front of the bathroom mirror and let my body act out the emotions that were surfacing. I made fists and began to punch in the air. "Get away" I tried to cry, as a silent scream escaped my tight jaws. My stomach knotted up, my arms flew together protectively in front of my chest, and I gasped for breath. Something told me I was experiencing the past life I had seen before—the one in which townspeople were dragging me away for some crime. The vision this time was powerful, poignant, and painful.

In my mind's eye, I saw myself being beaten. The men who had dragged me to the front of the village square were slapping me with a vengeance. I felt intense pain. I didn't even understand the so-called crime. They treated me as if I were an animal that they hated. I knew I couldn't let them see my pain because this fed their viciousness. I saw myself bring my arms inward in front of my chest and I steeled myself for the next blow. My jaw clenched and my face twisted in pain. My shoulder blades tensed and my body went through a physical spasm as the next wave of violence was aimed at me. I could barely continue to watch the vision. I wanted so badly to divert myself.

My awareness returned to the present and I stood there, shaken by the scenes I had witnessed. The body postures and the frozen muscle structures all paralleled the ones I carry in this life. The "what-have-I-done-to-deserve this, I-don't-understand" feeling is all too familiar. I didn't know what to think. What could I possibly learn from such horror? Perhaps this is why I am so terribly revolted by violence, bullies, and prejudice. Maybe this is the reason I wanted to lash out and hurt those who hurt others. I empathize now with a rage stored deep inside the human psyche. We've all felt the effects of fear and hatred. We've all longed to cry out in pain. How could we hurt each other so terribly?

At long last, I understand that even darkness breeds light. I saw this brutal vision, so I could understand forgiveness. I experienced the pain of the human condition, so I would not be arrogant. I reviewed this other lifetime so I could be compassionate in this life. I long for a day when there is no more prejudice, no more hatred, and no more hurting each other.

I shift my awareness back into the vision once again and I watch from a different perspective. The aggressors seem ignorant now. They don't even know what they're doing. They've strayed so far from their soul's purpose that they are like the walking dead. "Wake up," my soul cries. "See what you do—see the damage you inflict! WAKE UP." I call to those who forget who they are and what they are made of. I release the hatred. They do not know what they are doing.

I saw them as outside of me, yet we're all made of the same stuff—the dark and the light, physically and metaphorically, the beast and the beauty. All wrapped up in one package—all the same. We're all made of subatomic particles that have been in the universe from time immemorial. The atoms that flow through me may have belonged to a star system, algae, the ocean, a tree, or many other humans throughout time. We are fluid, living in a constantly changing field. The atoms that live in Ann now may have lived in her past life aggressors at one time. The knowledge is there.

"What lesson am I supposed to learn from this?" I asked my angel.

Ariel: To live with gentleness and compassion, to see what violence does to the human heart, and to learn forgiveness for those who continue to sleep in this dream called life.

Ann: Must I go through more pain to learn this lesson?

Ariel: That depends how much you learn each time. You've learned how to be human at the lowest of the low points, and now you can release and thereby transform that suffering. Each individual's shift in perception helps to release all human suffering and pain and thereby helps raise the masses out of the ignorance of their hypnosis. Do not hang on to hatred, for hatred bears no gift. Let go of that fearful emotion. See what hatred does? Hatred abuses and victimizes.

See what the illusions of separation can do. See with absolute unconditional love and clarity how the hearts of those men forgot. See them crying out in pain for forgiveness. They now are the oppressed, and you are free. Forgive, forgive, but do not forget or you will be forced to repeat the lesson. Love all with great compassion. Some will stay in their illusions and others will move on to see truth. Those on the spiritual journey must pack lightly and leave much of their baggage behind. You can no longer carry the pain of the centuries. Pain no longer serves you. Let the pain go.

— § —

Ann: Words pour into my head now. Scenes flash past my eyes...

I cry out in anguish, as the strangers break my human heart. To them, I am not even human. I am a beast—a sad projection of their anger, their hatred, and their violence. They lash out in hate at the portions of themselves they cannot stand to see.

I am part of them.

By what they do, they chain themselves to my wounded soul. Their guilt, their underlying terror at the hideousness of their fear causes them to bury their pain with anger.

Hurt, violence, hatred...
These qualities have no place in the light.
Like a wisp of smoke, they dissolve.
Like a dirty snow mound melting in the spring rain, they wash away.

Cleanse my soul. Bring me home to the place where the victim and the victimizer melt together in one loving presence in the light. We're all the same. The vine that chokes itself off dies. As we release our tenacious hold on our lives, we allow nature now to take her course. We are fluid, moving, always moving, always changing. To freeze ourselves in time is to fight the very nature of the universe. The universe will win

I melt into the rivers of life and let them wash my soul clean.

—— § ——

The next morning I felt strangely calm. The day was busy as usual, and although it was Sunday, I was scheduled to work the morning shift. I ran back and forth between my desk and the test lab, as always, making sure things were in order for the upcoming delivery. At my desk, something—a force, a knowing, a pressure that I couldn't feel—caused me to stare at my desk calendar. Then I heard the voices again, loud and clear, as if someone else spoke to me. *"Turn in your resignation tomorrow."* What? Instinctively I looked around although I knew there was no one else in the office. "Tomorrow?" I asked incredulously. I stared blankly at the calendar. *"Turn in your resignation tomorrow,"* the voices reiterated. This couldn't be right, I thought to myself. The project I was responsible for coordinating wouldn't be complete for another six months. I couldn't leave now. Everyone would hate me. I stared at the calendar again and argued with myself.

I could hardly believe this. For months, I had been asking to know the right time to leave engineering and to move on with my life. For months, I had been intending that the transition be easy and clearly marked. Now, here I was, hearing voices outside my head that were impossible to ignore. "I am going insane," I thought, but in the same split-second, I knew better. No, I wasn't insane; I was actually receiving the signs I had requested. I looked at the calendar and counted the weeks to the upcoming conference—the dates that would mark almost exactly one year since I had taken the Reiki training. If I gave my boss six week's notice before my resignation, I would have time to train people in my department who would take over my job, time to attend the conference that had changed my life only last year, and time to take some additional training in energy-work that I had wanted to sign up for but hadn't because the classes required too much time. I could enjoy Christmas this year. I would have time to enjoy the autumn season, time to hike, time to get my house in order, and time to start writing. I could eat meals at home and sleep in late on the weekends. "But everyone is going to hate me if I leave now," I heard the voice of my own doubt becoming weaker. The unseen force began to lift these concerns away from my heavy heart, and the path in front of me became increasingly clear. I finished my work as quickly as I could and, shaking all the way, drove home to tell John that I was ready to leave engineering.

We sat together at the computer and looked at our finances. My stomach did flip-flops when I totaled up my savings and found that I had stashed one hundred dollars more than the amount I had once said that I would need in my bank account before I quit. I was in shock. I reviewed the budget one last time to confirm that we could really continue to enjoy a decent quality of life after I left my job. I sat in silence and examined my intentions and my commitment to succeed in my new ventures. Still frightened, but ready to take the leap into an unknown future, I stayed up half the night writing my letter of resignation, shaking, and crying with relief now that the moment had finally arrived. "Who will understand the suddenness of this decision?" I wondered. I couldn't tell them about the voices. They would think I had gone crazy.

Oh my God, journal, I did it. I turned in my notice. I woke up with my stomach churning. I wasn't sure if I could go through with the resignation. What would people think? Would they be angry with me for abandoning them in the middle of the project? As if an unseen presence was helping me keep my resolve, I ran into my boss in front of the building as I was walking into work. "How did things go this weekend?" he asked. Before I had time to think, I blurted out my intention to leave and followed him to his office without even stopping by my desk. I was a nervous wreck. I shook from fear, so badly that I could feel my teeth clattering. I could read the lines on his face. "What a terrible way to begin a Monday morning," he was thinking. I knew the pressures I was creating for him. I knew he was already swamped beyond relief and that my leaving was going to make his job even more difficult. I felt terrible and responsible for that, but on the other hand, the time had finally come for me to live my own life instead of working to satisfy everyone else's needs. My boss understood. I felt unworthy of his kind response to my news, and I was deeply grateful for his empathy. He even joked with me, trying to cheer me up, or more likely to get me to stop crying.

Next, I went to tell the woman-friend who's become a sister to me. That was even more difficult. I was in morbid fear that she would think I was leaving to escape the pressures of the program; I had promised not to do that. I walked into her office and burst into tears again. Over piles of Kleenex I told her I was leaving and handed her a letter I wrote last night when I was calmer. I'm going to miss her so much. I'm going to miss everyone. I don't remember ever being so scared.

I walked around in shock, as the grapevine buzzed with the news that Ann Albers was leaving Honeywell. As if I was walking in a dream, I explained to one person after the next that I wasn't upset, that this really wasn't a sudden decision, that I wasn't leaving to escape anything but rather to pursue my crazy dreams of being a writer, a healer, and a teacher.

As I shared my truth with my managers and coworkers, I saw a side of them I had never seen before. Instead of seeing me as a driven career woman, they saw and acknowledged me as a human being. Some of them saw the real "me" for the first time—a woman with hopes, fears, and dreams just like theirs. They opened up to me and shared their dreams with me as well. I saw some people today whom I've known for years, for the very first time. When you're open and honest, when you're vulnerable, you finally allow yourself to receive the simply unbounded love of all those around you. You hear their stories and you connect with their hearts. I saw that I had been working all along in the company of angels.

A Boeing friend from Seattle arrived early for a meeting tonight. He joked that we could be friends now instead of vendor/customer, and his unconditional acceptance of my decision was a huge blessing. Oh God, this was all so difficult. Nonetheless, I was shown such incredible love and support all day long that I feel like am the luckiest woman in the world. I am surrounded

by such wonderful human beings. Why couldn't
I see this before?

My heart bursts.

I have been filled with so much love today,

it overflows.

I became human–vulnerable, scared,

and people opened up to me as never before,

telling me their hopes, their dreams, their stories.

We connected at levels I've never even known.

Difficult? Of course.

A window, an opening,

a portal into another way of being.

I face the fork in the road and choose my path,

never looking back, never regretting my decision.

It's only a choice.

All roads lead to heaven!

One must only pick the path that pleases the heart.

Dear angels, I am going to need your help and
support in the upcoming weeks.

Their response came easily. *My child, my little
one, of course we are always with you. We are*

very proud of you. You have come a long way. You have completed this round, this plane of the spiral, and it is time to wind your way up again! Rejoice, we are singing for your freedom.

Feel the love, feel all the emotions. Feel your human heart beat warm and vigorously through the crusty surface of the fears that have entrapped the light over the years.

Know that we are always with you. Never, ever, ever forget that.

I never knew, until my last month at work, how deeply connected I had become with the people around me. For a woman who had long considered herself unlovable, the outpouring of genuine warmth and good wishes for my future was almost too much to bear. One night the entire crowd of Boeing engineers who had worked with me on the program took me out to dinner. As I looked at the smiling, laughing faces on these men with whom I had shared a common goal, I thought my heart would burst again. Now that I was leaving, we dropped the professional masks and shared our thoughts and feelings about the program, my new ventures, and above all, about life.

Dear Journal - I really am the luckiest woman in the world. I am overwhelmed. Driving home from the dinner tonight, I listened to some exquisite music, with the car windows open wide and the starlight playing a visual symphony in the sky.

How did I get this lucky?

Life is rich.

Great pearls of wisdom are given freely to me

by people whose hearts open wide.

They open themselves to my heart.

They share with me.

Who am I to deserve such richness, I ask?

How did I get so lucky?

When they smile, my heart leaps in my chest.

I jump for joy.

For all the kings' riches in the world

are but a pittance

compared to this feeling inside.

I am rich. I am whole. I am loved.

Who could ask for any more?

Ann: Hey, Ariel, do you hear me?

Ariel: Of course I do Ann. I am ever near, beside you. Communication is so easy when you're in this state—so joyful, so freeing. I wait for these moments when our consciousness merges. I live through your eyes and know the incredible joy of being human. My being explodes in a million sparkles of delight now that you know so

much love. You have done well. We
congratulate you.

Celebrate with us. Step into a world much
larger than you've known, much larger than
you can dream even now. Step with us into
the dimension where your thoughts create
reality and your heart's desires become your
truth. Be with us, watch with us as the earth
unfolds its mystery.

Cry unto us and know the echo in your own
soul. Wait when it's time to be patient. Move
when it's time to rejoice. Come, call us and
we will be there. We live in your heart. Your
energy is expanding, making room for more.

Never, ever, stop believing in yourself. Never
stop believing in others. All relationships can
have the joy and satisfaction that you see
tonight. Rejoice, rejoice, rejoice. Life is just
beginning for you dear friend. You've opened
your eyes to see a universe filled with wonder.

— § —

My angel's words proved to be true. I went to work
each day filled with a sense of wonder and the joy of my
newfound connections. I didn't remember ever feeling
so happy while working so hard, but then again I had
never felt so free.

The synchronicities of my life continued to amaze
me. The friend who had been doing hypnosis with me
called to say that she had seen a vision that showed me
in a past life being severely abused, as if "someone were
striking me," she said. Her vision coincided one

hundred percent with the "past life" vision that I witnessed the day before the voices suggested I quit. I was amazed, but not surprised.

After work, at night, I was no longer tired. I sat outside by my pool area, looked up at the stars, and wondered about the nature of my existence. I wondered about this "other life" concept. I wondered, as I stared at the moon, whether or not I had stared up at this same sky in other times and other places...

Mother moon watches

from the diamond-studded jet-black skies.

I look up at her and peer with wonder,

through younger human eyes.

She's seen me here, on this planet

so many times before.

I've gazed at her with loving wonder

in centuries and places that exist no more.

Watch me from the sky, my friend.

Hold me in your heart.

Be there always by my side.

You know we'll never part.

Cycles turn, unending,

relentless like the tide.

Our lives are short. Our souls are long.

I've lived, I've loved, I've died,

but I go on and mother moon—

she watches in the sky.

Each time round she greets me,

mirrors the same soul

as it looks at her through different eyes.

One emotion-packed day was followed by the next. I was at work when I heard that the first Boeing 777 airplane purchased by United Airlines was going to land at Deer Valley Airport—a small commuter airport across the street from the building where I worked. I hopped in my car and drove over, just in time to see the huge airplane land on the small runway. The pilots allowed us to walk onboard, sit in the cockpit, and wander around the test equipment in the hull. I stood in line in front of a United Airlines pilot who said he was going to fly this plane someday. His excitement was contagious. I thought of all the people working at Honeywell and Boeing and all over the world. I thought of the lives affected, the dreams and hopes that were being played out as what began with a single thought took form and transformed into a miracle of modern technology. The plane had taken on mythic proportions for me. The 777 represented the power of what human thought could create, the power of what could happen when people communicate and cooperate with one another. I had poured my energy, heart, and soul into this for two years, and now I felt immense pride in the accomplishment. This airplane was the physical representation of the work of thousands of individuals all over the globe. We did this, I thought. We have much to be proud of.

> *The silver and blue bird soars.*
>
> *My heart leaps with every beat.*
>
> *The engines roar.*

> *The wings long and wide*
>
> *remind me I can fly.*
>
> *My life, my hope, my energy—*
>
> *directed to this dream.*
>
> *A tear falls down my cheek.*
>
> *I cry, and laugh for sheer delight.*
>
> *This plane, my love, my life has taken flight.*

> *Who says dreams must fade*
>
> *into the depths of night?*

— § —

Dear Journal - For fourteen more days I will be an engineer. I will pour the same power and passion into my job that I have over the last two years. Then, in the blink of an eye, life will all be different, yet the same. I get to take "me" with me. The voices whisper in my head and I hear them clearly. *"Be calm like the center of the storm while the winds rage around you."* Yes, be calm; be centered, I tell myself. *"Bring with you the*

*love in your heart, the joy in your head, the ability
to think, and the ability to act. Bring with you the
ability to be joyful with even the most difficult of
human beings, and the willingness to look for a
lesson around every corner. Do not leave these
things behind, for they were with you before you
started and they will be with you now."*

That was interesting. I was just typing and
the voices in my head took over. I let them
speak and they blend with my own voice. They
inspire me, goad me onward, and call me to be
bigger than I know I am. Tonight they are
impatient to speak to me so I'll continue.

*"Ann, Ann, Ann, do not forget who you are. We
are part of you. We are one Spirit. There is only
One. We rejoice in our ability to talk through you."*
"Who are you?" I ask. *"We're your guides, your
friends, the ones who have been assigned to you."*
"By whom," I question, smiling inside because I
feel unusual to be having this conversation while
reporting at the same time. *"Whatever you
choose to call Spirit, of course,"* they answer. I
feel a presence to my left side as if there is a
hand on my heart pouring love into me. I feel
supported and reassured.

I have come to love and cherish these joyful
beings. I no longer question whether or not they
are real. What is real anyway? Subatomic
particles whirl, spin faster than the speed of life
round one another. Enough of them spinning in
unison and you have an atom. Enough atoms
dancing in synchronization and you have a
molecule. Enough molecules and you have a
cell, then soon a body. We are all important
participants in one creation.

It's so difficult to tell people why I'm leaving. So emotional. So much feeling. I've been numb for so long, and now I have thawed. I am so lucky to be surrounded by people with such love.

— § —

The days of my last month in engineering seemed to fly by faster than I could flip the pages on my desk calendar. Each new day brought torrents of intense emotion pouring into my life experience. As I cleaned out my desk on the weekends, I discovered the difficulty in disposing of the things that had defined my identity for years—the old mail messages, the papers I had written, and the meeting minutes I had taken. I threw away reminders to myself. I filed notes of recommendation and praise to bring home with me, and I organized my educational certificates. I re-distributed materials into piles for the five people who would be taking over my tasks, and little by little, my office returned to its virgin state. I stacked my personal items in a box, took them home, and returned the next day to a barren desk.

As I emptied out my office, I found myself throwing out a sense of self-importance that I had filed in my psyche for years. As others transitioned to take over my jobs, I dealt with the feelings that accompanied what I already knew—no one is irreplaceable. Little by little, I gave away the authority I once carried in my job. I delegated the responsibilities and the burdens I had once shouldered. I began to feel invisible. People visited my office to say their good-byes at all hours of the day, "just in case they didn't have time later." I reminded them jokingly that I wasn't dying, or even moving far away, and yet I felt as if I did have some terminal disease and people were paying me their last respects.

My last Friday at work was a typical Friday aside from the fact that others attended my meetings, and I managed to delegate the remainder of my responsibilities. The fact that I was leaving engineering next Tuesday was beginning to feel real and by five o'clock, I was emotionally overloaded. At this unusually early hour, my coworkers and I left the office to attend a happy hour in my honor.

The small restaurant at Deer Valley airport was filled with its regular crowd of local airplane enthusiasts. About ten of us gathered around a few tables. Some of us watched the planes takeoff and land while others began to wash their concerns away with a few beers. Even though it was happy hour, I didn't really feel like drinking. "Odd," the thought crossed my mind. Perhaps, I was just tired from putting in such long hours, or more likely from the emotional highs and lows that beset me during the week. Big changes make for big stomach churning. I settled for a few colas and a plate of nachos.

As we joked and laughed, my stormy emotions gave way to calm. Perhaps they seeped into the atmosphere where bulky storm clouds were gathering to the east. Our windows were facing west so we didn't notice that we were in for one of those hell-raising, late-summer Arizona sky-breakers until the winds began to bend the few trees that bordered the runway. A friend and I went outdoors, admiring the approaching blackness that obliterated the evening sky and the jagged streaks of lightning that were beginning to slice across the heavens. The storm clouds were closing in on us as we watched. They were dark and threatening, swirling over the Phoenix skyline to the east and blotting out the last traces of sunlight. I loved storms. The energy they carried was palpable. We agreed to meet at my house for a movie and ran against the wind that was now driving dust into our eyes. I found and unlocked my car just as another gust of wind sandblasted the side panel.

I had been on the freeway a hundred times before in such storms. It's fast moving, exciting, and sometimes a challenge, but never, ever in my life had I felt the fear that was beginning to creep into my mind. I felt as if I had lived this exact moment before, like this was some déjà vu nightmare that I barely remembered. "Hmm," I tried to shake the uneasiness, chalking my queasy feeling up to a long day. "There have been many long days before storms," I reminded myself. "This is so unlike me." I was glad for the fact that I had skipped the wine cooler tonight. Something required my full attention.

The wind was ferocious now, and the clouds were scudding low above the ground. Normally I would have had my windows open to feel the wind on my face, and the radio would have been blasting a symphony to match nature's fury. Not tonight. This storm felt sinister, threatening in some vaguely familiar way and my radio was quiet.

The rain began to pour in torrents. "So what," I thought. I tried to talk myself out of the feeling. "I've been out in these storms every summer for eight years. I love rain. What desert-dweller doesn't?" Something was coming over me. A hazy memory from long ago, or perhaps some warning from a possible future edged its way into my normally calm mind. *"Stay alert!"* The command from within was urgent, insistent. I tensed up even more. "Maybe if I turn some music on," I thought, "I'll calm down." I flipped on the CD that was still in my car. Themes to Disney's "The Lion King" blasted as the rain pelted my little Dodge Daytona, and the wind pushed the car to and fro. This wasn't the typical stormy-night amusement ride.

I could no longer see, as the blinding rain coated my windshield faster than the wipers could clear it off. Red lights from passing semi-trucks swished by on my right, and waves of water from their wake washed over my car's hood and up the windshield as well. I was going forty miles an hour, with traffic, and I couldn't see a damn thing. This was the first storm in a few months and a sorry time to find out that my windshield wipers had finally dried to the point where they were useless. "Fool!" I thought angrily to myself, teeth clenched. I should have known to have them checked.

I was really scared now. This was no game. The storm, the traffic, and the danger were real. I couldn't stop on the freeway with a line of racing traffic on my tail. My exit was approaching in only a few miles, and I couldn't get over to the right because there were lines of trucks racing past. I could barely see where I was going, and the concrete barrier to my left was a blur. If I braked, the car behind me would slam into me, if the brakes worked at all. The concrete barrier in the middle of the freeway prevented me from moving left. If I tried to move right, I would have to dodge the fast moving semi trucks with no peripheral vision whatsoever and a rain-swept front windshield. The CD player boomed out a haunting melody, and for the first time ever, I prayed seriously for my life. Soon, I couldn't see at all. The evening turned instantly into the blackest night. Water sloshed over my windshield as the sheets of torrential rain continued to fall and waves splashed up the side of my car.

I found myself telling God that I wasn't ready to die. I had things to do, reasons to live, and contributions to make. I prayed to God, and begged my angels, guides, and dead grandfather to spare my life and get me off that freeway. I bargained, promising God that I would live my dreams to the fullest extent possible.

Be calm like the center of the storm when the winds rage around you. The voices I heard a few days before echoed in my head. I surrendered to fate.

I don't remember changing three lanes. I don't even recall getting off the freeway. The next thing I consciously remember was my friend, who had followed me in her truck, getting out at a stoplight and wading through six inches of water to ask me if I was alright. Still hyper-alert, with my fingers clenched to the steering wheel, I heard myself tell her I was fine. I thanked God for her and the other women who were following me home. We sat in the warmth of my family room at long last and shivered. We never did watch the movie.

I wonder still if that night weren't one of my opportunities to die. I wonder if we're given checkpoints in our life, where through accident or illness we can leave, start over and reset the cosmic clock. I wasn't ready. Yes, one life was nearly over, but there was a new one waiting to be lived.

In an overly emotional last day in engineering, I left everything I had ever known about success behind and walked forward into the unknown. Driving home, I had the "The Lion King" CD playing in my car again. I heard the haunting melody that had been playing that haunting night as I prayed in the darkness and the rain. Curious, I flipped over the cover to see the song's title. The song, track 7, was called "...To Die For."

Chapter 9
Initiation and the Shaman's Call

Shafts of light filtered between the shades and the glass on the French doors in the bedroom. They cast a warm glow on the spot where John had been sleeping just moments ago before the alarm clock interrupted our dreams. Instinctively, I started to rise until I remembered that I wasn't going to work today. "Hard to believe I'm never going back," I mumbled. Like a dream, the thought drifted out of my mind. I stretched slowly, yawned, and then rolled over on the crumpled sheets to position myself under the warm rays. Through the small windowpanes on the doors I could see the sun rising in an orange fireball on the eastern horizon. "Mm." I shut my eyes and reveled in the dawn's radiance as the streams of light crawled across my face and bathed me in a golden glow. "Would every day be this wonderful?" I felt like I was on vacation. Today was the first day of my new life.

I hopped out of bed, eager to greet the new day. "This is perfect timing," I sung at the top of my lungs. The annual mind, body, spirit conference began today. One year ago, at this very conference, my life changed utterly and completely. I wondered what changes this year's seminars would bring. I read the conference brochure while eating a leisurely breakfast. Many of the presenters from the previous year were returning and there were also some interesting new seminars being offered. I looked forward to one on shamanism and healing, and wondered if I'd have the good fortune to meet the person leading the workshop. I had wanted to meet someone who could journey in the sacred dream ever since I read my first book on shamanism.

As I hopped in my car, dressed in shorts and a colorful t-shirt, I couldn't wipe the grin off my face. I drove past people in suits and ties that looked as rushed as I used to be as they fought traffic to get to their busy jobs. "Yesterday that was me!" I thought wickedly. "Let's see," I reveled in my new freedom, "I would be in meetings now in a dark conference room if I were still at work." Instead, there was nothing but blue skies ahead. I walked into the great conference hall at the familiar Scottsdale resort and felt yet another sense of déjà vu. Had I walked into a time warp? Only a year ago, I stood in this same spot—a woman not too happy with her life, unsure of her future and just barely daring to dream that someday she might leave the safety of her success in order to pursue her dreams of a better life. I stood here today triumphant—a woman still uncertain of her future who had finally found the courage to take a leap of faith and follow her dreams. I felt a great sense of pride glowing inside as I looked back over the last year and saw how much I had changed.

I wandered the still-empty hallways, and watched the presenters set up their booths. The Reiki booth where I was going to work with Jessica this year was still quiet and empty. A man in a colorful tie-dyed shirt was unloading drums and rattles into the booth next to ours. His soulful eyes caught my attention, and I wondered briefly if he had anything to do with the upcoming workshop on shamanism. I didn't think about that for long. Unaccustomed to having free time, I meandered through the grounds of the resort enjoying the incredible stillness that contrasted with my busy days during the past year. I strolled through the gift shop, sat by the pool for a while, walked around a natural pond on the grounds, and finally settled into the comfortable seat of an overstuffed couch in the hotel lobby. When I looked up from the book I was reading and checked my watch, I was surprised to find that an hour had flown by before I even noticed. I tucked my book into my purse and walked back to the conference hall to meet Jessica.

I found her in the Reiki booth. She had already distributed her fliers and business cards on the tables, decorated the area with fresh flowers, and spread the nearby chairs in a small semi-circle so people could stop by for free fifteen-minute treatments. One person had already taken her up on the offer, so I tiptoed quietly past the two of them, and smiled my greeting. Her return smile was like the warmth of the morning sunshine that kissed me with the dawn. So many feelings welled up inside of me all at once. Here was the woman who had laid a gentle hand on my arm last year to quell my fearful shaking after my own Reiki treatment. This was the woman who lived a life that had seemed so far beyond my grasp last year, and yet today we stood side by side as friends, working together. Another conference participant sat down in front of me, asking for a Reiki treatment and interrupting my thoughts. I put my hands on the woman's face and felt the strong rush of life force flowing through my arms.

Person after person sat in our chairs. After giving my fifth treatment I felt as if my legs were floating in the air and my hands were my anchors in this reality as I gently touched the person who sat in front of me. Meanwhile, the gentleman in the tie-dyed shirt and shorts had finished setting up his drum booth and was sitting behind his tables. During a lull in my work, I snuck away from our booth to take a peek at the percussion instruments and learned that he was leading the conference seminar on shamanism that had caught my attention earlier that morning. "Not too surprising," I thought. He fit the description of every shaman I had ever read about—unassuming, older, and wise looking, yet young and spry with piercing eyes that focused loosely. Sometimes his gaze seemed to be focused elsewhere, but I could tell he heard every word that I was saying. He never called himself a shaman. In his words, he was "just a guy doing seminars." His simple appearance seemed to be a humble mask for the wisdom and power of the raw energy he carried with his presence. I could feel the life force strongly around him and felt privileged to be in his company. I asked him to teach me to drum and in five minutes I was ecstatic to be pounding a simple rhythm on a tall African walking drum. I couldn't play for long. There were people lining up to sample Reiki at Jessica's booth.

As I stood with my hands on one person after the next I watched Jim and his drums. He and I were both wondering how the setup would work—us with our quiet Reiki treatments, and him with his loud instruments. We needn't have worried. While I worked on a woman dressed in a beautiful green silk pantsuit, Jim began to play a slow and steady drumbeat. He watched us carefully out of the corner of his eye. The drum seemed to speak to my soul and resonate with my heart. I felt the percussive energy as physically as if a wave of water had washed over me and in my mind's eye I saw that my own energy field was dancing and pulsating to the drum's rhythm. I smiled again; the arrangement of our booths was perfect.

Later, long after the conference participants had retired to their meals, the poolside, or the comfort of their own rooms, I sat talking with the other Reiki people who were working at our booth. "Ask Jim to work on you with that didgeridoo," Jessica joked with me, "He'll blow your chakras out." I laughed at the energy-worker humor. Chakras, in the Hindu belief systems are energetic wheels located at various points in the human energy field. We engineers would call them transformers—mechanisms that stepped down energy from the surrounding environment so an appropriate amount can be taken into and metabolized by our physical system. To those who can see them, they look like colorful spinning vortices. I looked over at Jim's booth where a huge didgeridoo leaned against the wall in one corner. The didgeridoo is an Australian instrument, traditionally made of a long round tree branch that had been hollowed out by termites. By blowing hard in a certain manner at one end, a deep bass sound can be achieved and sustained for a very long time. I had been told that the instrument was a real trick to play.

I walked over to Jim and innocently asked him if he would be willing to trade a shamanic healing for a Reiki treatment. He squinted at me as if his look was measuring up the sincerity of my intention. "OK, sit here," he finally told me. He moved a stool out into the center of the empty conference hall. "I have this tension here, mostly on my left side," I told him, referring to the energetic blockage that I still felt, even after giving so many Reiki treatments. "Just shut your eyes and breathe," he replied calmly and seriously. I did as I was asked. I shut my eyes and began to take long, slow breaths. I didn't know what to expect, but I was incredibly excited. I had read so many accounts of shamans and their ways. I never believed I would actually get the chance to meet one let alone experience the healing power for myself. I breathed deeply once again and as Jim began to play the didgeridoo, I found that all my thoughts were quickly erased.

I heard the sound coming from the instrument as if the rhythm were being played directly into my mind. The music was loud, and as Jim circled me playing faster and faster, the sound took on a live quality. I felt

I was being stalked, circled by a large growling beast, and then the sound began to tug on my energy field. The sensations were beyond description. The beast growled, and where I should have felt terror, I felt only love and trust for this beautiful soul that was journeying with me on what I realized was some dark quest. Then I felt the claws, unseen hands ripping through a thick tar-like substance in my energy field about six inches away from my body on the left side of my back. The hands I couldn't see pulled and raked through my energy field, as the sound of the didgeridoo beast vibrated physically all around me. The sound was coming from all directions now, pulsating inwards toward my center. The claws pulled and pulled at the thick tar energy; and as I felt layers ripping off of me, not physically but in an altered unseen dimension where the invisible was tangible, I felt my physical spine spasm and jerk. Some vestige of rational thought caused me to wonder if I would fall off the stool, but instead I was glued to the chair feeling suspended in thin air, limp as a rag doll and being moved about by an unseen force. Later, I was told by those who watched that I was swaying in large circles and jerking about in the chair as if an electric current was being sent up and down my spine.

Again, I felt the smallest hint of fear, but I was soon bathed by another wave of powerful and yet loving energy. Something told me, "Trust, It's OK. You won't be harmed." To be so out of control of my own body and still not be afraid was the strangest part of the whole experience. Suddenly, the invisible beast stopped growling and I heard a whooshing sound like the wind. I heard a pair of wings fluttering away up and to the right into the ceiling, and then the playing stopped. I took a moment to rest as I realized I had been in a deeply altered state. I opened my eyes gingerly and looked at Jim. He was staring at me intently. "Wow," I said. What else could I say? There were no words. Jim was still breathing hard from the vigorous circular breathing. He slowly put away the instrument and the stool then stood and stared at me or, I should say, into me. I couldn't explain everything I was feeling. I felt a huge sense of relief, as if some burden had been lifted off my shoulders. I felt fragile, wide open, and very vulnerable. I was near tears with gratitude and I didn't even know why.

I looked at Jim again, feeling as if he had just been my guide and protector on a journey through some inner hell and back. I felt an unconditional love that had been present during the entire experience. My "Thank You" seemed inadequate. I left the great hall for the night and lay on a chair by the pool, under a waving, towering palm tree. A new age composer was also outside playing some of the tracks from his latest CD. I watched the stars overhead in the black sky and felt the tears of relief that Jim's treatment had unleashed begin to fall from my eyes as my chest rose and fell with easy breathing for the first time in years. "You can rest now," my thoughts seemed to be telling me. I took a deep breath and my body shook as if the remnants of my old life were leaving with each exhale. "Your old life really is over. Gone. Done. No turning back." I left the poolside and drove the hour across town, feeling as if I had been ripped wide open and sewn back together. My old life, and my whole way of being, was really gone. This wasn't just a vacation. I was never going back.

I attended Jim's seminar on "Shamanic Journeying" the next day. In a conference room that was lit by a large crystal chandelier, fifty people seated themselves in a large circle on the floor. A single green plate in the center of the room held a white candle that burnt slowly, releasing smoke that undulated in a rhythmic dance. I breathed deeply the smell of the copal incense that was burning in a small stone bowl next to the candle, and glanced around the room. A huge cowhide drum sat next to the candle, along with two large quartz crystals placed on a small mat. Jim arrived and seated himself directly opposite me. "He looks the part today," I thought, noting that his graying hair was neatly tied back in a pony tail and his face had the animated quality I had seen in people who carried a great deal of energy. The circle continued to widen as more people filed into the room. Jim explained the basic or "core" principles of shamanism. "A shaman," he said, "is one who can enter non-ordinary states of reality to bring back information or healing." "What a great, concise definition," I thought. My engineering training welcomed clear, concise definitions. I was less equipped to deal with the non-verbal, non-logical ways of knowing.

Jim continued by describing the core cosmology of the shaman's world—the Lower World where the animal spirits resided, the Middle World that represented our ordinary waking reality, and the Upper World where the more human-like spirits could be found. These were broad classifications, not entirely accurate in any one culture, and yet accurate enough across cultures that we could discuss them in relation to core shamanism. Today, Jim told us, we would be journeying in the dream to the Lower World where our intention would be to meet our power animal. The power animal, in the shaman's world, is a spirit ally—a non-physical helper and guide.

We passed a large abalone shell and a smoking wand of dried sage around the circle while Jim explained to us the importance of intent and trust. Before journeying, we were to intend to meet our animals, and then we were simply to follow the procedures, while trusting that the meeting would occur. The sage wand reached me and as I fanned the smoke over myself, I noticed I was already in a somewhat hypnotic state. The copal, still burning in the center of the room filled my lungs, and I swayed gently as deep relaxation set in. To raise the energy before our journey, we drummed. "Nothing mystical about this," I thought. A marvelous cacophony of sound filled the conference room as drums and rattles of every type merged their voices. The room itself appeared to be vibrating. My head was still swimming with the smoke and the rhythms when I began to feel that now-familiar sensation of floating in mid-air. My hands were on fire with the energy, and they buzzed with a feeling of static electricity. I felt waves of energy running up through my spine as if I were a fireman's hose channeling huge amounts of water. Suddenly, the sound ceased and we resumed our seats in the circle as Jim prepared himself to "call Spirit."

I looked around at the faces in the circle. Some were eager to enter the dream; others were a bit anxious. I was ready to begin; in fact, I felt as if I already had entered the space where I sat in this world while peeking into another unseen dimension. My eyelids were heavy so I let them drop. Jim played a monotonous cadence on a huge drum and then demonstrated a different beat that would be used to call us back when the journey was over. Next, the ceremony began in earnest. Jim's voice cried out in a song that was only part human. He walked around the circle, waving the shaking, singing rattle over each person in turn. With my eyes closed, the rattling sounded as if it were coming from every corner of the room and the voice was not always in the same place as the rattle. When the rattle passed over my head, I felt a presence yanking on my energy field, pulling my energy up through my head and out... somewhere. The sensation was much like what I felt with the didgeridoo. My spine was twitching again, or so I thought. In no time, I had entered into a non-ordinary state of reality.

I lay on the floor as instructed, with my head pointing toward the center of the circle. The drumming started again. "Boom, boom, boom, boom," the drum sang a song that seemed to entrain with my heartbeat. My mind wouldn't be still at first, so I pacified myself trying to think of an entrance to the Lower World. "Could I really do this?" I finally envisioned a crack in the red rocks of northern Arizona and then let my mind wander as the dream took over and I was sucked through the tiny crack into the blackness of a deep, dark cavern.

Walking between two worlds, I found myself in one that seemed very real, and the other surreal. In the everyday world, I knew still I was laying on a conference room floor with many others while the sound of the huge drum reverberated through my body and a single white candle cast dim shadows on the walls. In this world, I was still aware of the intense energies running through me. Like water being forced through a hose not quite large enough to accommodate the flow, the powerful waves of energy caused my body to jerk back and forth as if I were being shocked repeatedly. Surprisingly, I felt no pain or fear.

The other world of my dream was one of mythic proportions—a world where shamans and dreamers had journeyed over the centuries to meet their ancient animal spirit guides. In this shadowy world of the dream, I traveled through darkness until I found myself in a wide cavern room. The walls were moist and lit by small white candles placed on ledges in the rock. A black jaguar appeared—huge, strong, and sleek with glowing yellow eyes. He told me he wasn't my power animal, but he was my guide. He felt familiar even thought I had never seen him before in my nightly dreams. We walked down a tunnel, first on a gently sloping path then down an even steeper path to the left. The tunnel opened up into a huge cavern room where I could see the path sloping below us, and at the end, there was a bright white light. A gray furry mouse joined us, and together the three of us hurried down the path.

I'm not sure exactly when the jaguar and the mouse disappeared, but they were nowhere to be seen as I walked through an oval-shaped opening that was the exit to the cavern. Through this doorway, I entered an open area that was bathed in blinding sunshine. I felt my physical eyes, back in the room, scrunching up to avoid the glare in the dream. Physically my body was still having spasms on the conference room floor. Briefly, my attention returned to ordinary reality where I thought to myself that I must have been quite a sight twitching about while laying there. Then I returned to the dream. In the middle of the white light stood the wolf that I had seen in my dreams over the last year. I felt her presence in my poems that came, seemingly out of nowhere. She stood in front of me, mythical in size, gentle, yet immensely powerful.

She greeted me with a soft look in her eyes, and I hugged her huge furry head. Like two friends joined in joyful reunion, there was no need for words, or even thoughts of words. I moved in the dream easily now, knowing what to do and where to walk without speaking. I wondered where the hawk was and he appeared circling overhead. A hummingbird appeared in front of me and flew in counterclockwise circles three times over the head of the wolf. Together, we journeyed across a grassy plain to a circular clearing where a lone, dead tree stood at the center. The tree's bark was white and smooth and only the huge branches remained where leaves had once flourished. I knew that the tree wasn't exactly dead but rather alive in a different sort of way. For a few moments, the wolf and I played in the area around the white trunk. She raised herself high on her back paws to tussle with me in the grasses and for a joyful moment we romped like two childhood friends.

Then we went "back to business," although I still don't know what this business was about. The wolf and I circled the tree three times, counterclockwise. As soon as we completed the last round of the spiral, the scene changed and I was a wolf among the pack, eating a kill. I felt my strong jaws rip at the fresh flesh of some unknown animal and felt the raw power of eating the energy of the beast that had just given itself for our meal. I felt earthy, wild, and very much alive. There was a strong sense of connecting with the primitive element inside my own being. The portion of me that remembered myself as Ann wondered at the fact that I wasn't finding the scene disgusting and wondered further if the twitching in my spine would ever stop. I noticed also that the left side of the base of my skull was experiencing a splitting pain, but I soon forgot all sensation as Ann as I returned my focus to the dream.

The scene changed again. Now I was the one being eaten. I was human, and I saw the wolves tearing large chunks of flesh from my abdomen. I don't recall having arms at this point. Far from being frightened, or even disgusted, I was honored to be feeding them as if this was a privilege to give my life to a greater power. I felt no pain. Before the ordeal was over, I (the dreaming self, the one who was being eaten) fell asleep. Next thing I knew, I was floating headfirst, face-up down a sloping dark tunnel toward the light. Within seconds, I emerged from the tunnel and discovered I was a wolf puppy, newly born, lying in a litter with two other pups. I licked my young wet fur, and back in the room as Ann,

I was startled to feel prickling energetic sensations dancing along my arms. I saw the face of the mother wolf once again, an archetypal countenance filled with feminine power and love. Then, the dream began to fade away, and I heard the drum once again. The twitching in my back relaxed, and I (Ann) faded into a deeply relaxed state of consciousness where I saw the face of the wolf again, floating against a black void. For the next few minutes there was only blackness. Then I saw the wolf again—still gentle, still powerful, still watching...

"Boom, boom, boom, boom. Boom, boom, boom, boom." The drum cadence changed to the callback beat, and I groggily pulled myself off the floor and looked around the room in wonder. I had forgotten where I was. The death/rebirth theme of my dream was startlingly familiar. Death and rebirth were themes in my life as of late. I wondered what the dream meant and what I was supposed to learn from my journey. "*Appreciate all cycles of life*," I heard. I had been allowed to experience life as both the predator and the prey, and so I could appreciate the great dance of the energies in the natural world. I was directed to understand that there is only one God-energy, one Spirit; that the divisions are illusion; that there is no real "good vs. evil," but only different sides of the same coin. I felt very, very good but still a bit fuzzy headed as the words and teachings coursed through my mind. I took a few deep breaths and looked at the faces around me.

I sat quietly while the others shared their stories. Something deep inside of me had been touched or triggered—a memory perhaps? I had the sensation once again that I had done this work with the energy in the dream at some time, but when? Where? I yearned to learn more about shamanism. When I asked Jim what it meant to eat, be eaten, and then be reborn, he just looked at me with his piercing gaze, chuckled, and said ever so quietly, "that is shamanic initiation." He refused to say more. Instead, he referred me to a foundation that taught core shamanic practices. I gave up the notion of attending these seminars when I saw they were only offered in other cities. Secretly I wished for just an instant that I still had the money to travel at will. As I was telling Jessica of my dilemma, she said simply, "If an opportunity presents itself, don't be afraid to spend some of your savings." I wondered what she knew that I did not. I forgot about the incident, but not my craving to work within the sacred space of the dream.

— § —

After the conference, I adjusted slowly to my new lifestyle. At first I felt like a fish out of water. I was a woman with no identity. For the last eight years of my life I had introduced myself by saying, "Hi, I'm Ann, an engineer." Now I caught myself saying, "Hi, I'm Ann. I was an engineer for eight years, until I left recently to pursue my dreams." People were fascinated. Some wondered why I would leave such a lucrative career. Others gave me credit for having far more courage than I felt.

I was learning a new way of being. Some days I wandered through the shopping malls, testing myself to see if I really would be OK without the money. Strangely, I felt richer than ever before. I learned to listen to the needs of my mind, body, and spirit, and to honor them above all else. I started to open myself up to receive the abundance that was all around me. The garden grew, and my house began to look like a home once again. I slept for twelve hours a day, regaining the strength I had given away while working so hard for so long. My life flowed easily and quickly through days with no schedules. I worked joyfully to prepare my home, my office, and my attitude to begin writing. Things fell into place.

My mom called one day, inviting me to visit her and my dad in their home near Washington, D.C. They had frequent flier miles that I could use, and said they would love to see me now that I had some time. I had forgotten all about the seminars on shamanism as I prepared for my trip, but again the voices spoke to me. *"Check your brochure."* I dug through my files and found the flier Jim had given me, describing the workshops on shamanism. "October 15-16, Washington D.C." I got dizzy as a whirl of energy overtook me, and I sat on the floor with the flier still in my hand. My heart beat erratically in my chest, and once again I had the sensation that events were transpiring on a grander scale than I was consciously aware. The only seminar offered in the D.C. area during the entire autumn season was offered during the week that I would be visiting my parents. I accepted Mom's invitation and registered for the class.

Dear Journal - I'm in my parent's home in Virginia. Is this really me? Somewhere on a rainy freeway in a parallel universe about six weeks ago, Ann died. In this universe however, she lives joyfully, exuberantly, and with vigor.

Being at my childhood home is like walking into a dream or like the experience near-death survivors describe when their life flashes before their eyes in review. Memories flood me at a level outside of my conscious awareness. Emotional imprints are everywhere. I touch my brother's love-worn Winnie the Pooh bear, my little bunny bank, the old green desk lamp buzzing still by my old window in my old room, and for once I am swept into happy visions of my past. I feel as if I am a different person now looking in on someone else's childhood dream. In a way, I guess I am.

— § —

The alarm rang and I woke up in my brother's old room, staring down a street where the trees I had once hopped over were now fully grown, and neighbor's houses that once seemed immense were now just regular-sized homes. Even the eight-foot ceilings seemed small now that I was used to the wide-open cathedral-ceiling architecture of the southwest. I walked into the bathroom where I had spent most of my teenage years looking uneasily into the mirror, trying to figure out who I was and who I was becoming. Fifteen years later I stood here, doing the same. Only this time the woman staring in the mirror knew who she was and who she was becoming. I watched my face and wondered at the difference a month had made. Lines of stress that I had thought permanently etched in my countenance were beginning to smooth and the steely-confident glare of my professional eyes was relaxing into the vulnerable look of a woman who had stepped outside of her comfort zone.

I snapped out of my reverie and dressed quickly in the warm clothing I brought for the trip. Gathering up a blanket, notebook, pen, and a large rock I had carried from Phoenix, I rushed to hop into Dad's car. He was going to drive me halfway to the seminar. The seminar leader had graciously agreed to meet me and drive me the rest of the way. Life couldn't have been flowing any more smoothly.

At the interim stop, I could barely contain my excitement. Only a month ago, I thought my desire to learn more about shamanism was a foolish daydream— just another desire to add to my "sometime-this-lifetime" list of things I wanted to do. Now the daydream was coming true. A weekend workshop, or even years of study, wouldn't make me a shaman. Nonetheless, the work triggered memories for which I had no logical explanation. The energy in the dream was familiar, as if I had visited the territory of these other dimensions at some other time. I thought about the many times I conversed with "imaginary" friends as a child. "Were they my spirit guides," I wondered, "dressed in a guise that a child growing up in middle class America would understand?" I wondered how much of a child's imaginary world was fictitious.

The workshop was held in an old barn that had been refurbished to host seminars. The farm country surrounding the barn was beautiful. A huge grassy pasture led down to a forest that was ablaze with autumn color. There was a chill in the air but the fireplace indoors offered a comforting warmth. We seated ourselves in a circle and then proceeded to begin the class. Some of the exercises were similar to the ones I did at the conference. We journeyed to the shaman's Lower World by entering the dream through an opening we envisioned in the earth, and then we met with our power animals. We learned to journey to the Upper World where we met our human and angelic guides and where I experienced the otherworldly bliss and unconditional love that I was beginning to associate with the constant presence of my spirit helpers.

Perhaps the most amazing exercise involved finding a partner we didn't know and asking a single question.

Bonnie, a bright and beautiful woman from Maryland decided to work with me. "What is my book's title?" I asked her with no further explanation. She asked me to learn more about alternate careers she might pursue. As the drumming started, each of us entered the dream, asking our animal helpers to answer the question our partner had asked. We came back into ordinary reality and compared notes. Bonnie told me that she had clearly heard the word "Whispers." "Then," she said, "I saw an eagle, and then that fish symbol that represents Christ in some religious groups. I'm not quite sure what all this means. The book was about communication, about listening to Spirit." "SPIRIT!" I practically shouted. "Whispers of the Spirit!" Bonnie's eyes widened as we stared at each other in disbelief. I practically tackled her with a huge hug, and we laughed gleefully like two young sisters. I shared with her the information I had gleaned from my own dreaming and found that my advice was as appropriate as hers had been.

Around the room, partners who had been total strangers only half an hour before were sharing answers to some of their lives' most important questions. Before this exercise I had believed in the possibility that shamanic journeying might bring me answers to some of my questions. Now I knew beyond a shadow of doubt the value of this tool I was being taught.

The night after the workshop I had a dream of archetypal proportions. I watched scenes from my past flitting before my eyes. In the dream, I spread my arms and flew away in the direction of a future I couldn't yet see.

—— § ——

The remainder of my week at home turned out to be a time of great healing. The experience was both a completion and a catharsis. For the first time, I walked into my parents' house as an adult woman who no longer blamed her fears and limitations on her upbringing and was no longer willing to live anyone else's idea of a good life other than her own. I accepted responsibility for my feelings and my actions now, and for the first time felt no need to apologize for or be defensive about my decisions. Best of all, after the episode on my hike in Kauai, I knew my own worth and didn't have the burning need that I had once possessed for others' approval. I opened my heart again to the two people I most desperately longed to love, and I saw them as if for the very first time.

Dad was a healthy man in his mid-fifties, with the same crew-cut hair he had worn most of his life. His piercing eyes lit up with deep compassion and love for just a moment when he greeted me at the airport and we talked animatedly about my life choices. The emotions I saw were quickly shrouded again in the mask of his professional countenance, but the spark I had seen there behind the mask showed me there was love where I once thought there was none. I cried that night, burying my head under my brother's old feather pillow so no one would hear me. I didn't want to explain all that I was feeling. Ripped wide open and emotionally vulnerable once again, I allowed the feelings I had stuffed inside for so many years to surface, and they were almost more than I could handle. "All those years and I didn't even see what was in front of me." I wept with relief knowing I no longer had to carry the burden of illusions that said I was unlovable. I cried tears of gratitude for being able to feel once again that I had a family where I belonged. The flash of emotion I saw in Dad's eyes haunted me. The tears were waters that ran from my icy core as they warmed in the light of love that had always been present.

Then there was my mom. Always vivacious and energetic, she was now a beautiful woman in her mid-fifties, branching out to try new things in life for the first time in years, reveling in the playful opportunities life offered and urging her daughter to do the same. Was this the same woman with whom I had spent twenty-two years of my life? I hardly knew her. I realized she felt the same about me.

Mom had also been through many changes over the recent years. A dance with death had given her a new lease on life. While I was fighting, metaphorically to reclaim my life, Mom was fighting physically. Thyroid cancer had claimed three long years, and we were lucky that the illness hadn't taken more. Surgery, radioactive iodine treatments, hormone replacements, depression, and weight gains had taken their toll. Mom was a fighter though, and her persistent attitude carried her through the hard times. My brother and I had barely realized the severity of her illness because she had been reluctant to share the facts with us over the phone. We knew now how difficult the cancer had been. We now understood her anger and her sadness over the past several years. I looked with newfound respect on this woman who had managed to face fears that most of us avoid throughout our entire lives.

I cried each night under my pillow, wishing I could visit myself as I was fifteen years ago and tell the uncertain child that her parents did love her dearly and would do anything to see her happy. I longed to tell her that life would be difficult but that everything would all work out wonderfully; that in another fifteen years, she would be sleeping in the same house, fulfilling dreams she hadn't even dreamt yet, and embarking on a new and exciting career. I wandered through the house into my old room when I was alone and I talked to her. I lay down on the bed where she had spent lonely night after night, and in my mind I held her hand and told her she was loved, so very, very much. I cried the tears that the years had robbed from her and as I healed the old wounds in my own heart, I felt her healing too.

In the non-ordinary reality of the shaman's dream, my guides showed me pictures of my parents as souls. In this dimension, I knew them as friends and equals—deeply loving, bright beautiful beings who had agreed to the trials and the hardships that they would undergo in order to grow and learn. In the dream, I was told that the hard times I experienced were acts of love on their part that helped to mold me and motivated me to grow into the woman I had become. I blinked back the tears that were so ready to fall these days as I returned from what looked like a quick nap in ordinary reality. After spending several days at the house, I was now seated near one of the departure gates in Washington National Airport with my mom, waiting to embark on the next leg of our journey. I wondered if anyone knew where I went when I closed my eyes.

The flight attendant announced that our airplane was finally ready to board. Mom and I were traveling to a beautiful spa in the northeast where the trees would be as colorful as a king's ransom in gems, and the moonlit nights were advertised to be crisp and invigorating. We went together to forge a new friendship, to end our relationship as mother and child, and to learn how to be together as adults—two strong women who had each recently witnessed death of an old identity and birth of a new one. As I glanced at this beautiful woman beside me on the plane, I saw in her a strength I had never noticed before.

We landed late in the afternoon and checked into our rooms on the campus-like grounds of an old mansion that had been converted into a spa. Over herbal tea that night, we planned our agenda. There were so many choices: aerobics, hiking, canoeing, art, mediation, and massage. "What about past-life regression hypnosis?" Mom asked, "I'm going to try it." "My mother?" I thought. She just kept surprising me. "Yes," I replied. "I'll try that."

Chapter 10
Where Two Circles Meet

Dear Journal - Today I tried past-life regression
hypnosis. I don't even know how to describe what
I saw. I feel as if I've reached out to touch the face
of God and found myself staring in the mirror.
Incredible.

During the next three days, Mom and I got to know
one another intimately as we never had before. We
hiked, canoed, and ate fantastically healthy meals
together in the candlelit dining room, followed by long
moonlit walks. On the day of my hypnosis appointment,
I hurried across the courtyard. Leaves scudded in my
path, dancing in the wind. In my sneakers, black
leggings, and old oversized red sweatshirt, I hardly
looked like a woman about to embark on a mystical
journey that would be the experience of a lifetime.
Stepping inside the building, all I could think about was
how good the warm air felt compared to the chilly
outdoor weather. Too energetic to take the elevator, I
bounded up two and half flights of stairs and walked
through the doorway labeled "Behavioral Sciences."
"Ann Albers," I told the receptionist. "I'm here for the
past-life regression hypnosis." "Jill will be with you in a
minute," she replied pleasantly.

I took a seat on the comfortable couch in the waiting
area and fidgeted nervously. I knew suddenly, with that

curious foresight that defies logic, that this day would mark the end of one cycle of my evolution as a human and spiritual being. I couldn't shake the feeling. "Ann?" I heard my name called and walked slowly into the hypnotherapist's office.

— § —

I sank back into the leather recliner, adjusting the seat several times until I finally settled down in a comfortable position. "Sit still," I commanded myself impatiently. My mind was racing. What would happen within the next two hours? What would I see? Would the hypnosis scare me or unnerve me, or would the experience be wonderful? Would I get the answers I had asked for? Would the process even work? The questions flew through my mind as I tried unsuccessfully to settle down and listen attentively to the woman who was trying to put me at ease.

I glanced around the room. Sunlight streamed through two large-paned windows to my left and a comfortable couch sat to my right. "The psychiatrist's couch," I thought, still feeling antsy and a little bit odd. I had never talked to a counselor before. A scented candle burned on a small table. "Nice touch," I thought to myself. The fragrance relaxed me.

My mind wandered back to my "past life regression" experience at the bookstore only ten months ago. I felt like I was watching a dream back then—someone else's movie. I had a sneaking suspicion that today would be entirely different. For starters, there was no one else present but Jill and me so I would be allowed to enter very deep states of altered awareness. Furthermore, Jill was a permanent member of the spa's elite staff and reputedly quite skilled in hypnotherapy.

"Why are you here?" Jill asked warmly, interrupting my thoughts. She was asking me to set some intention for my impending journey. "Why indeed," I thought, searching for the truth. I really wanted to answer "just for fun." That reply would have been simpler, and at least partially true. But lately whole truths were begging to be told, so I sat and thought a bit. "I guess I feel somehow, intuitively, that in other lives or in some dimension I've been a healer. I want to remember whatever there is to know. I don't believe you can truly 'heal' anyone else. I believe real healers simply act as a mirror for others to see the power and beauty of their own spirit and to witness their own perfection," and, I thought silently, "to see themselves through the eyes of God." I wanted to remember how.

"My goodness, did that just come out of my mouth?" I thought, interrupting my own speech with a bit of judgment. "How eloquent." How unusual too, that the pesky inner critic portion of my mind should be complimentary today. "Funny how a good question can bring about an equally decent answer," I laughed inside knowing through my experience of the past several months, the truth of that statement. Jill smiled. I wondered if she knew the plethora of thoughts racing through my mind. "How can you fit so many ideas into one small head," I wondered. Arghh! Would I ever settle down enough to be hypnotized? I wasn't so sure.

I closed my eyes. I felt like I did many years ago when I was a little kid about to jump off the three-meter board at Fort Meyer swimming pool back in Arlington, Virginia. I couldn't wait to jump and at the same time I didn't want my feet to leave the board. I wanted to fly but the firm Plexiglas felt pretty safe. Now I wanted to leap into another unknown state of consciousness, but again, some small part of me still feared losing control.

"Too bad," I admonished myself. I've decided to do this, and now the time had come for me to take the leap.

"Ten. Nine. Eight. Seven. Six. Five," Jill counted. I was off the board now, going deeper and deeper. My eyelids were becoming heavier. "Four. Three. Two. One." I drifted backwards (or was it downwards?) into a dark, comfortable space. "Maybe this really is going to work." The thought drifted through my mind, not nearly so insistent as the others that had come before.

"Imagine a ball of light floating above you. Now see the light entering you through the top of your head." Jill's voice was calm, metered, and very pleasant. "What color should it be?" I wondered. "Oh great, now I've got to have designer light balls. Why can't I just settle down?" The chatter continued, while much to my surprise, a sphere of sparkling rose-colored light began to float about three inches above my head. My eyes were closed, and yet I saw this clearly as if imagination had opened a window through which I could see things that weren't really there. I felt the sensations from within, and yet my vision seemed to be centered a few feet away, as if I was watching myself from the outside.

The sphere was about sixteen inches in diameter, roughly the size of a child's beach ball. Now that I had something to focus on, the mental chatter began to die down. I watched, fascinated as this thing began to land on my head. "It's going to squash me," I thought wryly. "Wow!" The crackling light began to spark through my hair and vibrate ever so slowly into my head. I felt sensations that were difficult to describe—fuzzy, scrubby feelings as if I were receiving an internal cleaning with a water jet. I felt my forehead relax as the tension seeped away into the ethers.

The light tickled past my eyelids, smoothing any premature wrinkles, as if they were being caressed by an unseen hand. I felt my jaws release their strict hold on my face as the sphere descended, now completely encompassing my head. The rose ball of light continued to crackle, zapping any tension in its path. I sank back further in the recliner, savoring the sensations.

"See the ball descending past your heart area," I heard Jill's voice as if from far away. "While it rests there, two smaller balls break off from the main sphere and travel slowly down your arms." Mm. Delicious sensations. Two baby spheres of rose light split from the mother sphere that was still floating in my chest area. One of the smaller balls of crackling light began to travel down through my left shoulder and into my left arm, while the other ball mirrored its path on my right side. My shoulders, stiff from a canoe trip earlier in the week, let go and fell limp to the chair. The warm sensations continued to travel down my arms, and I felt my muscles releasing tension with tiny clicking sounds. "Could my arms have ever been stiff?" I wondered absentmindedly. They were becoming soft as cotton. My elbows relaxed, and then my forearms. They became heavier and heavier until I thought for sure they would sink right into the recliner. I felt the rose spheres in my arms splitting into streaks of light that crackled through each of my fingertips. My hands were buzzing as if I had put them too close to a TV screen that crackled with static electricity. They were very warm and very heavy.

The large sphere of light that had remained in my chest became a swirling whirlpool centered over my heart. The light seemed to merge with an energy of my own, dancing in a spiral of pinks, reds, and rose fuchsia, the color of fresh flowers carpeting a meadow on a spring morning. My chest expanded with a deep breath, feeling as roomy as if I had opened the shutters and pulled back the curtains after a long winter. Like a breeze, the breath flitted down my abdomen and throughout the cells in my body, filling each of them with life. Meanwhile, the light danced with my heartbeat. The feeling was exhilarating, exuberant, and extremely joyful. A floating sensation began to replace the heaviness I had been feeling, and I was no longer sure of my physical orientation. My thinking mind knew I was still laying face-up in the recliner, but some part of me wondered if I had drifted up a bit and floated away, as a balloon might have done.

The pulsating light continued its path down my abdomen, scrubbing away tension with sparkles and rose-colored lightning. Like waves, my breath pounded through my chest then retreated back into the ocean of air surrounding me. The light split again and traveled down my legs. I felt each of them release with a spasmodic jerk, followed by a feeling as if they were becoming leaden parts of the chair itself. Like the rest of my body, this was followed by a clicking sensation then a feeling of lightness, as if my legs had floated above my body to set me completely aloft.

I no longer remembered the room I was in. I was simply drifting, floating, filled with this rose color-of-love light. I no longer cared if the hypnosis would work. I just wanted to hang out in this space. A sense of well being permeated me to the core, as if I didn't have a care in the world. I might as well have been resting at the top of my favorite mountain or sitting by a pristine waterfall in paradise. I was mesmerized by the sensation of being completely weightless. With my inner vision I watched, fascinated as the light crackled, filling me and playing with me. Gently, sparks zipped up and down my form as I swayed to an unseen breeze.

I flirted with the feeling until with no apparent cause the light began to expand past the boundaries of my floating "body." I didn't remember the chair anymore. I barely heard Jill in the room, and I wasn't aware of the sunlight that had seemed blinding through the windows only a few short minutes before. I was light itself and I was expanding. I filled the room with rose-colored sparkles and then began to drift beyond. To where? I didn't know. I felt like butter being spread out over toast, or perhaps water seeping over parched land. I smiled inwardly, feeling deeply satisfied. The doubts were all gone. The hypnosis was working! Far away, I was reminded of my physical body as I felt Ann's face mimic my own feeling with a grin.

"What do you see?" The voice sounded muted as if it were coming from far away. Jill had told me beforehand that we would be able to speak to one another. Even from within the deepest trance, I would be able to hear her and respond. She would be asking me questions, and my job was to answer. In this manner we would be able to record the journey. There was no telling what I would actually remember.

I wondered if I really could command that voice to speak. I willed myself to do so, and far away I heard Ann mumbling my vague response. Strange. I was Ann and yet here in this dream-space I was also distinct from her. Who was I? I felt as if I was operating a brain attached to a mouth via some heretofore undiscovered remote control mechanism.

"I am in a forest," I heard the voice say. Who was talking? "I am Ann," one part of my mind insisted, while another suggested, that maybe, just maybe, there was more to the story. This wasn't making any sense at all. Luckily, before my mind got a chance to play with this brainteaser, the scenery pulled me back deeply into the dream. I would have plenty of time later to puzzle over the paradox of knowing I was Ann and yet feeling distinct from her. "It's autumn," I heard her/me continue in a monotonous voice. I couldn't make her speak the half of my experience. I found myself in a dream as real as the waking day.

I was deep within a forest. The tall oaks and ponderosa pines reached to the skies, where the clouds were gray but not foreboding. A sense of stillness pervaded in the quiet woods. "I'm in a circle of trees. It looks a bit like northern Arizona. It's very peaceful. I hear a hawk." While I worked the remote control voice, I was seated in a clearing—a circle of bare earth in the center of a ring of trees. The smell of fallen leaves was familiar, and the slight chill in the air was invigorating. I felt deeply peaceful here as if I were connected with the earth upon which I sat. The trees seemed to be wise ones surrounding me as I waited, relaxed and yet alert, for the dream to unfold.

I saw the Native American man who had gifted me with my symbol and whom I now considered to be one of my loving spirit guides. He was always somber and serious, yet deeply compassionate. I had never seen his face clearly, but his eyes were pools of obsidian, black as the night, with a sparkle brighter than the stars. I recalled with a start that I had "been" here before in a meditation. I remembered this place, this space, and this time! My spirit-teacher smiled ever so slightly, acknowledging my memory. With a nod he indicated a path leading away from the circle and then disappeared as quickly as he had come.

Slowly, I stood up and followed the short path to a rock wall. "What do you see?" Jill asked from another dimension. I began reporting more dutifully as the adventure unfolded. It was becoming easier to talk even though I could barely hear my own voice. The dream continued to become less dreamlike and much more real. "In front of me I see an opening to a cave." The gaping mouth of the cave appeared out of nowhere. "How could I not have seen this before?" I wondered. I entered cautiously. Stairs led down for a short distance, then the path gave way to rutted rock, worn smooth by the ages. "It is wet, moist, very damp in here," I reported. Water dripped from the stone walls, "plunk, plunk, plunk" in a hypnotic cascade as I continued onward. Surprisingly, deep within the dark womb of this dream-earth, the atmosphere was balmy and comfortable. Candles perched on tiny rock ledges cast a soft light along my path. The water on the walls shone black against their flickering glow and eerie shadows danced behind their flames.

I reached a fork in the tunnel. To my left a cavernous path wound out of sight. To my right, the tunnel plunged into a blackness deeper than the stormy sky on a moonless night. Which way to go? I chose the right-hand path and plunged into the darkness. The floor, although bumpy, was smooth enough to walk on, and the walls were easy to feel as I made my way blindly. Intuitively I knew I had chosen correctly although there were no signs of anything, anywhere.

"What do you see in the tunnel?" echoed the question from beyond. I looked up, startled. "There's a crystal embedded in the ceiling," I reported excitedly. The quartz point was about 6 inches long and had four faces at the pointed end. Through the crystal, I could see the silhouette of a large tree, shrunk to tiny dimensions in the small natural "window" that allowed me to peer out of the cave and into yet another world. I considered the situation. Maybe this was my way into the past-lives I had been expecting to visit. Maybe the crystal was one of those so-called dream portals. But how could I get through something so small and so solid?

Dream logic is a funny thing. You can do all sorts of tricks, expanding to immense proportions, or shrinking into tiny spaces. I tried to shrink, thinking that perhaps there was a crack in the crystal through which I could travel. To my surprise, I didn't get any smaller. Next, I attempted to imagine myself on the other side. Still no luck. I was becoming frustrated. I knew there was a world outside of the cave that I wanted to explore. Stubbornly, I refused to give up. "Maybe," I thought, "if I believe strongly enough, I can simply transport myself through the crystal."

I jumped upward fully expecting to travel effortlessly into the world I glimpsed outside of the cave. "Ouch!" This wasn't working. I was still 5'3" tall, and in the dream I was hitting my head on a crystal quartz point, trying to force myself through solid rock. The comedy of the situation struck me all at once. This was how I reacted in waking life when all else failed. Full speed ahead. Just do it. Go for it. The problem I found, both in waking life and in this hypnotic dream, was that circumstances didn't always cooperate with my zeal. I had to laugh at myself. I felt terribly foolish and yet I found myself reporting the entire incident. In another dimension, on a leather recliner, Ann laughed heartily with eyes still closed as she reported my useless endeavor. Jill laughed too, and for a brief moment, I was back in the room experiencing myself as Ann and enjoying the humor. I breathed deeply, and turned inward. Soon, the dream lulled me back into an entirely different reality.

I abandoned the crystal idea and wandered once again into the blackness. "Oh no!" My dream voice echoed through the cavern as the floor fell away beneath me. The haunting sound ricocheted off walls far above me as I slid down, down, and farther down into a chilly blackness. I was falling out of control, riding down a chute into nothingness. Just as I thought my descent would never end, I was tossed out of a gaping hole, high on a cliff side. For an instant, I was suspended in mid-air, terrified, expecting at any second to plummet to an untimely dream-death. I held my breath.

What was this?   To my astonishment, instead of falling, I was flying. I was a hawk! "Rrraaaww," I heard my own shrill cry as I rode the currents, ecstatically playing with the new sensations of flight. My wings were strong and sturdy. With only a few flaps I carried myself far above the cliff side, watching a waterfall plunge over its edge, cascading into foaming pools below as I circled ever higher.   Dancing in flight, I swooped downward, treasuring the spray, the air, the sunshine, and above all the sheer joy and freedom of it all. I was flying!

A stream wound away from the waterfall pools beneath me, gurgling past tree-lined banks, hopping here and there over boulders strewn in the water's path. I marveled at the scenery. The landscape was surreal, vividly colored, and sensual. I experienced everything around me with some heightened sense of awareness. The gentle breezes caressed the feathers on the back of my neck, while the wind spoke in whispered "swooshing" sounds. Smells from the creek wafted up through the thermals. I savored the sensations for a brief while, knowing they wouldn't last forever. I knew this flight had a destination. At a point that appeared to be pre-determined (by whom?), I veered off to the right and soared, flying above rolling hills covered with a lush green carpet of grass. "I'm above farmland." I reported. The scene shifted as I made my descent.

In an instant, day turned into night. I found myself floating, looking down on a campfire surrounded by a circle of Native American people. A round-faced elder-woman sat facing the fire, spinning the yarns of her story as the rest of the crowd sat entranced in her tale. Soon, I was no longer a hawk floating above the scene; instead, I was looking through the eyes of a human seated amongst the listeners in this nighttime story theater. I reported the change to Jill.

"Look at yourself," I heard Jill say. "What are your shoes?" I looked down. "I am wearing moccasins, pants, and shirt made of hide. There's also a grayish rabbit fur hanging from my left shoulder. I don't know if I'm male or female." This would remain a mystery for the time. "I have jet black hair and I am wearing two braids." "How old are you," Jill asked. I waited and then heard my Ann-voice answer, "I'm around twenty or so."

Back in my Ann-body, for just an instant, I wondered at the sensation of feeling as if I was floating upside down, feet pointed toward the ceiling, and head just above the chair where I had been resting. I returned my attention to the dream and looked around to see if there was anything more that would identify the person I had become. There was nothing on my hands, no decorations in my hair.

My logical mind began to intervene. I found myself thinking as Ann once again. "Was this it? Was this really a past-life of mine or was I tapping into some universal wisdom? Who is this? Was I male or female?" The questions poured through my mind without warning as if a mental floodgate had been unleashed. "Darn it!" I cursed inwardly. The mental chatter had disconnected me from the dream scene. I was just Ann again, sitting in a chair, still feeling a bit like I was floating, but more so, feeling cheated. I had been so close! Why was it I always thought too much, analyzed everything, and let my mind take over and rob me of the treasure of my experiences? Frustration oozed through my pores.

Jill, who seemed to possess eternal calm, must have sensed my unrest. She coached me, coaxing me back into the trance with her pleasant hypnotic voice. "You can go backward or forward in time to see more," she said simply. I wasn't going to give up so soon. I stilled my mind by silencing the thoughts that chained me back into my body and then focused on the sparkling light that had lulled me into the hypnosis. Holding my breath as if I was diving underwater for a second time, I returned to the dream. The transition was surprisingly easy.

I had moved forward in time. I knew now, without thinking, that I was seeing through the eyes of a Native American man. He was an older and much wiser version of the twenty-year-old who had sat listening to the old woman's stories in the previous scene. Time had worn deep furrows in his aging forehead and a heavy burden filled his heart with a great sadness. He was seeking advice from a tree that to him was very much alive, and very much a friend. "The people are restless," he told the ancient tree. "We do not prosper now." I heard his words echoed by me back in the chair in a voice slightly deeper than usual. I forgot myself as Ann and merged again with the dream.

The mighty tree began to teach the old man. I heard its words in my head as clearly as if they had been spoken by a master. "The people are restless because they have lost their connection," the wise old tree told the wise old man in a resounding voice. "They feel impoverished because they do not realize they are tied to the source of abundance. Everything goes in a circle. Life will return. See how I die? I drop my leaves and without fail, I come back to life again." The tree continued talking into my mind, its voice as deep and compassionate as the wise voice of a sage who had weathered the tests of time.

"Cut me down," the tree commanded all of a sudden. "Use me as a teaching in ceremony so the people will understand the cycles of life." The wrinkles on the old man's face became canyons as he laid my head in his hands. "No. I cannot do this," he replies. This tree is his friend, his advisor. This tree is older than he. He came to the tree for advice, seeking knowledge and understanding. Now the tree tells him he must kill it? NO! "I cannot cut you down, friend," the old man says. Tears of anguish fall from his eyes. I begin to sob quietly in the chair in the other dimension.

The tree persists. "Death, my friend," he reminds the old man, "is but an illusion. If you will not cut me down, you do not yet understand the nature of life. Let go of your notions of control. Life and death go on in cycles without end. Let it go. Cut me down. I give my life gladly for this teaching and," the tree paused for just a moment, then in a booming voice commanded the man, pleading with him to understand, "I DO - NOT - DIE." Gentler now, the voice continued. "My essence exists. Always. Period. I will become part of the earth and give life to another member of my species. See this. Know it. Teach it."

The old man is deaf to the logic. Ann sobs quietly, a choked version of the tears that flow freely from his eyes in the dream. He cries silently, proudly, somehow becoming aware of the profound teaching he is receiving. The tree is so beautiful, timeless, wise, and unselfish. The tree is giving up its life so the people, no, so he will understand. This tree belies the essence of the true martyr, the sacrificial lamb. Even in my hypnotic state, I understand in this instant the nobility behind the sacrifices of Christ, Martin Luther King Jr., and the countless others who knew their lives were but part of a larger teaching and a greater awakening.

In the dream, the old man also understands the tree's sacrifice but longs for reprieve. He doesn't want to cut down his friend. He looks at the gnarled trunk, pleading with soulful eyes for another option. In the chair, I wondered if this was how Abraham felt when God had commanded him to kill his own son. In the dream, the old man hoped that he would be given a new command. None came. Instead, he was overwhelmed with raw emotion. The tree was sending him feelings now, feelings of great love, of compassion, of trust. With a quiet voice, the tree said to the old man emphatically, one more time, "I don't die." I understood. I stilled my breath, deeply grateful for this teaching. The old man knew what he must do.

The scene changed abruptly. The trunk of the mighty tree had been cut and placed in the center of a dirt circle. Four dancers were tied to the tree with sinew attached via small wooden slivers piercing their abdomens. These were the holy ones, everyday men who were taking part in a sacrifice of pain to perpetuate the cycles of life. I was honored to be in their presence. I watched in reverent awe, not understanding the full significance of what transpired, and yet imbued by a feeling that told me all I needed to know. Somehow the dream found the old man in sacred ceremony, sitting on the sidelines—an elder watching in prayerful silence. In his ceremony I witnessed the timelessness of life. I saw that death is but an illusion to be crossed. Life goes on. Life does not die. The old man called upon the powers of Spirit to forever remove the curtains of illusion from his own mind and to do the same for his people. He asked that they never be allowed to forget. I watched through his eyes from within the hypnotic trance, in awe at the sacredness of the events that were unfolding.

Huge wings once again attached to my shoulders. I felt the brush of feathers as I rose above the scene. In one last glance, I saw the community below. A young man was pounding prayerfully on a hide-covered drum while the dance went on, slowly, rhythmically, like life itself. The spirits of the ancestors, the ghost people, and the wise ones stood around the perimeter of the community, watching. There were circles within circles of people in the sacred scene below as I took to flight. My heart was filled with gratitude, and I knew a deep sense of peace.

Abruptly the scene below disappeared. "Oh my goodness," I heard myself reporting breathlessly as I tried to take in the vastness of the new scenery. "It's so beautiful. I'm in outer space. There are stars everywhere. I'm sitting in the center of the universe. No, I'm floating above the earth now. There are mountains far below." Feelings welled up. I haven't felt these since... since when? I didn't know. Warmth spread throughout me in the dream and through me in the chair. Outside the dream, I was crying, tears streaming down my cheeks, moved by the sheer beauty that surrounded me. "Incredible love, it's almost overwhelming. I'm floating. I'm..." I heard my voice become quiet as I struggled for the words that would appear out of nowhere only a second later. "I'm cradled in the arms of the universe." The feeling was almost too much to bear—the blush of a first crush, the heart-melting warmth of a first kiss, the tender love of a mother gazing at her child, the beauty of a rainbow, and the orange-burst passion of a sunset, all focused on me. Love, incredible love, was filling each cell with each breath, buoying me in an invisible ocean of light.

"I'm being handed a gift," my voice told Jill excitedly. The voice was speaking faster than I could watch. There was no sense of time. "It doesn't make sense, but I don't care." Sometimes I saw first then reported. Other times, I reported, and then I saw. "I'm being handed a gift. It's a mirror." I become quieter now, reverent. "I'm at the edge of my knowing," my voice rings out. Yes, I was. "The mirror is taking the form of a perfect quartz crystal." I understand the purity and perfection of the crystalline structure to symbolize the white-light brilliance of our souls. In my body, tears of joy were still falling. This was so beautiful, so surreal.

The stars were moving now in a spiral all around me. I seemed to spin faster, out of control, until I stopped and found myself in a different time and place. This time I was in a long outdoor walkway. Stone pillars to my left supported great arches that connected with a massive building to my right. Farther to the left in between the pillars, a stone stairway led downward to some unknown destination. The long outdoor corridor stretched on far ahead of me, parallel to the building. I felt as if I were standing outside a castle and found myself, as Ann, trying to guess the location. "Not Europe," I reported, still trying too hard to make sense of the scene. I turned to study the wall and gasped. The artistry was breathtaking. A huge mosaic was laid out in tiny jewel-toned tiles. I couldn't yet see the pattern, but the colors were dazzling. "This isn't America either," my voice continued.

Jill's voice prompted me for more information. "Look at your shoes." I looked down. I was wearing green suede-like slippers with stones inlaid on the toe area in the shape of a beautiful flower. Silk harem pants billowed in the wind as I walked. "I am a woman from India, Egypt, or Nepal," I reported as I managed to slip into the role. I laughed as I discovered I was wearing a ruby in my navel. "I am quite manicured, and young, around eighteen. I have a dark complexion and my hair is tied back in a single long braid."

Assessing the situation, I remembered that I had snuck out of my room. I came here often to see the sparkles of the mosaic tile, laid out in a pattern I could now see. I was gazing at a monolithic puzzle of tiny stones depicting a huge black tree with a majestic orange tiger in the branches. "Do you see others?" Jill asked. I looked around. Ann is just a voice I am using to report now. "I am alone," I tell her. "I'm glad. My elders tell me what I can and cannot do." "How does that make you feel," Jill questions. I thought about this again. How does it make me feel? What a curious question, I thought. "It's OK," I answer, "that's just the way life is." As the dream-character, I accepted a life I would have balked at, as Ann.

"Why are you there?" Jill questioned. As the young woman, I considered her question. "My life is too formal in the main palace area," I respond. "My elders want me to act a certain way. I would be disrespectful if I were to disobey openly. I find that it is much easier just to sneak out every now and then." "Ask her what she has to say to you," Jill tells Ann. In the dream as the young woman I reply, "Value your freedom. You are lucky to have choice in all matters of your life." I am speaking to Ann casually as if people from different times and places were able converse all the time. Still thinking from the young woman's perspective, I comment to myself, "I have all the riches in the world in this life, and yet no freedom. Is that wealth?"

As the woman and the mosaic began to fade, I began to think as Ann once again. I liked the young woman's spirit. She treasured beauty and freedom and even in a lifetime without choice, she found ways to live her truth. Yes, I did treasure my own freedom. I had much to learn from her.

I took off again, my hawk-self resuming flight. Where to go now? I felt as if I had been in this dream for ... lifetimes! I laughed inside at the joke and waited to see what would transpire next. Things started to move again, swirling in the dream until a new scene stabilized in my inner vision. Far below, a cobblestone house on a green hillside came into view. I found myself floating inside the house, no longer a hawk and not a person either. A ghost? I didn't know, and I didn't seem to care. A plump fair-skinned and freckled girl with fiery red hair was baking pies in the kitchen. She had a thick Irish accent. I described her to Jill. "She's a bit prissy, fun-loving, Hm. She has a good laugh, but she's rather plain." "How old is she?" Jill questioned. "Sixteen," I replied, still speaking from Ann's point of view. "Her name is Molly. Boy, she's really working at those pies!" She seemed to me to be a little dense-minded, a simple girl perhaps wanting for a bit of attention.

"Ask her what message she has for you," I heard Jill as if she was shouting this time, even though I know she wasn't. I tried to get Molly's attention in all manner of ways, but how does a ghost attract attention? All of a sudden, despite my vain attempts, she looked up at me as if she had known I was there all along. "If ya kin appreciate the simple things in life," she said with a thick brogue, "you wouldn' hav' ta warry so much!" With that she went back to work and I laughed heartily. I understood. "She's a real tart," I thought, recognizing a mirror of myself in that last display of spunk.

At the precise moment of that insight, the house faded quickly, soon to be forgotten as I found myself once again floating in the great beauty of outer space. I was a being of pure light, expanding rapidly, growing ever so much larger than Ann. I found myself intricately intertwined with the scene, this time so much more than just a visitor. I was awestruck, overwhelmed, and nearly speechless. Without thinking, I began to relate my experience to Jill, as best I could via Ann's voice.

"Stars (or were they other beings of light?) glistened like diamonds in the blackness of space. Beneath me, the planet earth cast a soft blue glow into the void. All around me, the heavens expanded farther than the eye could see or the soul could sense." A warm, tingling feeling permeated my being as I waited anxiously and wondered what would come next. I had transformed into a soul suspended in a place between space and time.

"Soul." As Ann, I had always tossed that word around somewhat carelessly, never quite understanding what I implied. "My soul," I used to say, as if the soul were a smaller part of my identity as Ann. In a flash of instant revelation, I awakened to my true identity as part of this being of light—the larger and wiser being called "soul."

In the split second of remembering, I knew myself to be so much more than the woman lying in a chair in the northeastern portion of the United States, on the third planet from the star called sun. I was deeper in the hypnotic slumber now than I had been throughout the entire journey. My consciousness slowly merged with that of my soul, and I began to experience the vision through my soul eyes." Back in the chair, tears welled up in my eyes sneaking past my closed eyelids, while a warm feeling permeated my being. A voice echoed, "We wait for the adventure to complete."

Soon, the tides turned. Inaction gave way to quick movement. Peace spiraled into excitement. My anxiousness was replaced by my soul's expanded, overwhelming love for this tiny personality-portion of me awakening at last to the power and beauty of her spirit. As I watched in awed wonder through my soul's eyes, we transformed into a mighty archetypal oak.

Our roots embedded themselves into the very core of the earth and our branches thrust upward and outward, reaching to the corners of the dimensions. Crackling blue sparks of energy flowed through us carrying life, much like rivers of sap run through trees in the springtime and iron-rich blood flows through human veins.

As quickly as we became accustomed to ourselves as this Tree of Life, a disk of faces began to spin around our vast trunk. Against the darkness of a waiting universe they whirled, faster and faster until I became almost dizzy with their motion.

These were faces without names, people of every race, color, sex, and age group. To my soul's great delight, in a split earth-second, I understood that these faces represented different aspects of my soul-self, projections of my soul's consciousness into a reality called "space" and "time." These were the masks I had worn throughout the ages, the different personalities that comprised the totality of my being. As characters in the nighttime dream sometimes represent the aspects of a single human psyche, so too these characters were the players in the dreams of my soul. I understood myself to be one of these, so small and yet such an integral part of the collective whole that we are.

In the instant of knowing, flesh and soul reunited consciously for the first time this earth-life sending a seismic wave of ecstasy across the cosmos. Another circle was complete.

In the chair, in a separate space and time, I sighed with deep relief as the vision faded into blackness.

—— § ——

"Five. Six. Seven. You're feeling refreshed and wide-awake." Jill gently guided me back up from the deep hypnotic trance. My eyes were still closed, and I marveled one last time at the strange sensations. I was still buzzing, as if charged by an electrical current. The warm tingling sensations slipped into my torso, moved through my arms down to my fingertips, and then ran into my legs. I felt as if I were an energetic form slipping into my body, feeling warm and wonderful. I moved my fingers slowly, appreciating the miracle of my own two hands. "Eight. Nine. Ten."

Snap! I opened my eyes, startled at the brightness and the clarity of the scenery. Jill was smiling. She looked like an angel with the light filtering against the back of her blondish hair. I was grinning broadly as well. For a minute, I just stared, relishing the feeling of being back in my body while I rested in the bright and airy room. I rubbed my eyes, feeling as if I had just returned home after being away for a very, very long time.

My senses were super-alert. I soaked in the sights, sounds, and smells, as if I had never experienced them before. "Wow," I said at long last, startled at the depth of my own voice. "What a trip." As Jill and I talked, I noticed a shift in my thinking that startled me. No matter how hard I tried to do otherwise, I found myself referring to "'Ann" in the third person as if "'she" were a smaller part of my true identity.

I could hardly believe the events that had unfolded over the last ninety minutes. In a space of earth-time less than two hours I had become a hawk and flown above immense vistas, dipping down now and then into lifetimes that were relevant to my current quest. Had these really been lifetimes of my own, or had I tapped into some universal wisdom? I didn't know if I would ever have the answer.

I didn't believe in reincarnation in the traditional sense. Instead I believed that the soul might have different personalities living in different spaces and times all at once, much as several television shows can exist simultaneously among the different channels. Using this analogy, I identified myself as "Ann" because I only got to view one channel at a time. In altered states of awareness like the hypnosis, I got my hands on the channel changer and was allowed to flip through the other shows, witnessing bits and pieces of other "lifetimes in progress." To believe this metaphor as an intellectual curiosity was one thing; to experience different lives firsthand, and then to see the lives from a soul's perspective was a gift beyond comparison. Whether these lives were mine or others' didn't seem to matter so much. Each carried an important message for me.

I left Jill's office still trembling inside at the immensity of the visions I had just witnessed. The mighty tree stood out in my mind, larger than life. At the time, I had no idea that I had tapped into an archetype as old as myth itself. The cosmic Tree of Life, I read later, is an ancient symbol for the connection between heaven and earth. I didn't need to read that at the time. After becoming the tree, rooted on earth and reaching to heaven, the knowledge was stored in the very fibers of my being. From now on I would have no choice but to recognize myself as a being much larger than Ann. I had seen through my soul's eyes. I knew who I was. I remembered.

"I remembered!" The words echoed in my mind. "Yes!" I remembered who I was, why I was here. My heart was full of ecstatic love—not narrowly focused on a single person, but reaching out to all of creation. I swam in an ocean of feeling welling up from and spilling over my heart. I felt light as a feather and thrilled to be alive.

I kicked up the fallen leaves in my path and laughed aloud. Amazing! The pieces of the puzzle of my life were all coming together to form a beautiful picture. I knew now, without doubt, that part of my life's work was to reach upward, asking Spirit for its help in pulling us all toward heaven and more joyful living here on earth. I was to reach outward too, branching beyond the safe core of my identity as Ann and sharing the life that runs through my own "veins"—the experiences and wisdom I have been privileged to learn along my path. I was overwhelmed, humbled, and filled with gratitude. Still living through the eyes of my soul, I re-entered my world with a much-broadened sense of who I really was and why I was here. Bliss filled my being.

"Could there really be a heaven on earth?" Looking around, I thought I might possibly be there. The sky was a sullen gray with low cloud cover, but the maples were bursting with fiery red and orange foliage and the bright mums surrounding a fountain punctuated the dimness with splashes of color. The colors were so bright I had to blink. The air seemed crisper than usual too, or was my imagination simply playing tricks on me? The pungent smell of leaves and the clean scent of a creek drifted up from the forest below.

White painted trim on the buildings glistened like alabaster. The sparkling glass windows threw off hints of shimmering light that reminded me of the stars that had glistened in the night sky of my dream. The afternoon was eerily silent except for the whispers of a soft wind. There was a surrealistic quality to the landscape that I hadn't noticed before. I hurried along the path, surreptitiously pinching myself just to make sure I had indeed transitioned back into real, waking life.

My thoughts were interrupted when I reached the doorway to my building. I wound my way up a spiral staircase surrounded by long glass paned windows, then wandered down the softly carpeted hallway and turned on the lights in my room. Outside I could hear a soft rain starting to drip off the leaves of the trees that snuggled against my windows. The temperature was getting chillier, but inside I was warm and cozy. A soft glow radiated from the desk lamp chasing away the gathering gray shadows. I laid down, resting my head on mounds of soft pillows, and stared out the window.

"Cycles and Circles. Circles and cycles," I chanted a bit hypnotically, wondering at this theme that had appeared many times throughout the dream journey. Just as the thought drifted through my mind, a leaf fell off the tree outside my window, drifting lazily on the wind into the gathering dusk. The scene reminded me of the dream-tree that spoke to me during the hypnosis of life in its many forms and its never-ending cycles.

"Life really is a series of cycles and circles," I thought at long last. I flipped onto my back to stare at the ceiling and remembered the many times life had taken me in circles. The people had changed, or the circumstances perhaps, but time and again I had found myself faced with the same issues, the same concerns, and the same questions, worries, and fears. Like a broken record, the themes had repeated until recently, when I had finally been able to move on to the next song. One circle path was complete and the next was just beginning.

"Mm," I sank back into the luxurious pillows, wallowing in warmth and comfort. In just a few minutes I would meet my mother and some new friends for dinner in the candlelit dining room of the spa's restored mansion. After that, perhaps we would stroll for a while in the dark silence of a rainy night and then duck inside to dry off and enjoy a warm cup of herbal tea. How incredible I felt, at age thirty, to be starting a new adventure in this manner. How magical life had become.

A few years ago, if someone had told me my life would be this wonderful, the thought would have been as far removed from my reality as the lives I had just witnessed in the hypnotic dream.

I would never know the woman I would have become had I stayed in engineering and continued to ignore my dreams. That woman was gone—erased from existence. Somewhere along the line, Spirit had thrown the switches, changed the tracks, and the train of my life went quickly along another course. I would never know the destination of my original paths, and for this I was deeply grateful.

The Whispers of the Spirit had guided me home.

IX. Epilogue

In the time that has passed since I began this book, my life has changed even more dramatically. A few months after leaving engineering, I decided to begin a year-long apprenticeship to my Reiki instructor, so I could learn to do the energetic initiations that allow others to heal. The year was one of great personal challenge, growth, and change.

During my apprenticeship, I spent my time quietly—writing, doing energy work, and delving deeper into my mind, body, and spirit to heal aspects of myself that I hadn't even known required healing. I spent the year learning more about who I am as a soul and what purpose my life is here to serve. I watched the energy help people change their lives after they completed the Reiki training, and I began to understand the patterns of growth and spiritual development.

Shortly after my Reiki master attunement in January of 1996, I became a full-time Reiki teacher, professional channel, angel communicator, and spiritual instructor.

John and I did reclaim the unconditional love we've always had for one another. As we did so, however, we realized the truth of our lives, namely that we had chosen different paths, different belief systems, and had formulated different goals for our futures. After spending months in quiet contemplation, with open, honest, and loving communication, we decided to separate. We're still privileged to care about each other as friends, and we've never lost the deep love, respect, and honor that we have for one another.

In the process of separation I learned that the greatest gift you can give another is to unconditionally accept his or her life path, although it may be different from your own. The greatest gift you can give yourself is to listen to the whispers of your own soul and to live your own truth.

I now know the essence of my life's purpose. I am here to help people discover the power and beauty of their spirit, to help connect them with the love and wisdom of their guides, and to help them reclaim their passion for living. I know my life will take more radical turns. I may never fully know my future, but now I trust and have evidence that each step will be given to me along the way. Each time I have a question, I now know I have the tools to turn inward and listen to the whispers of the Spirit as they continue to guide me along life's journey.

You too can listen to the whispers. You too can follow your heart and lead a life better than you could ever imagine. Yes, this journey requires courage, but you *do* have the strength and you *will* be given the help if you only ask.

Check deep inside to find your own truth. In painful circumstances, look for the lessons. Start to pay attention to your dreams. Look for recurring themes in your life. Notice objects, signs, and symbols to which you are attracted. Ask yourself what they mean. Trust your own answers. Ask to be given information on your soul's purpose in this lifetime, and like a child putting together pieces of a puzzle, take delight in your search for self.

Look at the mirrors that life presents you. Who are your teachers—both those who support, and those who trigger you? What do you have to learn from the people in your life? What can you share with them? If you are inclined, ask your angels and guides to start working with you and pay attention to their subtle whispers in your life—an unexpected turn of "luck," a piece of information you need coming from an unlikely source, a helping hand when you thought none was there. Try bodywork, energetic healing, and massage to help you release stuck emotions. Be willing to let the stuck emotions flow and then let them go. Be willing to give up a comfortable identity for one that will bring you bliss.

Explore the many realms and dimensions that life has to offer. Immerse yourself in the human experience. Engage your senses. See the beauty all around you. Feel the textures. Delight in the sounds. Only when you start to pay attention to the everyday dimension do you get to experience the others. Be where you are first. Be willing to work with all you've become. Be willing to release the past and dare to dream of a future beyond what you think you can create. Your soul whispers at first, then calls to you in an unmistakable voice.

Your soul asks you to become holy, or *whole*, to reclaim the parts of yourself that you've left behind along this road of life, and then to stand in your power and your truth, to let your life be blissful and an inspiration to others.

Yes, the whispers are subtle at first, but they can be heard. I honor you on your path and encourage you to step beyond who you know yourself to be.

Spirit speaks to you, in you, and through you. You *can* hear the voices.

A Note from Ann

As I finished the final edit of this book, the angels crept into my head once again. *"Look at today's date,"* I heard them giggling as I read through the last few paragraphs about the cycles and circles of life. It was October 26, 2007. "What's so special about that?" I questioned them. *"Look in your journal,"* they instructed me. *"You'll see."* More laughter. I dug out my journal.

On October 26, exactly thirteen years ago to the day, I returned home from my spa vacation with Mom. The day I finished the final edit of this book marked the anniversary of the first day of the rest of my life.

There is so much more I have to share with you. Stay tuned...

About the Author

Ann Albers graduated from the University of Notre Dame in 1986 with a Bachelor's degree in Electrical Engineering then worked in the avionics industry for 8 years before leaving to pursue her spiritual calling.

She is now a popular author, lecturer, angel communicator, spiritual instructor, and traditional Reiki master/healer. Her life is dedicated to helping people find the power and beauty of their spirit, and a practical deep, abiding, and joyful connection with God, their angels, and guides. She lives in Phoenix, Arizona, with her two dogs and host of heavenly helpers.

For more information on Ann's books, tapes, and classes, or to sign up for her free weekly email newsletter "Messages from Ann & the Angels," visit her website:

www.VisionsOfHeaven.com

If you liked this book...

Visit Ann's website for other books and CDs such as:

Love is the River:

Learning to Live in the Flow of Divine Grace

Bridging the Gap Between

Christianity & Mysticism

Love Letters from Ann & The Angels

Aura Hygiene: A Guide to Keeping

Your Spiritual Energy Strong & Positive

Angel Meditation CD's

And more...

www.VisionsOfHeaven.com

Printed in the United States
113046LV00003B/148-162/A